Evidence for Truth: Science

From: The Right Reverend Bishop Michael Marshall
Lambeth Palace, London SE1 7JU

I heard Prebendary Pearce lecture the Christian Broadcasting Council at the end of last year and was most struck by the importance of what he is saying. There is no doubt in my mind that there is a kind of 'academic mafia' around Biblical scholarship which resists and resents any traditional and radical reappraisal of Biblical scholarship. Prebendary Pearce is a glorious exception by his singularity. He is a scholar of amazing and substantial ability and experience and needs to be taken seriously in this whole quest for the recovery of our scriptural nerve for the Decade of Evangelism.

From: the late Dr John W. Wenham
Vice-principal Trinity College, Bristol
Warden of Latimer House, Oxford
Co-founder of Tyndale House, Cambridge

Victor Pearce has a great breadth of knowledge in theology and science and has great courage in relating them to one another. His particular strength is in anthropology, a subject about which few Christians are well informed, but one in which he has specialised. He does not indulge in cranky or unsubstantiated scientific ideas, but sorts out the sound scientific conclusions from the notions based on secularist philosophies. He works from an unashamed acceptance of Scripture as God's Word (in the way that Jesus himself did) and robustly and straightforwardly relates secular knowledge to this basic truth.

Evidence for Truth: Science

Victor Pearce

Series Editor: David Page

eagle

Guildford, Surrey

Other books in this series by Victor Pearce:

> *Evidence for Truth, Vol 2: Archaeology*
> *Evidence for Truth, Vol 3: Prophecy*

Other titles by the same author:

> *Who Was Adam?*
> *Origin of Man*
> *The Science of Man and Genesis*

Copyright © Victor Pearce 1993 and 1998

Printed 1998. Reprinted 1998

The rights of Victor Pearce to be identified as author of this work has been asserted by him in accordance with the Copyright, Design and Patents Act 1988.

British Library Cataloguing in Publication Data. A catalogue record for this book is available from the British Library.

Published by Eagle, an imprint of Inter Publishing Service (IPS) Ltd, St Nicholas House, 14 The Mount, Guildford, Surrey GU2 5HN.

Scripture quotations: unless specified, Bible quotations are the author's own translation from the Greek or Hebrew text

Typeset by Eagle Publishing
Printed by CPD Wales
ISBN No: 0 86347 263 X

CONTENTS

List of Illustrations   13
The Principles Behind this Series   14
About the Author   15
Preface to the First Edition   16
Preface to the Second Edition   17
Foreword   19

Introduction:
Scientific Discoveries Anticipated in the Bible   21
The Concept of this Series   22
Objectives of this Book   23
Darwin's Alarm and the Evidence of his Conversion   23
Wellhausen (1844–1918): the Darwin of Theology   24
The Death of Faith   25
Scientists Return to Biblical Concepts   26

1. Correlation of Genesis 1 and Science:
Cosmic Origins of Life   27
The Order of Life   28
The Climax of Creation   28
The Method by which Genesis 1 is Set Out   29
The Physical Order   30
Atmosphere Clears   31
The Biological Order   32
Insects and Flowers   33
The Land Animals   33
Modern Mammals   35
Three Basics Created   35
The DNA Genetic Life Code   36
Correlation of Science and Scripture   39

2. Space Probe Finds a Beginning:
The Big Bang Theory   41
Genesis and the Big Bang   41
Seeking to Avoid the Creator   42
The Confessions of a Scientist   44
Lumps in the Primeval Soup!   45
Leading Scientists Confirm the Bible   47
St John's Amazement   48
Scientists Acknowledge God   48
'I Am the Alphabet of Life'   49
NASA Spacecraft Discovery   50
Let There Be Light!   50
Quark Soups – Six Flavours   51
Invisible Reality   51

God and the Big Bang   52
Anthropic Universe   53
Science and the Invisible   54
The Great Scientific Myth   55
The Propagation of False Ideas   55
Prophesied Proof   56

3. God's Timing of Creation Events:
   An Assessment of Prevailing Views   58
Changing Fashions of Biblical Scientists   58
Prevailing Creationist Views   59
Earth Days or Galaxy Days?   59
Age-day Interpretation   59
Thousand-year Day Theory   60
The 24-hour Day Theory   60
Chaos Theory   61
Seventh-Day-Not-Ended Theory   61
Revealed in Six Days?   62
The Tendency to Give the Earth a Great Age   62
Signs of Rock Ageing   63
Dinosaur Paluxy Footprints Re-examined   63
Modified Evolution   63
Timing and the Methods of Science   64
A 360-Million-Year Day?   65
Biblical Arguments for the Age-day View   66

4. Moses in the Time Machine:
   An Imaginary Space-Time Journey   71
Time in Space   71
All Aboard the Time Machine!   72
Relative Time   74
Blue Hot Stars   75
Elemental for a Fisherman   76
The Mysterious Three-in-One   77
Charming Stars   78
The Anthropic Principle   79
The Second Day of Creation   80
The Third Day   81
The Fourth Day   82
The Fifth Day of Creation   83
The Sixth Day   84
The Sixth Day Afternoon   85
Operation Hominid   86
Enzymes Piece Man Together   87
Adam Speaks in Day Six   88
Watching God Make a Woman   92
The Busy Afternoon Continued   94

5. God's Amazing Word-processor:
The Genetic Book of Man 98
Genetic Sub-editors 99
Female Copyright 99
Translating the DNA Code 101
The Book of Man 101
The Cell 103
Can Man Create Life? 103
'Black Box' Evidence of the Creator from the Cell 105
Using God's Tools 107
Genetic Engineering and Mutations 109
Enzymes for Engineering the DNA Instructions 111
More about God's Words in the DNA Code 112
God's Word-processor 112
Space Fiction or Creator? 112
God's Code Breaker 113

6. The Missing Missing Link:
The Fossil Evidence 116
The Absence of Link Fossils 116
Life Appears Suddenly 118
Darwin's Own Witness Against Evolution 118
Supposed Links 119
Living Fossils! 119
Brain-wash Fiction 120
God's Creation by Words 120
A Recorded Absence of Links 121
Leaps or Links? 122
No Links for Hominids 122
An Assessment of Anthropological Finds 123
Meet Lucy 123
How Old Was Lucy? 124
No Stooping Ape-men 125
Powerful Fossil Evidence 126
Geology Founded before Darwin 126
Witness with the Fossils 127
Overlaps Reverse the Order 127

7. The Great TV Cover-up:
Media Promotion of Evolutionist Frauds 130
Barren Rocks before Creation of Life 130
Ancient Sea Creatures and Old-fashioned Theories 131
Design in Creation 132
Insects and Symbiosis 133
The Butterfly 134
Peacock's Feathers 134
Migration of Birds 135
Evolutionist Frauds 135

Engineering Trusses   136
Pterodactyls   136
God Recodes the Instructions   137
Flying Mammals   138
Sonic Sight   139
The Human Flying Machine   140
Eyes as Eagles   140
Devolution   141
The Miracle Human Eye   141
Jesus Creates Eyes   143
Evidence Captured in Amber   144
Mutant Mistakes   145
Variations Within Species   145
Can a Crocodile Lay a Bird's Egg?   146
Those Black Holes   147
Scientist Believers   148
Truth at the British Museum   148
Fraudulent Museum Displays   149

8. The Conversion of Charles Darwin:
The Evidence Some Seek to Hide   151
Testimonies to Darwin's Conversion   152
A Horror of Alcoholism   153
Lady Hope's Report   154
Details Confirmed   155
Darwin's Revival Meetings   156
Fegan's Orphan Boys   157
Darwin's Second Thoughts   157
Darwin and the Occult   159
The Wedgwood Potter's Vessel   161
Darwin's Support for Christian Missionaries   162

9. The Garden of Eden:
The Origin of Farming   165
Where Was the Garden of Eden?   165
How we Know that Farming Started Here   166
The Spread of Farming   167
Moses Gets it Right   167
An Answer to Doubters of Eden's Location   169
World Conference of Prehistoric Archaeologists   169
Adam's Dry Farming   171
Eden's Granaries   174
How Did Farming Begin?   174
Surprise in Denmark   178
Man's First Friend   178
They Came From Eden   1809
The Uniqueness of Human Speech   182
The Ecology of Eden   183

Evidence for the Dispersal of Farming from Eden   183
What about the Americas?   184
Leguminous Plants   185
God's Story Unfolds   186

10. Evidence for 'The Fall':
The Purpose of Animal Sacrifice   188
An Age of Innocence and Belief in One God   188
The Consequences of the Fall Become Evident   189
The World Views of Primitive People   189
Mistaken Scientists with no Experience of Fieldwork   189
Atheists Feel Need of Religion   190
Anthropology Supports the Bible   191
Fieldwork Evidence for Primitive Belief in One God   191
Returning to God   192
Expulsion from Eden   193
Farmers Migrate from Eden   194
The First Wave of Peaceful Farmers   194
Evidence of First Lamb Sacrifices for Fallen People   196
The Spread of Domesticated Animals from Eden   196
European Farmers Follow in the Steps of Abel   197
The Mystery of Cain's Rejection   198
Origin of Primitive Sacrifice   198
The Eastward Migration   199
Worldwide Degeneration   199

11. Cain's City and Culture:
The Bible and Cultural Evidence   202
A New Stone Age City   202
Neolithic Refuse Collectors   204
A Great Trading City   205
Roof-top Highways   206
Early Farming Development   207
Cain's Wife   210
Wall Paintings and Women's Dress   210
Jubal's Pipes and Harps   211
The Technological Succession in Genesis   211
The Genesis Cultural Succession   212
What Lessons Can we Learn?   212
Unlikely Items in the Bible, but Proved Later by Science 213

12. Noah's Flood:
The Bible and Science Agree   215
What Caused the Flood?   215
The Earth's Inner Core   217
Oceans Rush over Continents   217
The Evidence of Paleomagnetism   218
The Old Axis   218

The Mysterious Core   220
How the Earth's Crust Separated from the Core   220
How the Axis Change Caused the Flood   222
Evidence of New Sea Levels   223
The Changes in Global Features   225
The Angle of the Coral Beds   225
The Mountain Range Angle   225
Bible Clues   226
Frozen Mammoths   226
Different Sun Rise   227
Ancient Nations Give Evidence   227
Conclusion: Science Vindicates Noah   229
A Word of Caution   229

13. Worldwide Evidence of the Flood:
Scientific Facts Agree on an Axis Change   232
Mystery of the Mammoths   232
Pre-Flood Animals in North America   233
Worldwide Disappearance of Life   236
'Dirty Shame' Site Examined   237
Fort Rock, Oregon   237
The Mysteries of South America   238
Tiahuanaco of the Andes   239
Extensive Agriculture and a Sea Port   242
Changes in Climate and Calendar   242
Axis Change Adds more Days to the Year   243
Post-Flood Mathematicians   243
Noah's Calendar   244
Calendars Throughout the World   244
Conclusive Evidence   245

14. Unravelling the Ancient Records:
Tablets and Cultural Clues Give Evidence   247
The Flood Beyond Doubt   247
The Akkadian Tablets   250
Genesis: the Original Version   251
Mythology versus Reality   252
The Danger of Subjective Theories   252
Words Uncover the Truth   253
A Ship's Log Book and Ancient Song Writers   254
A Complete Record of Events   254
The Chronology of the Flood   256
Agatha Christie Clue at Nineveh   257
Conclusion: a Perfect Correlation   259

15. Repopulation of the Earth after the Flood:
Evidence in the Middle East and Europe   261
Migration from Ararat to Iraq and Babel   261

Ubaidians After the Flood   263
Post-Flood Pottery   263
Pre- and Post-Flood Soundings in Mesopotamia   265
Evidence of Metallurgical Progress   267
Cultural Succession and Hiatus: the Real Clues   267
Building Sites Before and After the Flood   268
Egypt After the Flood   269
Sequence of Cultural Phases in Egypt   270
A Fundamental and Abrupt Change   271
Mesopotamian Influence and Egyptian Ingenuity   272
The Flood Solves Scientist's Problems   273
Skulls Change in Egypt   273
The Flood Hiatus in Europe and Elsewhere   273
Deposits at Shippea Hill, Cambs.   274

16. The Tower of Babel and Nimrod:
Further Evidence in Mesopotamia   277
Ambitious Building Projects   277
Mysterious Destruction of the Tower of Babel   278
Reed Boat and Basket Builders   281
The Greatest Sports Hero of Old   281
Excavation of the Ziggurat Site   282
'Chariots of Fire'   284
Mesopotamian Town Planning   285
A Trader Sends His Delivery Bill to Sodom   286
The Copper Stone Age Ice Man   286
A New Start in Europe   287
A Five-Thousand-Year-Old Haircut   287
The Importance of Incidentals   288
Correlation of Genesis with Archaeology and Culture Sequences   288
The Religious Significance of Such Remarkable Records   290
Agonising Questions   290
The Supreme Demonstration   291

17. The Bible Speaks for Itself (1):
Understanding the Torah   293
The Influence of Attitudes   293
The Five Books of Moses   293
The Old Testament Writings   294
The Authorship of Moses   295
Archaeologists Teach Wayward Theologians a Lesson   297
Theories of Primitive Religion   298
Wide of the Mark   298
An Israeli Scholar Points to the Truth   300
Exciting Discoveries of the Ebla Tablets   300
God's Direct Message to Moses   302
The Siloam Inscription   302
Samaritan Clue Supports Authorship of Moses   303

18. The Bible Speaks for Itself (2):
The Prophets and the Sacred Writings   306
Contemporary Writers   306
The Bible and Israel's Secular Records   307
The Latter Prophets   308
Were there Two Isaiahs?   309
The Unity of Isaiah   309
Were Daniel's Predictions a Fraud?   311
Daniel's Choice of Language   311
The Seventy Weeks   312
The Four Empires   312
'For Ever Learning But Never Understanding'   313
Jeremiah – the Greatest!   313
The Sacred Writings   314
David's Royal House   315
Summary of Human Authors of the Old Testament   316

Conclusion   318
Subtle Deceptions   318
He Was Taught Criticism   319
Guidelines for Truth   320

LIST OF ILLUSTRATIONS

Fig. 1.1	The original super-continent	31
Fig. 2.1	The Big Bang theory	43
Fig. 2.2	Ripples of matter in space	46
Fig. 2.3	Varieties of Quark	52
Fig. 3.1	The Milky Way Galaxy	65
Fig. 5.1	Human genome	98
Fig. 5.2	Machinery in our cells	103
Fig. 5.3	The cell's automated factory	105
Fig. 6.1	Fossil record of life	117
Fig. 6.2	Row of stooping 'apes'	125
Fig. 6.3	The overlap effect	128
Fig. 6.4	Reversed fossil order	128
Fig. 7.1	The bat	138
Fig. 7.2	Trilobites	142
Fig. 8.1	Down House	156
Fig. 8.2	Cartoon of Charles Darwin	158
Fig. 8.3	Collection of adverse opinions	160
Fig. 9.1	The Mountain of Ararat	166
Fig. 9.2	The headwaters of four rivers	170
Fig. 9.3	Neolithic dry farming	172
Fig. 9.4	Wild grasses of the Mid-East	175
Fig. 9.5	The tools Adam used	177
Fig. 9.6	Photographs of tree-felling	179
Fig. 9.7	Skeleton of a Neolithic dog	181
Fig. 11.1	Room in Catal Huyuk	203
Fig. 11.2 (a)	Oldest example of textile	204
Fig. 11.2 (b)	Berber woman spinning	204
Fig. 11.3	Hatchway at Çatal Hüyük	207
Fig. 11.4	Çatal Hüyük: 5th layer	208
Fig. 11.5	Archaeological remains of wheat	209
Fig. 12.1	Ancient Chinese compass	216
Fig. 12.2	The dynamo of the earth	221
Fig. 12.3	Diagram of magnetic axis	224
Fig. 12.4	Inclination of natural features	226
Fig. 12.5	Twentieth-century BC cylinder	228
Fig. 13.1	Mammoth from Siberia	233
Fig. 13.2	Newspaper record of mammoths	235
Fig. 13.3	Oblique diagram of stratigraphy	238
Fig. 13.4	Elevated parts in the Andes	240
Fig. 13.5	Elevation of monolithic gate	241
Fig. 14.1	Record keeping 5,000 yrs ago	248
Fig. 14.2	The Tartaria tablets	255
Fig. 14.3	Cave strata in the Mid-East	258
Fig. 15.1	Racial family tree	262
Fig. 15.2	Pottery before and after Flood	264
Fig. 15.3	Deposits at Shippea Hill	275
Fig. 16.1	Ziggurat in Mesopotamia	278
Fig. 16.2	King Djoser of Egypt	279
Fig. 16.3	The stepped pyramid	280
Fig. 16.4	Ubaidians after the Flood	283
Fig. 16.5	'Nimrod's palette'	285
Fig. 17.1	Egyptian murals	296

THE PRINCIPLES BEHIND THIS SERIES

THERE IS MORE EVIDENCE today that the Bible is true and accurate than ever before, but the facts have been denied to the public and even to many church people. Evidence and the Bible text have convinced Dr Pearce that the Bible is true from the beginning. It is his purpose to reveal all the undeniable facts:

• That the Creator of the world is also the Author of the Word. He fully inspired all the 41 writers of the Bible who contributed to the sacred Scriptures over a span of 1,500 years. This is the only explanation of the accuracy and cohesion of the Bible.
• That the message in the Bible concerning spiritual truth is true, as is also its history, prophecy and science. All are completely true, reliable and factual. This has been confirmed by research.
• That those who doubt, do so because they do not have the facts, or do not wish to have them or believe them.

Those who have attended the author's lectures have included atheists and agnostics who thought that they had explained everything without God, but as a result of his teaching, have become convinced and converted and blessed.

Dr Pearce has made it possible to explain science, archaeology, and prophecy in simple ways which thrill the student.

• Psalm 119:160 'Your Word is true from the beginning.'
• Psalm 119:18 'Open my eyes that I may see wonderful things out of your law.'
• Psalm 119:42 'Then I shall have an answer for him who taunts me.'
• 1 Peter 3:15 'Be ready to give an answer to everyone who asks you for a reason for the hope that is in you.'

The Creator is seen in his works and has spoken in his Word.

ABOUT THE AUTHOR

DR VICTOR PEARCE had factory experience as an apprentice and later as a personnel officer and so knows the type of discussion typical of the factory floor and in the office. His experience as a teacher in comprehensive and grammar schools, also his training and lecturing in universities, gives him additional insight to academic views on science, theology, anthropology and philosophy. He became an honours graduate of London University in anthropology, through University College, then specialised at Oxford in prehistoric archaeology. He travelled for archaeological digs and research around the Mediterranean including Turkey and The Levant and also in the USA. He read theology at the London College of Divinity; is a Prebendary of Lichfield Cathedral; was Rector of one of the largest Anglican parishes in England; has had 25 curates, built two churches and several halls (one by voluntary labour). He was a member of the Diocesan Synod; was chairman of an *ad hoc* committee of the Education Council for a new religious syllabus and a visiting lecturer in two Bible colleges. Because this combination of skills with geology and fieldwork is unusual, Victor Pearce is able to offer a unique ministry. He has been much used of God in the conversion of atheists and agnostics who become surprised and fascinated by the facts which previously had been denied them.

He is author of *Who was Adam?*, *Origin of Man*, *The Science of Man and Genesis* and a contributor to the *Dictionary of the Church* and writes in various periodicals. He has lectured on evidences for biblical truth in university unions and schools. He was a broadcaster for Hour of Revival and Transworld Radio for 18 years and now broadcasts daily throughout Europe for United Christian Broadcasters. His main subject is the accuracy of the Bible as corroborated by the science of man (anthropology) and archaeology.

PREFACE TO THE FIRST EDITION
WHAT THIS COULD DO FOR YOU

LET ME ASSURE YOU from the outset that there is abundant evidence available which can establish you in a triumphant faith in God and help you to convey it to others. In this series, I recount **evidence for truth** from science, archaeology and fulfilled prophecy and relate this evidence to the Bible in considerable detail.

In Volume 1, I consider the abundant evidence of **science** in relation to Scripture. There is much scientific background in the Bible which can only be accounted for if the author of the Bible is the Creator of the universe. In speaking of science, I mean that science which has general consensus of agreement arising out of empirical investigation, not changing theories. I give many examples.

Likewise, **archaeology** has confirmed that all the written history in the Bible is true, accurate and factual. Tablets, mounds and pottery dug up from past civilisations confirm this, especially when the Bible dates for events are accepted. All this is covered in Volume 2.

Above all, the Bible contains the **prophecies** by God of future history right from the beginning. God foretells to the prophets at each stage all that is to happen and why and all that will happen. In this way, God proves that he is unfolding a remarkable plan for the future happiness of the world and for you. This plan could have unfolded without suffering had not mankind rebelled against God, but now, even by suffering, especially that of Jesus Christ, those purposes will be fulfilled. In Volume 3, we discover the evidence for Bible prophecy past, present and future.

The facts which will be brought before you can give you a firm, practical faith to face life and to convince friends.

Victor Pearce
Kidsgrove, England, 1993

PREFACE TO THE SECOND EDITION

All three books in the *Evidence for Truth* series quickly sold out in their first printing and a deluge of requests for reprinting followed. I rejoice in the opportunity of this revised text published by Eagle which has been endorsed by my co-directors at United Christian Broadcasters. It now means that many more people will have access to true facts to counter sceptical propaganda about the origins and destiny of mankind which assails the public. Also, it gives me the opportunity to add further information.

Concerning creation, this volume on science informs you that scientists discovered evidence through their improved radio telescopes that, right from the beginning of the universe, the creation of man was the central objective. Stephen Hawking in a TV series acknowledges this. I quote from his book *A Brief History of Time* (OUP, 1993, p 127):

> The initial state of the universe must have been very carefully chosen indeed if the hot big bang model was correct at the beginning of time. It would be very difficult to explain why the universe should have begun in just this way, except as an act of a God who intended to create beings like us.

Meanwhile, more and more books by scientists are questioning Darwin's Evolution Theory and what others deduced from it. Darwin knew nothing about genetics or the DNA code and so made wrong assumptions. Because of what others (including theologians) came to believe, Darwin died distressed by the way the Church and the world in general 'made a religion' of his 'unformed ideas'.

Concerning the Flood, spectacular discoveries have been reported in *New Scientist*. There is more water under the earth and in its interior than there is in all the oceans, and these 'waters of the deep' could cover all the continents if they burst out. Compare Genesis 7:11, 'All the fountains of the great deep burst forth'.

Concerning genetic engineering, I make reference to my predictions in 1967 which stated the feasibility of cloning as demonstrated 30 years later in Dolly the sheep clone. This gives insight to God's cloning of Adam when he created Eve 'bone from bone, flesh from flesh'.

I present here my first volume of authenticated evidence in the fields of science, archaeology and biblical prophecy. It is a compilation of 60 years of study, research and on-site investigation and is presented in simple English, enabling the general public to judge for themselves the *Evidence for Truth*.

Victor Pearce, Kidsgrove, January 1998

FOREWORD

From: Kenneth Kitchen
Professor of Egyptology in the School of Archaeology
& Oriental Studies, University of Liverpool

It gives me great pleasure to commend to you these writings of Dr Victor Pearce. I share his concern that scientific and archaeological research is not getting through to young people in schools and colleges. Particularly all the evidence supporting the reliability of the Bible.

In some circles there even seems to be a deliberate withholding of such information, yet, it is the fruits of leading scholars. The late F. F. Bruce was internationally acclaimed as a fair-minded scholar of the first rank and president of leading learned societies. Professor D. Wiseman is an Assyriologist and Semitist of international standing, likewise such colleagues as Professor Alan Millard and Dr Terence Mitchell, formerly of the British Museum. These men are known for their restrained, moderate, factual presentation of their researches, as indeed Victor himself is in his books and lectures among us. Victor has brought his own special area of research to bear upon the Bible accounts, namely anthropology and prehistoric archaeology.

Victor refers to me in his works. For myself I have gone for facts not party opinions. Consequently, as does Victor, I have gone for source material and translated from tablets written thousands of years even before Christ: Hittite, Elamite, Sumerian, Aramaic, Egyptian, Ugaritic, Akkadian and Eblaite.

Yet many critics ignore most of this evidence which establishes the accuracy of the Bible text, and sadly it is neglected in many certificate courses sanctioned by some of the mainstream churches. Victor has given us the fruits of his own researches which have taken him into many universities, museums, laboratories and archaeological sites in many parts of the world. This has enabled him to contribute original source material himself.

I encourage you to read thoroughly every page which has flowed from his pen – a distillation of years of work in this field. Do not discount the simpler bits nor baulk at the technical pieces: allow this work to purge out the deceits and suppositions that may have settled in your mind over the years regarding the world's view of such fundamentals as creation, the Fall and the Flood and other episodes in the biblical narratives. While there is room for more than one opinion at various points, the overall trend is clear.

INTRODUCTION

SCIENTIFIC DISCOVERIES ANTICIPATED IN THE BIBLE

Welcome to this series *Evidence for Truth*. Today, Christian truth is essential from every viewpoint. Young people are taught so much unbelief and older folk hear the faith attacked through the media: and yet there is more evidence for Biblical Truth than there ever has been; but it has been kept from the public.

Hundreds of letters addressed to me during my years of broadcasting, often from young people and their parents, testify to the need for *Evidence for Truth*. The general public need to have the facts which have been denied them. It was this expression of deep need which made me see that this series must be prepared. Just a few quotations from these letters will suffice:

- 'Can you help me in answering folk in a concise way about Genesis? The Bible says that God created the world . . . but science says the world and animals came from evolution. Please explain.'
- 'I have been a Christian for three years and would like to know more of the Bible truths to do with creation and evolution.'
- 'If only the evidence you present had been available when I was 15, perhaps I would have stayed firm in my faith. I've spent 18 years re-finding the Lord.'
- 'I've been a Christian for two years and the programmes by Victor Pearce have opened my eyes to how much anti-biblical theories I used to believe and accept as fact, especially that which I was taught at school. And now I find the science which I thought disproved the Bible only strengthens the dynamic fact that God created the heavens and the earth and everything in it.'
- 'Your [information on] science and prophecy were very, very valuable, enabling me to answer many questions from non-believers.'
- 'Your subject of 'Human life and genetics' was really exciting. I am a biologist.'
- 'Dr Pearce has, from his tremendous experience in the scientific and archaeological field, helped me to examine the Bible teaching and explain it.'

Fortunately, my training in the sciences at the universities and research in various countries over many years have given me facts which can establish your faith in Christ and in the Bible and at the same time fill your life with blessing. So often, when I have given talks to house groups, schools, colleges and larger meetings, people have been fascinated and filled with joy on hearing facts to support their faith.

The evidence for God's truth which I reveal to the reader is not just to support the Bible in the light of today's knowledge – the Bible stands alone on its own merits and does not require support in that way. It is to reveal truth which answers genuine queries from knowledgeable young people and their parents and teachers. At the same time, it counteracts false teachings accepted by three or more generations of churchgoers and clergy who readily believe media stories about evolution and fossil remains.

THE CONCEPT OF THIS SERIES

In this series, the evidence for truth will be given from science, archaeology and Bible prophecy. The information will be explained simply with the Lord's help. You don't have to be clever to understand, but if you are knowledgeable in these areas, your understanding will be enhanced. The Lord Jesus himself said, 'Thank you Father, Lord of heaven and earth, because you have hidden these things from the philosopher and intelligent, and revealed them to babes' (Matt 11:25).

Concerning **prophecy** (Volume 3), Jesus Christ was able to go through all the Old Testament and show all that was prophesied concerning himself had been fulfilled or would be fulfilled. This substantiated his claims.

Concerning **archaeology** (Volume 2), if you follow the Bible's dates for events, you find that everything fits in as impressive evidence for scriptural accuracy. This is an effective answer to media misrepresentations.

Concerning anthropology, **the science of man** (this book), I have had special training and bring you information not often available in one binding to give answers to those questions you may have asked which dispel wrong ideas promoted by the media and even the Church.

I find there is no contradiction between true science and the Bible because the author is the same, i.e. the Creator, who fully inspired the Bible. This is why we find the Bible is true and accurate from beginning to end.

OBJECTIVES OF THIS BOOK

I find the most effective way to give evidence to a doubter is to use what science already accepts in the order of creation, then reveal that this correlates with Genesis chapter 1. This then prompts the question: 'How did it get into the Bible in a non-scientific age unless God revealed it?'

I quote scientists to show how new facts are bringing leading scientists back to accepting a Creator, and that science shows that mankind was the object of his creation. Scientists call this the **'Anthropic Principle'**.

I then deal with the question of timing in the creation process. The data concerning several fashions of application are set out and show that the correlation of creation in both science and the Bible is not diminished by the time factor.

I then show that the order and nature of life-forms was the result of God's instructions in the DNA code of life, an astonishing new science which demonstrates that, as Genesis says, each new order of life was the result of God's words – the chromosomes and genes recorded them. We go on to outline the basics of all forms of life cells and show that the agnostic is faced with severe unanswerable problems if he maintains that there was no Creator.

I demonstrate how to analyse critically the many nature programmes on television and expose the plausible explanations which are substituted for the proper scientific method. This is to give you effective answers for your friends who discuss with you the overt nature of media promotion of evolution, particularly on TV.

We also look at fossil evidence for creation and the evidence against evolution which was even admitted by Darwin and whose principles now actually argue for creation.

Darwin's Alarm and the Evidence of his Conversion

Many books on Charles Darwin usually omit what gave rise to his alarm at the misuse made of his theory. That alarm has been fully justified.

I give in Chapter 8 the evidence, from many sources, of Darwin's conversion to Christ. Why? Because many are out to deny it. This reveals that they feel the impact of its implications, especially since his favourite book was Hebrews in the New Testament.

We discuss the evidence which my training as an anthropologist has given, for the Garden of Eden and its location given in Genesis chapter 2, and confirmed by leading scientists.

Further on in the book, we show the effect of the Fall (into sin) on faith and social order portrayed in the Bible and proved correct by field research. Anthropology finds that religion did not evolve. It degenerated from the original revelation of the Creator God.

Then we look at the abundant worldwide evidence for Noah's Flood and the probable method God used to bring it about. The new paleomagnetic sciences help here.

We show how life developed after the Flood from all the scientific evidence available today and consider the way the Bible speaks for itself in support of all this evidence.

Wellhausen (1844-1918): the Darwin of Theology

Before closing this Introduction, there is a further related matter I must deal with briefly.

Although there can be no question as to the reality of Darwin's conversion at the end of his life, unfortunately this did not alter the enormous damage done by his Theory of Evolution (*Origin of Species*, published in 1859). It not only affected people's attitude to the origin of life – becoming the greatest stumbling-block to belief in the Creator, but it also affected the way many theologians went about interpreting the Bible.

The greatest damage done by Darwin's theories was that it caused many theologians to reinterpret the Bible in an evolutionary way. Religion, too, must also have evolved, they thought, so Wellhausen reshuffled the Old Testament to make it an evolutionary picture.

It is strange that many theologians hang on to this concept, ignoring the later evidence from archaeology and anthropology. I shall be able to share with you the fruits of information my researches have gleaned from many of the world's most scholarly archaeologists and anthropologists. The closing chapters show that the weight of evidence fully supports the Mosaic authorship of the Pentateuch and the accuracy of the gospel accounts of the life of the Lord Jesus.

Wellhausen claimed that God could not have spoken to Abraham in 2000 BC – as Genesis says – because the Abraham stories could not have been written until religion had 'evolved' into monotheism many centuries later. Because of this, he argued, Abraham must have been an animist worshipping sticks and stones. Likewise, Moses could not have introduced the advanced priestly system, so Leviticus must have been written a thousand years after Moses, in about 400 BC! The Bible, critics say, was therefore man's idea about God, not God's revelation of himself to the prophets, as claimed in Scripture. Therefore, they continue, the early chapters of Genesis were myths and folklore derived from Babylon.

This attitude is still featured on TV and attempts to reply have been blocked. We shall see in due course that not only is Genesis scientific, it is the original pure account and that it is the Babylonian versions that were idolatrous corruptions of the truth.

The Death of Faith

R. K. Harrison says the critics, 'went so far as to reconstruct the history of the Israelites on to what amounted to an evolutionary pattern. Wellhausen . . . adopted the evolutionary concept . . . when the intellectual climate was dominated by theories of evolution.' Wellhausen played a similar role in destructive criticism of the Bible that Darwin unwittingly played to destroy faith in the Creator.

The result for Wellhausen was to be that for many since. 'Before his death, in 1918, Wellhausen conceded that the rationalism that he had embraced so avidly in earlier years had made havoc of his own faith in the authority and authenticity of the Old Testament' (R. K. Harrison, *Introduction to the Old Testament*, IVP).

Unfortunately, Wellhausen's theories are still pressed upon theological students and there is an amazing intolerance of any who would dispute the theory or if the discoveries of archaeology and anthropology are used to show that the literary methods of the Ancient Near East are quite contrary to Wellhausen's theories. In fact, Harrison says that 'a close watch was made to keep out from academic posts in universities or theological colleges any scholars who did not teach the Wellhausen theory'. That is also true of many of the older established churches which press this destructive criticism upon its lay reader's courses.

Truly, St Paul prophesied that 'the time will come when they will not endure sound doctrine . . . they shall turn away their ears from the truth and turn to myths'. This is why this text is so necessary for you to follow. A. H. Sayce began at Oxford as an enthusiastic supporter of Wellhausen but, when he became an archaeologist, he changed to a distinguished champion of the Bible's truth and accuracy.

As I wrote in my book, *Origin of the Bible*, archaeology has contradicted Wellhausen's assumptions by revealing that all the cultural background and customs of 2000 to 1500 BC are faithfully portrayed in the five books of Moses. A later writer could not have known of them. The Bible presents that God revealed himself, at the outset, as the one true Creator and that belief in many gods was a corruption which came later.

Jesus himself indicated that the errors of the Sadducees would come into the Church. 'Beware of the yeast of the Pharisees and Sadducees' (Matt 16:6). The disciples understood that he warned them of their teachings.

What did the Sadducees teach? It was that miracles were impossible, that there was no resurrection. Wellhausen's assumptions were similar; therefore he reasoned that Moses' miracles must be myths and Christ's healings hallucinations. Christ's correction to the Sadducees is the appropriate one for Wellhausen and his followers: 'You do not understand the scriptures or the power of God' (Matt 22:29). 'Had you believed Moses' writings, you would have believed me' (John 5:46).

So we see the damage Darwin's evolution theory inflicted on sound faith in the Bible. Sadly, his conversion in later life could not undo what was already done.

Scientists Return to Biblical Concepts

Had Darwin, with his new-found faith, lived today, he would have welcomed the news that scientists were revising their theories of origins. This is revealed by Richard Leakey who has given many a scientific programme on television from an agnostic viewpoint, yet in his book *Origins Reconsidered* (L. Brown & Co, 1992), he sums up the drift of opinion among scientists towards biblical concepts. He says that they are divided in opinion between a Garden of Eden origin and a Noah's Ark replacement model. Those who advocate the former are called 'The Gardeners' and those favouring the latter 'The Sons'. It is an attempt to explain why the human race falls into distinct groups, and yet has only one origin, according to gene frequencies. Leakey sums up in the following words: 'My anthro-geological colleagues are equally divided in their assessment of the fossil record, half supporting a form of regional model, half a form of the Noah's Ark Hypothesis.' Then he quotes the *San Francisco Chronicle*'s heading: 'The Mother of us All – a Scientist's Theory' which refers to Eve as the one source of the human race.

To understand why Eve's name has been married to such a high-sounding appellation is explained in my chapter on the cell's mechanism. Scientists are now saying that Genesis 2:21–23 is a perfectly scientific account of how God cloned a woman from a body cell in Adam's rib marrow, allowing the reproduction of the human race to take place.

But let's start at the beginning . . .

1 CORRELATION OF GENESIS 1 AND SCIENCE
COSMIC ORIGIN OF LIFE

Many people are often ready to chat about popular science, especially that which has appeared in the media. Therefore it is very useful if one has a few interesting answers ready. This may open up curiosity on more important issues which they would otherwise avoid. This book will provide you with many answers and, if you can remember only a few, it will help you to make interesting and helpful conversation. The summary at the end of each chapter will help you to recall the salient points.

Many will question you about issues in the first twelve chapters of Genesis. Let us start with chapter 1, which records how God created the universe and all the living matter which supports mankind on Planet Earth.

Q How are you to help a person believe that Genesis 1 was given by the Creator?

I have found that it is more effective to be positive. It helps someone to believe the chapter by pointing out its remarkable correlation with science.

Many doubters have been surprised when I have shown them the British Museum book, *The Succession of Life Through Geological Time*, by Oakley and Muir-Wood. I've put the chapter and verses of Genesis down the margin of this science book. They see that the order of events are the same. Green vegetation to **supply oxygen**, life in the waters, land animals and finally man (see my detailed correlation at the end of this chapter).

Dr Rendle Short made this comment in his book, *Modern Discovery and the Bible*:

These considerations bring to light a perfectly amazing accordance between the Creation narrative and the discoveries of modern science. When we remember the wild guesses as to the ultimate nature and origin of the earth that were current amongst other ancient people, the accuracy of Genesis stands out in solitary grandeur. Geology is a young science; the classification of strata is not much older than a hundred years; we may be sure the author of the Creation narrative derived none of his information from fossil hunting. Neither guesswork nor intuition taught the writer to arrange events in the correct order. This narrative bears the marks of a divine inspiration.

A doubter may try to avoid the force of your case by bringing in a point of contention, just as the woman of Samaria did when she debated with Jesus in John 4:19,20, but don't be side-tracked on to some favourite topic of yours, such as how long ago creation took place. The Bible gives no dates, but says 'In the beginning'. We are told not to add to God's Word, but some have tried to add dates.

With a non-Christian whose schooling has been mainly sceptical, the evidence for truth loses credence with him if he is pressed for certain interpretations. If I see that a person has been brainwashed on the evolution question, I do not tell him that I find that the fossil record does not support it. Not to begin with anyway. Why? Because he has seen the museums, seen TV nature programmes, had it in school and for just little ol' you or me to say it's untrue would probably remove any desire he may have to listen further. No, I first get him convinced on things he already consents to. So let's start!

THE ORDER OF LIFE

A number of atheists and agnostics have been won to faith and then to Christ by being shown the correlation of Genesis 1 with science. It is worth doing this. Some controversial questions need not be touched at this stage.

It is sufficiently impressive that **the order of life's appearance** on earth is similar between the Bible and the evidence of science, namely: Genesis sets it out simply, starting with matter, light, then with green things, then marine creatures, next the land animals and, finally, man.

Let's look at that in more detail. Why did 'green things' come first? Science says that green algae were necessary first to produce oxygen for the air so that creatures could breathe.

Next in the Bible order is life in the waters. Science has found that marine creatures of about eleven classifications appear at this time. Then the Bible refers to very large sea creatures.

Both science and the Bible put land animals next. School children get very excited about the amphibians, especially with the huge towering dinosaurs.

The Climax of Creation

Finally, God creates man in his own image. Science finds that man is last to appear on the earth. There is much argument about man's origin and, as an anthropologist, I have investigated the various theories, but no one is able to deny that he is last on the scene and that both Bible and science agree. They also agree that no new species have appeared since and the Bible tells you that God rested from making anything else after he made man. In fact, Hebrews chapter 4 tells you that he still rests and uses the fact to invite you into a spiritual rest of faith in the finished work of Christ for your salvation. That God still 'rests' is an interesting application of the fact that there is no statement in Genesis to say that 'day seven' – God's rest from creation – has ended.

The Method by which Genesis 1 is Set Out

The order in which life appears is similar to the order of occurrence of fossils in the rock strata. But it is important to note that, when each order of life is mentioned, the whole succeeding history of that order is then included. This is similar to many science summaries. They give a column to plant life, but starting with green algae. They give a column to marine invertebrates (non-backboned), then a column to marine vertebrates (with backbone), from the first fishes to the amphibians. Then a column to land animals from the first to the last. Then there is a column for the mammals from first to last and finally man.

Thus, Genesis 1:11 says, 'Let the earth bring forth greenness' (*deshe* = green matter, referring to chloroplasts to put oxygen into the air – algae being the first). But then the succeeding column of plant life is given as 'seed-bearing herbs, trees, propagating by seeds'. This refers to the two main plant groups. First were the non-flowering ferns and mosses (cryptograms) and then there came the flowering plants and trees (phanerograms) with their varying seed-bearing methods, like the naked seeds of the Devonian and Carboniferous pines and cyads.

Likewise, the marine life was created next. This starts in verse 20 with 'swarms and swarms of small creeping things'. The original Hebrew word '*sherets*' aptly describes the trilobites, molluscs and other non-backboned marine life, which appeared suddenly in great swarms and have left their fossils in thick strata. This is in great contrast to the absence of life and fossils in the rock bed below them. This made Darwin admit that it looked more like sudden creation (*Origin of Species*, chap 10, pp 305, 308). The Genesis 1 marine column then describes later marine life (v 21), with large sea monsters called Tannim, which could include the dinosaurs. Winged creatures are next mentioned according to their various kinds which would include insects, winged reptiles, birds and bats, all of different phyla or kind, i.e. 'every winged creature according to its kind'.

Next came the land animals (v 24), 'Let the earth bring forth . . .' (v 25) animals in general, mammals and creepy-crawlies (*rames*). Finally, man, created in God's image.

THE PHYSICAL ORDER

The first physical event in Genesis is God's command, 'Let there be light'. Such a concept was contrary to primitive ideas, and the casual observer today sometimes remarks that this sequence of events seems unlikely. Yet science agrees that the intense visible radiation that was present at the beginning of the universe is in accord with God's command, 'Let there be light'. So we see that those words in Genesis were given by the Creator himself.

In order to make the text in this book easy for you to read, some will be in the style I use in my broadcasts. Over the years, many have written to ask for these scripts so that they can have this information to hand. This fruit of years of research is now being made available for you. I want you to feel that you are in personal contact with me, so when the script is in question-and-answer style, you may put yourself in the place of the questioner – even if the question is not one you would ask.

Here are some questions you might ask or get asked.

Q You say that there is a remarkable harmony between science and Genesis. How do I know that you aren't imagining it?

By comparing a secular scientist's book with the sacred Scriptures. If you correlate them page by page, you can see that the order of events is the same. As I said, I have written down in the margin of a science book the individual verses of Genesis chapter 1, because each event tells the same story.

Now Genesis chapter 1 was written 3,500 years ago, long before scientific knowledge. How is it that the Bible has the order of creation correct? The only explanation is that the Creator of scientific events is the same as the author of Genesis chapter 1.

Let's look at what science says on how things began, using this British Museum book *The Succession of Life Through Geological Time*. The book begins by stating that it is first dealing with the opening period, '. . . from the origin of the earth to the beginning of the Cambrian'. The Bible likewise sums up briefly the events before the days of creation as in verse 1. 'In the beginning, God created the heavens and the earth.'

The science book then says, 'The earth started . . . possibly as a whirling globe of hot gases. It passed through a liquid stage'. The Bible is similar. It reads: 'The earth was without form and void.'

The science book then says: 'For long ages the earth was surrounded by a thick, steamy atmosphere'; while the Bible states: 'And darkness was upon the face of the deep'. The envelope of vapours surrounding the earth brought darkness to the depths beneath it.

The science book then says: 'As soon as the surface became cool enough, the water vapour condensed as rain, producing rivers and seas'. This again harmonises with the Bible: 'God said, 'Let there be an expanse (atmosphere) in the middle of the waters and let it separate the waters from the waters,' so God made the atmosphere separate (by evaporation) the water clouds from the sea waters.

God said 'Let the waters be gathered into one place and let the dry land appear.' Science agrees. The original single continent is called Pangaea which then broke up into the individual continents we know today (see Fig 1.1).

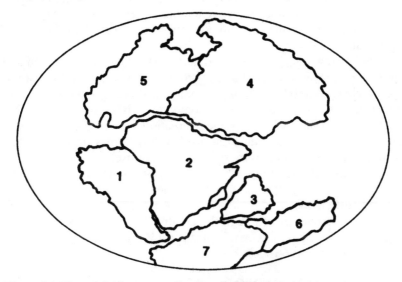

Figure 1.1. The original super-continent, called Pangaea
The continents have broken away and drifted apart to their present positions.
1. S. America 2. Africa 3. India 4. Eurasia 5. N. America 6. Australasia 7. Antarctica

The science book says: 'The atmosphere lacked oxygen . . . most of the free oxygen present in the air has been produced by the activities of green plant life'.

While the Bible continues: 'And God said, "Let the earth bring forth greenness." ' Note that the Hebrew word *deshe* should NOT be translated 'grass'. It means something green. Not surprisingly, the science book says, 'blue-green algae'.

That is remarkable harmony so far between science and the Bible, given by an unsolicited scientific source.

Atmosphere Clears

Another instance of this harmony is that science says that originally all the continents were joined together as one land mass. When you look at a globe, you can see how the continents fitted together like a jigsaw puzzle. Moses could not have had a spaceman's view of the earth and yet he wrote in Genesis chapter 1, 'And God said, "Let the waters . . . be gathered together into one place and let the dry land appear." '

Q The science book says that after the condensation of the thick, steamy atmosphere, the sky could be seen and the sun and the moon and the stars. Where does this fit in with Genesis?

The Bible places this in the fourth day of creation. 'Let there be lights in the sky . . . so God made two great lights . . . He made the stars also.' But does this mean that God did not create the sun until the fourth day of creation?

The Hebrew historic tense used here means that the sun, moon and stars were already created, but they could not be seen until the atmosphere cleared in the fourth day of creation. It is important to be clear about this. One man who was very dogmatic with his ideas told me that the mention of the sun at this stage in creation showed that the sun was created **after** the earth. But even a schoolboy knows differently, that man would bring unnecessary ridicule upon himself by saying that the sun was younger than the earth. As Professor Rendle-Short said, 'The record does not say that God now made the sun . . . but the clouds now cleared sufficiently to allow the sun, moon and stars to be seen from the earth's surface. All through the creation narrative, the observer is regarded as being on the earth's surface' (*Modern Discoveries in the Bible*, IVF, 1943, p 66).

THE BIOLOGICAL ORDER

Your questioner may want more details about the biological order. Our science book gives the next event, 'By the beginning of Cambrian times, a considerable variety of non-backboned creatures came in the seas . . . All the main divisions existed in the seas.' The seas filled with swarms of them.

The Bible states, in Genesis 1 verse 20: 'And God said, "Let the waters teem with swarms of living creatures." ' Those of us geologists who have chiselled out the fossils of this period, know how suddenly swarms of marine creatures of all kinds appear without the trace of any before them in the layers of rock below.

Q Doesn't that look like sudden creation rather than a gradual evolution?

Yes, all these creatures are complete and perfect. The trilobites for example, have jointed legs, breathing gills, articulated bodies and an advanced type of eye. Levi-Setti says (*Royal Anthropological Journal*), 'How such an advanced creature appears suddenly from nowhere, is a puzzle to the scientist.' He should have said that they are a puzzle only to any scientist who does not believe in the Creator, because there is a high percentage of scientists who acknowledge that a Creator is the only explanation.

Insects and Flowers

It is a pity that translations of Genesis chapter 1 are not done by Christians trained as scientists. A lot of wrong impressions would be avoided if they were. For example, Genesis 1:20 in some translations says, 'Let **birds** fly above the earth'. The Hebrew word does not say 'birds' but 'flying creatures'. This would refer to winged insects. In harmony with Genesis, their fossils appear at this period of Upper Carboniferous times.

The Hebrew word '*oph*' means 'to fly' and is used about insects as in Leviticus 11:23. This shows how the inspired Hebrew of so long ago is more accurate than a modern translation. Science shows that insects were the first flying creatures and appeared at this point.

It is remarkable how insects appear at the same time as pollen-bearing flowers (angio-sperms) in the geological record of fossils. One could not exist without the other for longer even than one summer. The British Museum pamphlet on the geological record remarks upon this. 'The spread of insects was probably associated with the appearance of flowers, for many flowers and insects are mutually dependent, the insects pollinating the flowers and being repaid by nectar.' They would have to appear at the same time or at least in the same season, yet the evolution theory depends on millions of years' development. How could two entirely different kingdoms of flora and fauna evolve separately, at exactly the right speed, so that they would both be ready to sustain each other at the very same moment in time?

Think of the miraculous mechanism of insects' wings beating hundreds of times a second at adjustable angles! It is impossible to say it was by chance. What a remarkable accident to happen in one season and just at the right moment for the arrival of a new kind of flower – the angio-sperms!

The Land Animals

Another instance of a misleading translation is in the Old English of verse 21. It speaks of whales. 'God created great whales'. Well whales are sea mammals. The Hebrew actually says, 'great sea monsters' (*tannim*) or 'great sea creatures' as in the New Kings James Version. And so we find the next thing our science book says is that land animals appeared. It says that geologists call this the New Life period. Why? Because a large number of new kinds of creatures start together. The Bible stated this quite clearly long before science did. On the sixth day of creation, in Genesis 1:24, it reads: 'God said, "Let the land bring forth the living creatures after its kind." '

Next, I read here, comes the age of the mammals, as our science book calls them. Does Genesis agree with that? Sure enough, Genesis says, 'Let the land bring forth cattle and creeping things and beasts of the earth according to their kinds'. You will notice that Genesis is fairly general in its terms. That is because it is very concise. When it speaks of cattle and beasts, it refers to all mammals, in general terms, speaking to a non-scientific age.

Now here comes a difficulty for Darwinism. The science book does not mention the Creator.

Q Ought the science book to have mentioned the Creator?

Yes, because whales and other sea mammals appear near the beginning of the age of mammals, not at the end, as an end product. If they were there by evolution, they would have needed many millions of years to have undergone such remarkable developments, but instead the sea mammals appear among the early mammals.

The Darwinians believe they must have started as mammals intended for the land, because they suckle their young at the breast. Mammals started life on land where breast feeding suited the environment, but to breast feed in water would be difficult and would need special, immediate readjustments. Also whales are air-breathing for land life, so the Darwinians suppose that this underwent a lot of adaptation for life under water. A vent hole would have to appear in the head 'by accident'. The legs of a mammal are meant for land, but would have to undergo a great change to become flippers. For whales, the body would have to grow into monstrous proportions and develop protective blubber. Sea mammals would have to be 'fitted' with valve-closing nostrils.

And for all this supposition, there is no fossil record, neither is there the time for such huge changes because their fossils appear soon after those of the land mammals. Also, whales themselves have so many different varieties. There are 14 different kinds. The balleen whale has a grill in front of its mouth because it eats only small fish and sprats. The Mediterranean cachalot whale has no such grill. It can swallow whole sharks, even people!

The Bible tells us that Jonah was swallowed by a 'big fish' in the Mediterranean, so it must have been a cachalot whale. Jesus refers to the special significance of Jonah's whale in connection with his resurrection. Mediterranean whales were created with the ability to swallow a man, and in the stomach to have plenty of air for the man to breathe, although it was extremely hot air.

How do we know that the air is extremely hot? Because other men have been swallowed by this type of whale in modern times. Although it was very hot, they could breathe and they came out alive! The name of one was James Bartley. He was in a whale's stomach for a whole day. When they cut open the whale, he was still alive. He had plenty of air, he said, but it was so hot that it made him faint. But he came round all right when the seamen threw a bucket of cold sea water over him!

Modern Mammals

We come now to recent times, geologically speaking, and we discover that the science book tells us that our modern mammals are very recent. The farm animals and the domesticated animals are no older than man himself. This is the picture also in Genesis chapter 2.

Later on that same sixth day of creation, God said, 'Let us make man in our image . . . so God created man in his own image . . . male and female created he them'.

Q Victor, you are an anthropologist, so what about the many scientists who say that various types of human have been on earth for the last four million years?

Whether they are right or not does not alter the fact that mankind appeared last, just as Genesis 1 says. But the fascinating question you have raised is one I shall be discussing with you in succeeding chapters.

Three Basics Created

In this correlation of science and Scripture, other striking features emerge. No one could accuse Professor Julian Huxley, who is grandson of Darwin's great advocate, as biased towards Scripture, yet as an atheist, it was in all innocence that he made a statement about origins which illuminates our understanding of Genesis. He said that there were three basic phases required for the universe to come into being – the inorganic, the organic and the psycho-social. Huxley could not have guessed that he was supporting Scripture, where we also find three stages of creation.

When we make something, we usually obtain certain basic materials from which the product is put together. The word 'create', in Genesis 1, refers to such basic materials. It is the Hebrew word '*bara*'.

It is the only Hebrew word to mean 'create from nothing'.

This word *'bara'* is used in the text in connection with three origins. The first concerns the creation of **matter**, 'God created the heavens and the earth' (v 1). The second concerns the origin of **living creatures**, 'And God said "Let the waters teem with living creatures" ' (vv 20, 21). The third is of the origin of man's **spiritual** nature, 'God created man in his own image and man became a living soul' (chapter 1, v 27 and chapter 2, v 7).

Thus God's basics, matter, life and soul, match Huxley's requirements of inorganic, organic and psycho-social. Following the creation of these raw materials, so to speak, from nothing, a process is spoken of. It is from these three basics that God 'moulds', 'makes', 'forms' and 'brings forth'.

The DNA Genetic Life Code

When you have demonstrated that the order of events in creation is similar to that which science has discovered, you can then turn to the origin of that order. Genesis says that it was the result of God's speech (Genesis 1:1,6,9,11,14,20,24 and 26).

Each time God spoke, a new order of life resulted. The DNA genetic code now reveals that all life forms are a result of a code of instructions.

When God said, 'Let the earth bring forth greenness,' God put his instructions in the form of DNA codes into all plant cells. Now plant cells are more complicated than animals cells. Each cell contains 20 to 100 chloroplasts. Each chloroplast has about 45 sun traps. They are rather like house-top solar panels, to receive and convert the sun's rays into energy, absorb carbon dioxide, and then to give out oxygen into the air for animal life later. Each solar panel in the plant contains a green pigment called chlorophyll. This greenness soaks in the sun's energy. That is why God said, 'Let there be greenness'. So, contrary to evolution, the more complex systems come first. Animal cells don't have these complicated sun-converting panels. Yet, without that, animal life could not have started or survived.

Then God spoke again, 'Let the waters bring forth swarms of creatures which move.' So the first marine life is the result of God's creating words.

The next main order is also the result of God's speech: backboned fishes.

Then God again uses his 'language of life', as the scientists call it, and says, 'Let the land bring forth land animals and mammals'. The fossil record bears this out as my diagram shows (Fig 6.1). There are no evolutionary links between these main orders; it's only God's speech recorded in the DNA code which brings these main orders into being.

Finally, God said, 'Let us make man' with his own unique DNA coding.

The DNA code – a familiar expression throughout the media – is a most staggering discovery which is making many think again. It is the language of life. We will be discussing this in Chapter 5, but let me say that scientists now see that all life is the result of a language which is put in code form in our bodies and in all plant and animal life.

Dr F. Jacobs says in *What is Life?* (BBC Publications, 1968): 'Life is a language and a programme.' Dr George Beadle in *Language for Life*, (Gollancz, London, 1967) adds: 'It is as old as life itself. Its words are buried deep in the cell of our bodies . . . and of all plants and animals.'

Suddenly, this sparks meaning into a phrase in Genesis repeated between each act of creation: 'God said'. That expression occurs between each new order of life. This is why I believe that what God said is recorded in the DNA code of the cell of each plant, animal and human.

Supposing there is, in the room with you, a trained scientist, eminent in his field and an ardent believer in Darwin's theories, used to setting up and testing hypotheses in order to prove theories. Supposing he is convinced that he has proved that God does not exist. How would you help him to find God and lead him to trust in Christ for redemption?

As a trained scientist myself, I would welcome the opportunity. This is because he would know the scientific method and would be used to logical investigation.

It is because of this that there are now more scientists who are believers in God than those who are unbelievers.

Q That's surprising! I thought it was the other way round, that most scientists don't believe in God?

It is propaganda which gives the wrong idea. The famous scientist, Sir Bernard Lovell, did a survey and found that a huge majority of scientists thought that the evidence required a Creator. Actually, I have been able to bring a number of atheistic scientists into faith by presenting all the evidence we have today. With some, it has taken two years, with another, one year and, in some cases, quite quickly.

There was one scientist, who was a university biologist, who rang me on the phone to say he had read my book *Who Was Adam?* He explained that he had been an aggressive atheist for 40 years, but he knew my book was correct. He was converted without any more proof and asked if I would pray that his son would be converted. He was so sorry that he had misled him.

So, what about the scientist we mentioned who took two years to be convinced? He thought that he had explained everything without God – as in our question. I had to go through the evidence for creation and redemption step by step. He was very thorough. At last he said, 'I am convinced on all the points, but the next step is the most difficult for me – it is the step of faith. I have to take Jesus Christ as Saviour by faith'. He took two weeks over that and then he asked Jesus into his life and accepted the free gift of salvation. Immediately he knew Christ was real and that he was saved from his past sins.

Q Well, how do you set about helping scientists to a point of under-standing and salvation?

I show them that the order of events in Genesis chapter 1 is the same as that which they accept as a scientist. Then I show them that the next ten chapters show the exact same succession of cultures and civilisa-tion as the anthropologists have found.

Concerning Genesis chapter 1 itself, it is important to realise what the purpose of this section is. Although it correlates so remarkably with science, the object is not actually to teach science, so its details are selective.

What then is its purpose? Look at the clues! There is that repeated phrase after each act of creation: 'God saw that it was good'. We are told that six times and, to emphasise it, the summary at the end states: 'God saw everything that he had made and behold it was very good'.

This opening chapter of Genesis prepares the Bible's answer to the question: 'Why is there so much evil and cruelty on the earth?' Chap-ter 2 then tells you that everything, including the first man and woman, were created 'good' (and innocent), but the rest of the Bible reveals what spoilt it all; and how God undertook to remedy it; and how in the end 'God will make all things new, so write this down, for what I tell you is trustworthy and true' (Revelation 21:5). 'The glory and honour of all nations will be brought to God's throne. Nothing unclean will be permitted or anyone who practises immorality or dishonesty. And there will be healing for the nations', as it says in the last two chapters of the Bible.

How will this be brought about? My third volume *Evidence for Truth: Prophecy*, expounds the Bible's solution in its historic fulfil-ment in Jesus and in the coming glorious climax to which today's events are leading. So with these purposes in mind, the creation

CORRELATION OF SCIENCE AND SCRIPTURE

(By giving the order of events, we do not necessarily substantiate the timescale sometimes suggested.)

Science	*Genesis chapter 1*
Before the days of Creation	
The universe begins with the explosion of the primeval atom	'In the beginning God created the heavens and the earth' v 1
'Streams of light quanta from . . . the Big Bang' (Gamov) diffusing light protons throughout the universe	'Let there be light' v 3
Our galaxy begins to rotate	
Pre-Cambrian Eras	
Condensation into oceans and vapours above	2nd day of creation 'Let an expanse separate the waters from the waters
Early Pre-Cambrian Schists with rocks oxidised by chloroplasts and blue-green algae to put oxygen into the air	3rd day of creation land emerges v.9 'Let the earth bring forth green matter (Hebrew *deshe*) v 11
Dense vapours clear to reveal sun, moon and stars	4th day of creation 'Let there be lights in the sky' v 14 God had already made (historic tense) the sun, moon and stars v 16
Post-Cambrian Eras	
Marine fossils swarm the strata	5th day of creation Let the waters bring forth swarms of life' v 20
Insects and angio-sperms (Upper Carboniferous)	'Winged creatures' v 20b
Amphibians and Reptiles	'Great sea monsters' (Heb *taninim*) v 21
New Life Eras	
Land animals Age of mammals	6th day of creation (first part) 'Let the earth bring forth living creatures'
Mankind	6th day of creation, latter part, 'Let us make Man'

account speaks of an original good at every level of origin – physical, biological and human. The fact that scientists find that it gives a correct order of events, is purely because the information was given by the Creator himself.

Just look at that first chapter of the Bible again! What a wonderful majestic and poetic statement it is. But as a scientist I find it is fully factual as well. Note the balanced repeated phrases: 'God said'; 'God made'; 'God moulded'; 'and it was so, God saw that it was good and there was evening and there was morning, the fourth, fifth, or sixth day'. Then the great dignity with which man was introduced – the crown of God's creation.

Note that the Bible stands alone without the need of supporting evidence from science and archaeology. Yet it provides a wonderful account of incidental scientific, cultural and historical evidence which modern students are eager to understand. The evidence for biblical truth captured in my books will not only convince and convict these same enquiring minds about man's origins and destiny, but will help to focus on his yearning for a Creator and Saviour.

S U M M A R Y

Science and Genesis Correlation

Correlation between Science and Genesis chapter 1.

- **Order of life** is similar:
  Algae, marine life, vertebrates, land life, mammals, man.
- **Physical order** similar.
  Three basics (*bara*): matter, life, soul.
  A beginning, from formlessness to gravity, cosmic light, life and soul. One original continent, enshrouded earth.
  Hebrew historic tense re sun, moon, and stars, means they were already there but unseen.
- **Biological order:**
  Chloroplasts, advanced marine life (trilobites). Symbiosis of insects and flowers, sea mammals almost contemporary with first land mammals.

British Museum's Succession of Life through Geological Time shows same events as above.
Dr Rendle-Short's quote on 'Who taught the writers to arrange events in the correct order? . . . divine inspiration.'
'More scientists believe than disbelieve' (Sir Bernard Lovell).

2   SPACE PROBE FINDS A BEGINNING
THE BIG BANG THEORY

Imagine with me that stentorian voice, 'In the beginning God created the heavens and the earth'. These were the first words Colonel Borman uttered from the moon. He had reached it in 1969 and spoke these startling words when his spacecraft came round from the backside of the moon.

'In the beginning God created the heavens and the earth.' All the world heard it. It was written into the planned space programme. They are the first words in the Bible. Why? Because they are written into God's planned space programme, too. They are the opening to both the science story and Bible story of God's plan for the universe.

Why science and the Bible? Because science agrees that the universe **did** have a beginning. All the radio telescopes of the world combined to give evidence. They convinced the European Physical Society's Conference in 1969 that the universe did have a beginning.

Why was that? Because they found that all the universe was flying away from one central point at a terrific speed – currently at the speed of one-fifth of the speed of light.

'*In the beginning.*' Yes, there was a beginning. But some scientists missed out the next word – '**God**'. It was God who did it. '*In the beginning, God.*' Yes, God who created it! '**Created**' – some left that word out of their science as well. '*In the beginning, God created.*'

This newly-created universe was 'flying away' from God. That is also the description at the other end of the Bible. It is in Revelation 20:11, 'And I saw a great white throne and I saw him who sat upon it, from whose face the heavens and earth fled away.' So it was God who made the heavens and the earth 'fly away', and it was God who was at the centre of it.

Who was it who saw this? Was it a scientist looking at his radio telescope? No, it was John, the beloved disciple. God was showing it to him in a vision. 'Look,' said the angel, and John looked and what did he see? He saw God at the centre of the creation of the universe.

Genesis and the Big Bang

It is sometimes asserted that as Genesis is a religious account, we should not expect it to support any particular scientific theory. This cannot be said concerning the origin of the universe, which involves the question of the origin of matter. The opening verse clearly states that the universe had a beginning. 'In the beginning Elohim (God) created the heaven and the earth.'

Science had two theories on this question. One was that the universe did have a beginning. It was popularly called, 'The Big Bang' theory (Fig 2.1). A dense primeval atom containing primitive atomic elements exploded to rush at great speed into space. Proponents of this theory maintain that all the chemical elements with which we deal today must have been formed within the first 30 minutes of the life of the universe and time, in the sense of being measured by any clock, did not exist before that moment and space, in the sense of being measured by any yardstick, was contained entirely within the 'primeval atom'.

Le Maitre was the astro-physicist who formulated the concept and calculated that the beginning was 13,000 million years ago. **Whether we agree with such a timing is not so important as the evidence that creation had a beginning.**

Fred Hoyle, a popular scientist of Cambridge, produced a contrary theory that the universe had no beginning but that it was creating matter all the time. This model, called the steady-state theory, meant that instead of matter emanating from a centre in the universe in the distant past, it was being produced all the time equally throughout space and so the universe had no beginning. This theory was tested by the radio telescopes of the world. They found that matter was flying out from a centre into outer space and that it was not being produced equally all over the universe. So Hoyle's model was pronounced wrong.

These findings of the European Physical Society's Inaugural Conference were reported in April 1969 in the *New Scientist* as follows:

> The sum total of work on radio source counts and quasars now argues strongly against the steady-state theory of Hoyle, Bondi, and Gold and, attractive as this may be from a philosophical angle, it now looks as if it must give place to a version of the Big Bang model of the universe.

Seeking to Avoid the Creator

Hoyle's concept that the universe had no beginning was admitted to be a philosophical one. 'His reasons are essentially philosophical,' commented Dr Peter Stubbs. In other words, 'a spontaneous creation of matter' dispensed with the need of a Creator.

Another astro-physicist is Professor C. Boyde of London University. Although this could not be a valid reason for Professor Boyde who is an ardent believer, he too confesses, 'Personally, I rather like this so-called 'steady-state' theory – mostly for aesthetic reasons.'

Unwilling to accept that the universe had a beginning, Hoyle and

60   EVIDENCE FOR TRUTH: SCIENCE

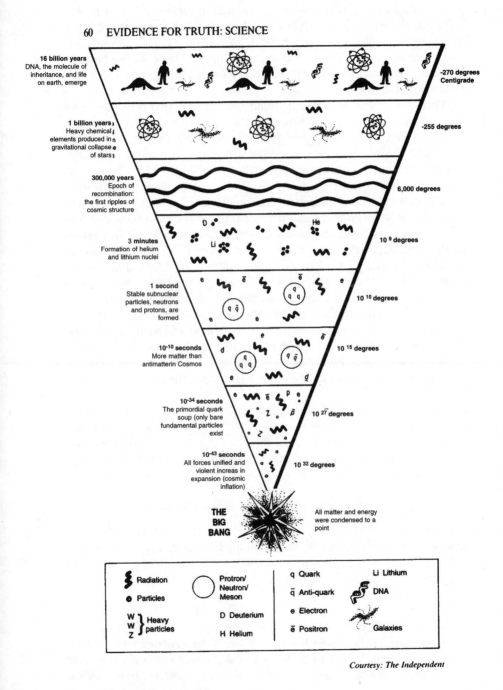

Figure 2.1. The Big Bang theory
Adapted by the author from a drawing in *The Independent*

others readjusted their theory to an 'oscillating universe'. This postulated that the expanding universe reached a climax at which the force of gravity began to slow down the expansion and pull it back into contraction until the universe collapsed in on itself. This collapse became another dense 'primeval atom' which exploded again to become a new expanding universe.

This theory was tested and found wanting on two premises. The mass of the expanding universe was too small to pull it back and the velocity of expansion too great to arrest its speed. Indeed, the visible 'red shift' showed that the outer edge was increasing speed faster and faster until it would ultimately equal the speed of light.

Dr Paul Wesson reported to *New Scientist* that there was 'insufficient matter in the universe ever to arrest its continual expansion'. He says, 'Three independent and different lines of research have resulted in a very puzzling and apparently inescapable conclusion.' This effectively terminates the long-continued conjecture (following Hoyle, Wickramasinghe, V. C. Reddish and others). 'It shows that cosmic dielectric dust between the galaxies cannot provide enough matter to seriously slow down the present expansion of the universe, which is therefore probably destined to carry on increasing in size for ever.'

These conclusions have since been confirmed and reinforced by the discovery that the current speed of expansion also cancels the possibility of contraction. Perhaps this is a cosmic comment on Revelation 20:11. 'The great white throne from whose face the sky and the earth fled away.'

We cannot avoid philosophical considerations on origins because the human mind is unable to understand or test unending time and unending space. This is why, also, that we cannot understand how God was and is always there 'who inhabits eternity' (Isaiah 57:15). 'I am he, the beginning and the end' (Isaiah 48:12, Revelation 22:13).

The Confessions of a Scientist

It is significant that Dr Hoyle has since written a book (in 1982) and reported widely, in which he has completely changed his outlook and believes in a Creator. He further declares that as a young student, in common with many others, he was 'brain-washed' into accounting for everything without God.

It is a pity that the agnostic atmosphere in our culture jeers at the cleric Archdeacon Usshur of the 17th century (who dated creation and Adam at 6,000 years ago) and conceals that our greatest scientists have been men of faith, some of them clerics.

Le Maitre was a cleric. He was the physicist whose Big Bang theory, that the universe had a beginning, was pronounced correct by the Conference of Scientists. Malthus, who first predicted the population explosion, was a cleric. Mendel, the pioneer geneticist was a cleric. The Abbé Breuil, who corrected crude ideas about primitive man, was a cleric.

The opening sentence of the Bible is remarkable in its implication that God existed outside of time. God was there before the beginning in order to create the universe. This concept is constant throughout Scripture. To Moses he was revealed as the eternal present, 'The I AM'. To Isaiah, he announces, 'I am the Lord who inhabits eternity', and 'I am the beginning and the end'. To the Jews, Jesus said, 'I am the Alpha and Omega, who is and who was and who is to come, the Almighty.' It is difficult for the human mind to conceive that time and space are creations and that God is a reality outside of time and space. Yet this is the essence of Einstein's equation, $E = mc^2$.

Lumps in the Primeval Soup!

There was great excitement among the scientists when the NASA space probe sent back pictures of the first ripples in the universe (Fig 2.2). 'Wow! What an exciting discovery,' said one scientist from Durham. What caused those ripples? It was the force of gravity. Scientists use a funny language today. They said, 'There were lumps in the primeval soup!' Yes, that is how they put it – 'lumps in the primeval soup!' And do you know what some of those scientists said?

The strength of gravity shows that it was intended to lead up to man. Man was in mind. Why? Because 'the strength of gravity was just the right strength for the size of the earth to support man'. Dr Nigel Calder said, 'For man to walk on this planet with 12,000 kilometres of the earth beneath his feet, man had to have the two gravity balances in his head rightly tuned.'

Many scientists call this '**The Anthropic Principle**'. Isaiah 45:12 puts this principle in a nutshell. I quote, 'God said, I made the earth and created man upon it.' Those first ripples had man in mind. It was written into the space–time plan!

Q In what words was that space-time plan written? What words were made possible?

The nucleic acids are used by God to contain the genetic instructions for man. Deep in the hot interiors of big massive stars, they are created amidst terrific heat – the primary elements. The quarks (more about these later) cohered into usable material for the language of life anticipating that instructions for life would be placed on that material fused together in the hot stars!

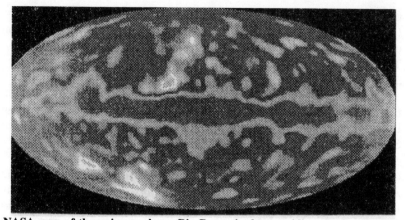

NASA map of the universe shows Big Bang ripples providing the first historic evidence of creation

Figure 2.2. Ripples of Matter in Space – press cutting

THE FIRST definite evidence of the Creation has been discovered by astronomers.

Traces of 'wispy ripples of matter' were found at the edge of the universe by the American space agency NASA's Cosmic Background Explorer orbiting radio telescope (COBE) which showed how, 15,000 million years ago, matter began to coalesce into stars and galaxies.

Dr Michael Turner. of the University of Chicago, said yesterday: 'This discovery is unbelievably important. Its significance cannot be overstated. These astronomers have found the Holy Grail of cosmology. They certainly will have to be considered for Nobel Prizes.'

Prof. George Smoot, of the University of California at Berkeley, and his colleague Dr John Mather, COBE's chief scientist, said they had found the 'missing link', sought for the last 28 years, between the Big Bang which created the universe and the solid matter of which it now consists.

Dr Mather said: 'We have revealed the primordial seeds that developed into the modern universe. They tell us how the cosmos developed from a gigantic explosion, in which nothing had any density, into today's huge clusters of galaxies.'

Although the ripples occurred 15 billion years ago, radio signals of it are only now reaching the Earth, having been travelling towards it for all that time at the speed of light, 670 million mph.

The Big Bang has been known since 1964, when astronomers found continuous radio disturbance that was the last remaining trace of that explosion.

But the mystery until now has been how the matter thus flung out in all directions gradually coalesced from scattered subatomic particles into hard matter.

Dr Rod Davies, director of the Jodrell Bank radio telescope, said yesterday: 'These newly-found ripples show the first small density variations of matter in gradually increasing fluctuations. which were caused by gravity, about a million years after the Big Bang.
Courtesy: Daily Telegraph

'In the beginning'. Science has confirmed *that*!

'In the beginning God created the heavens and the earth'. The Bible has confirmed *that*!

'The universe fled away from the great white throne of God's presence.' St John saw that in Revelation 20:11.

But where was the plan written into the space–time programme? It is John again who tells us at the opening of his gospel. 'In the beginning was the Word and the Word was with God and the Word was God. The same was in the beginning with God.'

Leading Scientists Confirm the Bible

Le Maitre, the mathematician who first worked it all out, said this: ' "Let there be light!" correctly described the origin of the universe.' That other leading physicist, Professor George Gamov, said that the Divine command, 'Let there be light!' was completely scientific. Here are his words: 'All the chemical elements which we deal with today must have been formed within the first 30 minutes of the life of this universe, and it accords with the Divine command, "Let there be light". There certainly was light through this intense radiation.'

And who was there in that beginning? John wrote in his gospel that it was Jesus. What! Jesus? Yes, 'In the beginning was the Word . . . Without him was not anything made that was made . . . that Word became flesh and dwelt among us and we beheld his glory . . . full of grace and truth. In him was life and the life was the light of men . . . and the light shines out into the darkness' (John 1:1–5).

Now the scientists say that early in the universe, nucleic acids were formed and that shows that **life was the purpose of the universe**. Why? Because upon those nucleic acids, the instructions of life were to be coded or written. All the instructions on how to make an animal are imposed upon nucleic acid tapes. All the instructions on how to make men and women are on nucleic acid tapes. The alphabet of life, as it has been called, is contained in the alphabet of 64 letters or codons.

'In the beginning was the Word,' wrote John. 'I am the Alpha and Omega,' said Jesus in Revelation chapter 1 – the alphabet of life. 'The beginning and the end,' said the Lord. 'In him was life,' said John, 'and the life was the light of men.' So John takes the physical universe and says that same Jesus can create the light of understanding in you and me as well.

It is sad, isn't it, to see so many walking in darkness. They don't realise that Jesus can give them light. He, the Creator, can tell you the reason for it all.

To obstinate philosophers who preferred to walk in their own theories, Jesus said, 'I am the light of the world. He who follows me will not walk in darkness, but will have the light of life' (John 8:12). The puzzle is then, why doesn't everybody rush to the light? John explains in his gospel, in chapter 3, v 19, 'And this is the judgment, that the light has come into the world, but men loved darkness rather than light.' Why? 'Because their deeds are evil. For everyone who does evil hates the light, lest his deeds should be exposed. But he who does what is true comes to the light, that it may be clearly seen that his deeds have been wrought by God.'

St John's Amazement

Can you sense the utter amazement of John, as he thinks about it? He had **looked** upon the One who had created everything by words. He had actually **seen** the creating Word with his own eyes. He had actually heard him **speak**; he who spoke the creating words at the beginning of the universe, 'Let there be light!' But even more amazing, he, John, with his own hands, had actually **touched** the One who had created life by words. More so, with his own hands he had actually handled the creating Word. His head had rested upon the chest of the Word made flesh at the Last Supper (John 13:23).

John did not realise at the time that this wonderful man with whom he talked and walked and leant against, was the Creator who spoke the creating words. All he was conscious of was that here was the most gracious, kindly, amazing man he had ever met. He had been drawn to him, he loved him and this man loved him.

Then he turned out to be the Creator himself who had created life by words. 'Our own hands have touched the Word of Life' (1 John 1:1).

John's words were fully scientific. He had put his finger on one of the most amazing discoveries of our time. It is that all life is created by words. And John had touched the author of the DNA code in Jesus Christ!

The first ripples on the dark matter of the universe were photographed by the NASA probe (Fig 2.2). But did not the opening words of the Bible describe the Holy Spirit of God moving upon the waters, making those ripples in the early universe? It is the ripples of the Holy Spirit drawing together by gravity the elements and then making the nucleic acids upon which the words of life were to be written.

Scientists Acknowledge God

Many scientists have given up trying to explain the beginning without a Creator. Crick and Watson, the first discoverers of the ribbons of life's code, quote Salvador Dali, 'For me this is the proof of God!' Others have struggled to explain how substances like phosphates and sugar could provide a double ribbon upon which nucleic acids could come together with God's creative instructions placed on them. In the instructions to create man, this ribbon, if unravelled, would be long enough to go twice around the world! Agnostics have struggled to explain how those words could come by intricate mechanical instructions to make the clever machinery of life. Instructions enough to fill a whole library. Then they discovered that those words needed to be translated. The code had to be cracked. The translator is called a ribosome and there is a ribosome in every cell of your body – many ribosomes. They take this secret code of God and change it into the alphabet of 64 letters – 64 codons (see Chapter 5). Then the instructions begin to make sense. The machines in your body can read them, obey them and produce specific proteins to make your blood cells, your muscles, your bones, with all those mechanical joints, your heart and even that wonderful brain of yours!

'I am the Alphabet of Life'

'I am the alphabet!' declared the risen Jesus, in the last book of the Bible. 'I am the alpha-beta, I am Alpha and Omega, the first and the last, the beginning and the end.' You will find him at the beginning of the Bible and at the end. You will find him at the beginning of creation and at the end. He is those words which said:

- 'Let there be light!'
- 'Let there be atmosphere to cause evaporation.'
- 'Let the waters gather back to reveal the one big continent.'
- 'Let that continent bring forth green algae with chlorophyll, chlorophyll to put oxygen into the air for animals later.'
- 'Let the atmosphere clear to reveal the sun, moon and stars.'
- 'Let life start in the waters!'
- 'Let life next start on earth.'
- 'Let us make man – male and female.'

Jesus was the living Word uttering these things. God then let the layers of rocks record this order of life by its fossils, as evidence to man that Genesis chapter 1 is correct, and that science and Genesis agree.

'I am those words of life,' said the risen Jesus. He spoke those instructions. He provided the ribosomes to translate them and the machinery to make the products.

'I am the Word of Life. If anyone believes in me, he will live. If anyone obeys my words, he will live spiritually.' His spirit moves upon the dark waters of your mind and says, 'Let there be light.'

'If my gospel is hidden, it is hidden to those who are lost. Satan has blinded their minds lest they should believe the glorious gospel and be saved' (2 Corinthians 4:3–4).

NASA Spacecraft Discovery

I stated before that many secular scientists are now admitting that the way matter and gravity were formed in the early universe indicates that it had man in mind. This, of course, is what the Bible says also!

Since the discovery of the ripples in outer space by the NASA probe, people are asking, 'Why are the scientists so excited about this discovery in the universe?'

Well, it was to the American Physical Society meeting, early in 1992, that the satellite discovery was presented. Scientists today have a homely way of expressing what they feel about this discovery. Let me ask you; would you be embarrassed if you hiccupped and somebody heard the echo?

That is the language scientists use. The spacecraft heard the universe hiccup – that was when it got 'lumps in its quark soup'. The universe hiccuped 14 billion years ago, say the scientists, but the echo has only just reached the spacecraft satellite.

Are we saying that the universe was created 14 billion years ago? I am only quoting the scientists. Whether we agree with their time-scale or not, the point is that basic particles were exploded out into space, but there seemed to be nothing to coalesce these particles to form matter and eventually to form galaxies and planets. To return to the simile of the soup, it accounted only for 'thin gruel' at the beginning of creation. Thin gruel would not form into anything. Matter would not form and galaxies would not form, nor suns and planets. But now NASA detected ripples of matter forming, they think, just 300 thousand years after the creation. There were lumps in the soup! Some force had drawn the particles together to form matter. This was the force of gravity. The same attraction which made an apple fall off a tree and knock an idea into Newton's head. But who created gravity?

Let There be Light!

The answer is God, of course. He created everything. Let us look at this from a Bible viewpoint. The world's scientists now agree on the scientific truth of the first three words of the Bible, 'In the beginning'; but as we have learnt, they have left out the next word, 'God' and the next words, 'created the heavens and the earth'. The heavenly bodies, the galaxies and stars, were all the result of gravity coalescing the 'gruel' into 'lumpy soup'. Scientists still don't know what gravity is. Obviously, Jesus Christ knew. He had control of gravity when he ascended into heaven. The thin gruel stage of the universe left it without form and void, until God said, 'Let there be light!' Dr Nigel Calder says, 'Newly-formed atoms gave off a great glow of visible light'. Radiant energy was particles of light passing from electrons to anti-electrons. That is why, in Genesis, light was created long before our sun.

Quark Soups – Six Flavours

I like the popular cookery terms the scientists used about the thin gruel at the beginning of creation coalescing into a lumpy soup soon after creation. This space probe gave the first evidence that it had actually happened. Dr Michael Turner said the discovery was 'The Holy Grail of Cosmology'. The satellite had sent back pictures of the ripples which were forming into matter. The Bible adds that it was God who was doing it.

Another scientist asks, 'But how did the lumps get into the porridge?' (to use a different culinary term). The matter of which the earth is made and of which your body is made was formed by gravity pulling together all kinds of primary particles. Science has been finding that matter is more complex than anyone thought. At one time, matter was thought to consist only of protons and electrons and neutrons, but this soup, as the analogist has called it, consists of lots of simpler elements called quarks. Yes, don't laugh, but what that satellite has discovered is the formation of quark soup to make up the material needed for galaxies and planets and life.

There are different kinds of quarks with interacting forces to hold things together. There are 36 different kinds of quark in the universe's quark soup, some of which are shown in Figure 2.3.

There are up quarks, down quarks, charmed quarks, strange quarks, top quarks and bottom quarks. And all these in turn have anti-quarks, and anti-ups and downs and tops and bottoms and so on! This is all to keep matter from falling apart. Do you remember what Colossians 1:17 says, that 'God created all things by Jesus by whom all things hold together', also Hebrews 1:2–3 says 'God created the worlds by Jesus who upholds the universe by the word of his power'.

By the way, your lumpy quark soup is in six flavours and each flavour has three colours – red, green and blue!

Invisible Reality

These are the terms scientists use to describe the basics of created matter. But here is an astonishing statement in the report of NASA satellite's discovery. All this is only 1% of what exists in the universe. Why? Because 99% is invisible. Science knows it is there because of mysterious interacting forces, but they are all invisible! Are you one who believes only what you can see? There is 99% of reality which is hidden from your eyes!

Yes, 'Satan has blinded the minds of those who don't believe . . .' (2 Corinthians 4:4).

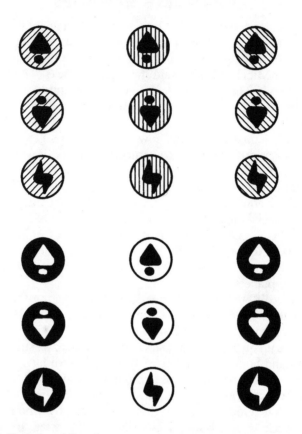

Figure 2.3. Varieties of Quarks   *Adapted from an article in the Daily Telegraph*
Sub-atomic particles are made up of 18 quarks (plus 18 anti-quarks) which serve the
function of holding matter in a stable form, without which so-called 'solid matter'
would vanish!

GOD AND THE BIG BANG

I have heard some preachers give the Big Bang theory a knock, if
you'll forgive the expression, but there is nothing wrong with it unless
you say that the Big Bang created the universe without saying it was
God who created the big bang.

Actually, the theory has made all the scientists agree with Genesis
that there was a beginning to the universe. Some confessed it was
against their wish to agree. They preferred to think that the universe
was always there and that nobody created it. The theory was against
their atheistic philosophy, but they could not deny that all the radio
telescopes showed everything in the universe was rushing away from
one centre. The Bible says that centre is God.

I have shown how, in Revelation 20:11, there is a good description of the Big Bang theory, but with a difference. It corrects the idea that it could happen without a divine cause. In that verse, God is the cause. John records, 'I saw a great white throne, and him that sat upon it, from whose face the earth and the heavens fled away . . .'

But does this verse describe the creation of the universe or is it another Big Bang to come at the end of the world when God creates a new heaven and a new earth, as the Bible says he will? Whichever it is, it certainly describes a Big Bang. St Peter himself says in 2 Peter 3:10, 'The day of the Lord will come like a thief when the heavens will pass away with a loud noise, and the elements will melt with fervent heat.'

The original Big Bang was so hot that only elemental particles existed. Peter's use of the word 'elements' was fully scientific. The word in the Greek is '*stoichea*'.

But there were people who could not fly away from God. The next verse says, 'And I saw the dead, great and small, standing before the throne and the books were opened. Also another book was opened, which is the book of life. And the dead were judged by what was in the books according to their deeds. And if anyone's name was not found in the book of life, he was thrown into the lake of fire.'

Anthropic Universe

Many leading scientists are now seeing that the early formation of the universe was leading up to man. Where the earliest particles and quarks were formed, they had man in view, says Professor Calder. As I told you before, scientists have called this 'The Anthropic Principle'. It merely means that from the earliest weak force called 'charm', to the subsequent gravity of the universe and size of the earth, creation had man as its object.

Of course, the Bible says this also. The reports sent back by NASA satellite which excited the scientists and were widely reported in the papers, proved that gravity was bringing together the materials to make the atoms. What is important is that universal gravity is just the right strength for man and for planet earth. If gravity were stronger, it would crush earth in on itself. The size of the earth also gave just the right strength of local gravity for man.

Professor Calder says, 'Gravity detectors in man's head enabled human beings to walk upright, and the thickness of their bones . . . oppose the gravity prevailing 6,000 kilometres from the centre of the earth.' (The hollow design of the bone combines strength with lightness). Also the heat and distance from the sun are just right for man. A star bigger than the sun would burn too fiercely and too quickly. Yet the bigger giant stars were necessary farther away, their greater heat 'increasing the protons and adding to the succession of elements needed by man and earth' – elements such as hydrogen, helium, carbon, oxygen, sulphur, silicon and iron. These are now part of our earth, resulting from activities in outer space.

So then, man needed a small place like the earth in a large universe before he could be created. The ground contains these elements and from them God made man from the dust of the ground and scientists are now saying, '**Every atom in the human body was fashioned in stars** that formed, grew old and exploded most violently before the sun and the earth came into being, and scattered their fine dust to form planet earth. And from earth's rocks, atoms were incorporated into living things; carbon, nitrogen, oxygen, phosphorus, sulphur, calcium for bones and teeth, sodium and potassium for nerves and brains.'

All this is what Genesis chapter 1 says in verse 24, 'God said, "Let the earth bring forth living creatures according to their kinds." ' And then chapter 2:7 reads, 'The Lord God formed man from the dust of the ground, breathed into his nostrils the breath of life and man became a living soul.' Yes, it was the dust that had formed in those huge exploding stars (novae).

So this man-oriented (anthropic) principle is supported by many leading scientists. God had man in mind from the outset. But the Bible goes further. Did you know God had you in mind? You were created to serve him. Romans 8:29 says, 'Those whom he foreknew, he also did predestine to be conformed to the image of his Son, that he might be the firstborn among many brethren.'

Science and the Invisible

Q Have the recent discoveries by science and satellite projects proved that God is the Creator?

Yes, even Richard Dawkins of Oxford admitted that he favoured his 'Selfish Gene' theory because the obvious alternative was an intelligent Creator. The great excitement among scientists about what happened just after creation has also shown the truth of Hebrews 11:3, 'The things which are seen were not made by the things which are visible.' The search into deep space has revealed many mysteries acknowledged by scientists, including that about 99% of the matter of the universe is invisible to us. Calculations prove there ought to be far more matter around for today's galaxies to have formed than they have observed.

Q Is it a mistake to think that all evidence comes by science?

It is a mistake! Science can observe or test only what is visible or material. The spiritual causes behind the creation of the material of the universe can be known only if the spiritual source reveals it. This is the realm that God has revealed to mankind. He tells you in the Bible and through Jesus Christ that he created and made all things. In Isaiah 45:12 God says, 'I have made the earth and created man upon it. I, even I, have stretched out the heavens and all their host I commanded.'

Some scientists go no further than assuming that matter and energy were in existence for the Big Bang to happen. If there was no Creator, then the logical result would be nothing. Nothing leads to nothing, but in the universe there was matter and energy. Stephen Hawking admitted the difficulty of who supplied the message on the DNA genetic tapes. Life and animals are machinery more complex than anything man has made.

Evolution is quite inadequate to explain all this; so the visible can be explained only by the invisible Creator. Unless the invisible Creator speaks up, science is left with 99% unexplained – and invisible to science.

The wonderful fact is that the Creator has spoken up. He says in Hebrews chapter 1, 'God, who at various times and in different ways spoke unto the fathers by the prophets, has in these last days, spoken unto us by his Son . . . by whom he created the universe.'

THE GREAT SCIENTIFIC MYTH

Having spoken of the beginning of the universe, now look with me at the beginning of the earth's history, particularly on how life began.

There is a phrase which is used concerning the first formation of life which can confuse people. It is the 'primeval soup theory'. This has nothing to do with the 'lumpy quark soup' early in the universe before the earth was formed. This particular soup refers to the condition of the early oceans of the earth. The theory was that the early oceans were 'very soupy', and that from the soup life appeared accidentally.

This supposed possibility arose in the 1920s, when it was thought that life was simple and uncomplicated. As Dr G. Chedd said, writing in *The New Scientist*, this led to concepts which were hazy and distinctly unsatisfactory scientifically.

The Propagation of False Ideas

Some determined materialists are still so obsessed with the simple to complex outlook that they mislead both themselves and others by describing things as simple when they are not.

Oparin, a Soviet scientist, propagated this theory that simple life arose from soupy seas of early earth. His theory went like wildfire through the universities. Since then, the complicated mechanics of early life has been revealed. It has also been demonstrated that the early seas were different from what Oparin thought.

Consequently, Dr L. R. Croft, a lecturer in Biological Sciences at Salford University, has called Oparin's theory 'The Great Scientific Soup Myth'. He is referring to earth's early history, not to the early universe, as I have said, so do not get confused. Dr Croft says that life could not arise by accident and adds, 'I am astonished that **Oparin, a dedicated Marxist, could have succeeded in converting most of Western society** to his belief in the so-called "primeval soup" ' (*How Life Began*, Evangelical Press, 1988, p 113).

The physicist, Freeman Dyson, remarked in 1985, 'The Oparin picture . . . was popular, not because there was any evidence to support it, but because it seemed to be the only alternative to Biblical creation.'

'This view,' says Croft, 'was echoed by Sir Fred Hoyle. It is remarkable that over the past half century, the scientific world had almost, without exception, believed a theory for which there is not a single supporting fact.'

'It is true to say,' says Dr Croft, 'that no other apostle of Marx has been so successful in the promulgation of his gospel of materialism . . . It comes as no surprise to find that Oparin was awarded the greatest honour of the Soviet Union.'

The Soviet Union financed Oparin's books to make them cheap for universities around the world. It was this atheism which led to the collapse of the Soviet Union. It is in danger of leading to the collapse of Western society.

Schools are turning out agnostics. It is typified by a young teenager whom I caught breaking a church stained-glass window. 'Why do you do such things?' I asked. He replied, 'There ain't no God mister! That's why!'

As a university biologist, Dr Croft goes on to show how it was quite impossible for life to arise without a Creator. Certainly, 'The primeval soup theory has been the greatest scientific myth of all time.'

Prophesied Proof

Here is an opportunity for you to turn this man-made myth into a prophesied proof. That word '*myth*' is a Greek word and it occurs in 2 Timothy 4:4. Mark it in your Bible for use, and learn it by heart. Paul is talking about conditions in the time when Christ's return is getting near. He starts in chapter 3 verse 7:

People will be '. . . ever learning but never able to come to the knowledge of the truth.' Why? Because, '. . . the time will come when they will not tolerate sound teaching, but to excuse their own lusts, they will heap up to themselves teachers saying what they want to hear; and they shall turn away their ears from the truth, and turn unto myths' (2 Timothy 4:4).

S U M M A R Y

FACTS FROM THE NASA SPACE PROBE

1. NASA feedback was like a video run backwards catching up with the beginning of the universe. Rev 20:11 describes a 'Big Bang', but God causes it. Gamov and Le Maitre who worked it out, quoted Gen 1:3 'Let there be light'.
Scientists use culinary terms:
First elementary particles were like thin gruel.
Ripples proved gravity operating (lumps in the quark soup).
Universe hiccupped and NASA heard the echo.

2. Man-centred: strength of gravity proved man was in mind.
Anthropic principle – required small earth but big stars. Why? Any planet bigger than earth would crush man. Yet huge stars were needed to fuse the quarks into atoms, required for man's body make-up. These novae stars then exploded the dust into space for man's body (and planets).
Prof. Calder (BBC science broadcaster) says, 'Gravity detectors in man's head' . . . are rightly adjusted for earth's mass. Anthropic principle supported by leading scientists. Is 45:12, 'I made the earth and created man upon it.'
DNA acids for man created in the hot interiors of exploding stars. St John was overawed that he had actually touched the 'Word of Life' (1 John 1:1).

3. Reality is invisible.
Scientists find that what is detectable in the whole universe is only 1%. The other 99% is invisible. Heb 11:3, 'The worlds were framed by the activating word (*hreemati*) of God, so that the things which are seen were not made by the visible.'
Stephen Hawking of Cambridge is attempting to combine Quantum Physics with Relativity to give a Theory of Everything. He wonders whether we shall know everything without the mind of God. Solution: The mind of God is given in his Word (Heb 1:1).

3 GOD'S TIMING OF CREATION EVENTS
AN ASSESSMENT OF PREVAILING VIEWS

It is helpful to realise that there have been fashions of interpretation among Bible-believing scientists when it comes to relating Genesis and science. By Bible-believing scientists, I mean scientists who believe that the Bible is fully inspired by the Holy Spirit and therefore is true and accurate in all that it says. The term I shall use for such a person is 'Biblical scientist'.

During the last 200 years or so, the fashions of interpretation have changed or rather, one fashion has gained support over the others, particularly in interpreting Genesis chapter 1.

Changing Fashions of Biblical Scientists

In the 19th century and in the early 20th century, most Biblical scientists believed that the days of creation were age-days and that the earth was of a great age. Many still think this.

Later it became popular to regard the days of creation as 1,000-year days. When Usshur calculated that Adam lived 6,000 years ago, the seventh millennium would be the day of rest spoken of in Revelation chapter 20.

More recently, there has been a big upsurge of those who take the days of creation to be 24-hour days. There are at least three varieties of this interpretation. There are 'young-earthists' who confine the creation and the age of the universe to being six 24-hour days in length, before Adam. There are those who allow a great period of time before those six days of creation. Then there are those who think that creation was revealed to Moses in six days, but the actual creation itself was of unspecified time-length.

There is still another group of Biblical scientists who accept the theory of evolution, but in moderation. They stipulate that evolution was the method by which God created, but that no aspect of evolution should be held which is in contradiction to the Bible.

I am setting out these fashions of interpretation in order to show that the Bible test of sound faith is not whether a scientist adopts your favourite interpretation, but **whether he believes the Bible to be the unerring Word of God**. This is necessary if only for Christian brotherliness as, lately, those of one particular interpretation have shown considerable intolerance towards the others. This has not helped the gospel witness.

PREVAILING CREATIONIST VIEWS

It will be helpful if we consider each of these interpretations, the scientists who support them and the reasons why they correlate science with the Bible in the way they do. Each reader can then favour what appeals to him, but should not condemn another who is sound in faith according to the scriptural test of soundness.

As I have said, the scriptural test is whether a person believes the Bible to be God's fully inspired inerrant Word, not whether he accepts your chosen interpretation.

Earth Days or Galaxy Days?

'And there was evening, and there was morning – the first day.' 'And there was evening, and there was morning – the second day' (Genesis 1:5,8 NIV). The Hebrew *aered* (evening) literally means 'conclusion' and *diger* (morning) literally means 'beginning'.

It is important to understand that the correlation between the creation story and science is not dependent upon whether we regard these days as earth days of 24 hours or cosmic days of geological ages. The fact that the succession of events both physical and biological is similar stands indisputable. The timing factor is a separate issue.

First we note that the days of creation do not commence until after the initial cosmic events, 'in the beginning'. All the heavens, i.e. the universe in its earlier stages, were created before the days begin to be recorded so that no timescale can be assessed from the Genesis account, except that it was from the beginning onwards. This is followed by void and darkness of verse 2, into which many primeval processes can be fitted. The days following are then measured by the end of one day of creation and the beginning of the next. It is the end which marks the first day of creation – a significance you should note.

Concerning the time factor, I now give a summary of attempts to correlate the days of creation with the findings of science.

Age-day Interpretation

First then, the interpretation that the days of creation were age-days. Great names which took this view in their apologetics were Dr Merson Davies, D. Dewar and Professor Ambrose Fleming (these three were founders of the Evolution Protest Movement); Professor F. A. Filby, senior lecturer in organic chemistry, Dr R. E. D. Clark, former editor of *Faith and Thought,* Walter Beasley, who ran a Bible Truth Museum in Australia, Professor Rendle-Short of the Inter-Varsity Fellowship and others such as Dr Hugh Ross of California.

Thousand-year Day Theory

Secondly, the interpretation that each day of creation was a thousand-year day became quite widely accepted among many Bible believers. There were several clues to strengthen this interpretation. One was Archbishop Usshur's calculation in the 17th century. By taking all the genealogies from Adam to Christ, he calculated that Adam was created in 4004 BC. As there have been nearly two millennia AD, the 'Millennial Sabbath' should start soon. Thus, it is deduced, the days of creation would also be a thousand years each. It would harmonise with St Peter's statement that a day with God is as a thousand years and a thousand years as one day.

A difficulty raised against this viewpoint was that Usshur should not have linked dates together in linear fashion as there were three or four breaks in those successions. Indeed, Campian calculated that the date for Adam would be around 10,000 years ago which, incidentally, is the date which anthropologists give for when farming commenced, and Adam was a farmer.

The 24-hour Day Theory

The third interpretation that the days of creation were 24-hour days was strengthened by Exodus 20:11, 'For in six days the Lord made the heavens and the earth . . . and rested the seventh day. Therefore the Lord blessed the Sabbath day and hallowed it.' In reply to this, others have said that we should expect that God's days would be longer than man's days, as Peter says in 2 Peter 3:8. Also in the Bible, a day is made to represent various lengths of time. In Ezekiel chapter 4, God makes each day represent a year. Sabbath rest for the land was one year in Exodus 23:11. The Lord Jesus referred to his three-and-a-half year ministry as being three-and-a-half days long (Luke 13:32). The reference to Adam's day of life would appear to be a thousand-year day. Why? Because Adam was told that the day in which he sinned he would surely die. If a thousand-year day was referred to, this was fulfilled because Adam died soon before he was a thousand years old, as did all the other patriarchs.

The names associated with the 24-hour day interpretation are H. M. Morris who wrote *The Genesis Flood*, Dr D. T. Gish who speaks to colleges around the world, D. C. C. Watson, J. C. Whitcomb who wrote *The Early Earth*, Dr A. J. Monty White who wrote *What About Origins?* and Professor H. Enoch of India who wrote *Evolution or Creation?*.

Professor Enoch makes strange statements in his book. On pages 40–41, he says that the sun was created after the earth. This appears to be an application of Genesis 1:14–19 where the sun, moon and stars appear on the fourth day of creation. Such a view, however, seems to overlook a characteristic of the Hebrew tense. The Hebrew historic tense means that the sun, moon and stars were already in existence. (Genesis 1:16, the verb 'made' is in this historic tense), but they could not be seen from the earth because up to this time the earth was wrapped in swaddling bands of vapour and cloud, as God said to Job in chapter 38:9 of the book of Job. In Chapter 5 of his book, Professor Enoch claims that the earth looks old because God made it to look older. Dr Hugh Ross's reply to this is that God is not dishonest or out to deceive.

Chaos Theory

Others have allowed for greater time span by a chaos theory in verse 2: 'And the earth was without form and void and darkness was upon the face of the deep.' They suggest that God's original creation was spoilt and that the six days were a rapid restoration. However, the Hebrew tense does not mean, 'The earth **became** without form'. The meaning is rather that this was a stage of creating formless matter into shape. Derek Kidner comments in the *Tyndale Press*, 'If verse 2 were intended to tell of a catastrophe as some have suggested, it would use the Hebrew narrative construction, not the circumstantial construction as here.'

If one wants to hold to the 24-hour day and yet to allow a greater age for the earth, note that time before the first day is open-ended. Only the end of the first day of creation is mentioned and no date is given for the beginning. For Usshur of the 17th century to have added a date to the words, 'In the beginning God created . . ' was wrongly adding to God's Word.

Seventh-Day-Not-Ended Theory

Observe also that the seventh day is not said to have ended. All the other days ended but not the seventh day. This means that we are still in that seventh day because God rested from making any more species after man. That is a scientific fact. Nor will God create again until he says, 'Behold I create a new heaven and a new earth', when even carnivores will become herbivores (Romans 8:19–23, Isaiah 65:17–25). Hebrews 4:3–4 agrees that God's Sabbath rest continues until now. 'His work has been finished since the creation of the world for he has spoken about the seventh day in these words, "On the seventh day God rested from all his work".' So the seventh day has not ended but still continues. Moreover, Moses who wrote Genesis 1 says in Psalm 90, 'Before the mountains were brought forth, or even thou hadst formed the earth and the world, even from everlasting to everlasting thou art

God . . . for a thousand years in thy sight are but as yesterday when it is passed and as a watch in the night.'

Revealed in Six Days?

Another quite different concept is to say that the six days were the 24-hour days during which God told Moses about his creation. In other words, it was the telling of the account to Moses which took six days. This was suggested by P. J. Wiseman and is supported by his son, Professor Donald Wiseman of London University in *Science and Christian Belief*, April 1991. A similar suggestion was made by Professor van der Spuy in 1992 in his paper, *A Six-Day Programme for a Billion-Year Future*. Six 24-hour days were Word-days, when God worded his creation programme. 'What God said', which then took a billion years to operate.

The Tendency to Give the Earth a Great Age

Why are so many anxious to make room for a great age for the earth? Let me remove some misconceptions. First, it was not because of radiometric dating. One hundred and fifty years before this method, geologists thought that the earth was ages old. Long before Darwin, the annual varves or sediment layers in lakes had been counted and also what is called geological superposition had been worked out across Britain by Geo Smith and others. Also the existence of conglomerate pebbles revealed geological strata in them even before they became part of a later strata.

Second, it was not to accommodate evolution as some assert. Geological data was collected 50 years before the theory of evolution was launched.

Third, from the outset, the geological data and fossil succession were against evolution, not for it. Even Darwin acknowledged this in *Origin of Species*, Chapter 10.

Fossil evidence at the time was that all new orders of life had an independent start as if they had been created. **Darwin merely hoped that evolutionary links would be collected, but they have still not been found**. The fossil picture is even more definite today in favour of creative acts. The order of the fossils is similar to that in the creative acts of Genesis chapter 1.

Dr Arthur Frazer is a born-again Bible-believing Christian of the Department of Geology, Hull University, who gives the following reasons why rocks are old. Rocks are the product of processes, he says, under laws of sedimentation: 1. Superposition; 2. Initial horizontally; 3. Biotic succession. These were estimated long before the evolutionary theory was postulated.

SIGNS OF ROCK AGEING

Rocks give the following indications of old age:

1. Pre-Cambrian, NW Scotland – deformed, distorted intrusions pressured under weight (mica schists, distorted microetues intrusions).
2. Garnet nodules form from chemical change under pressure.
3. Dykes intruded after first rocks, then further distorted.
4. Intrusions folded in six periods of crushing (Lewisian).
5. Younger rocks on top of Lewisian in Scottish Hebrides.
6. Fragments of old Lewisian in younger (old) Torridon.
7. Beaches in Torridon in rounded stones. On top of Torridon another system, tilted.
8. Ground and milled rocks.
9. Deformed fossils by pressure.
10. Alps overthrust, as in Fig 6.3.
11. Conglomerates.

Dinosaur Paluxy Footprints Re-examined

This geological succession was confused when some maintained that humans lived at the same time as dinosaurs. They produced footprints in the Paluxy River bed which appeared to show human footprints alongside the dinosaur's footprints. It is to their credit that they have acknowledged their error in this. The footprints going alongside those of the dinosaurs are not human and drawings in their books of human footprints are misleading. I quote their acknowledgement from *Faith and Thought* (The Victoria Society).

The young-earthists,

> to their credit, have done considerable research on the site of the Paluxy footprints in the USA and, as a result, have now withdrawn the claim (and the film *Footprints in Stone*). The supposedly human prints are apparently modified dinosaur prints. We congratulate those concerned for their integrity and willingness to go public in announcing their retraction. Would that all scientists were so willing to admit an error.

Modified Evolution

Another interpretation of the days of creation is by those who accept a modified evolution. They are often called Theistic Evolutionists. They accept what Darwin said in his *Origin of Species*, 'There is grandeur in this view of life, with its several powers, having been originally breathed by the Creator into a few forms or into one . . . and from so simple a beginning endless forms . . . are being evolved. To my mind it accords better with what we know of the laws impressed on matter by the Creator.'

If this was so, then Genesis should have spoken of one day of creation and six days of rest! For God needed to do nothing after the original launching of life. Theistic Evolutionists agree that the succession of events is similar to that found by scientists, but point out that there are words used which could be evolutionary, e.g.

- 'Let the waters *bring forth* . . .' marine creatures.
- 'Let the earth *bring forth* . . .' land animals.
- 'God *formed* man from the dust of the ground.'

The discovery of the DNA code, however, has shown how impossible it was that such a complicated language of instruction could have happened by a series of accidents in the cells of animals. The DNA code supports the Bible which says that God created each order of life by coded words.

Timing and the Methods of Science

If the days which follow this untimed era are taken to be 24-hour earth days, or 1,000-year days, then because the succession of processes is the same as that recorded in the rocks, it is the timing methods of science which must be questioned. If, however, there are indications in **the text** that the days of Genesis are ages, then the timing parameters of science need not be questioned.

What are the arguments professed by age-day believers? They say that the Hebrew word '*yom*' (day) is used in very general ways as well as when it means a precise day of the week. As often as it is used in a precise way, it is used just to mean an unspecified length of time or an occasion. In fact quite often, they say, the word could be substituted by the phrase 'at the time of'. Such an instance is chapter 2:4 which reads, 'In the day that Yahweh-Elohim made the earth and heavens'. This is translated in NIV as 'when the LORD God made the earth and the heavens'. If the word '*yom*' here, were taken other than an unspecified time, it would imply that the six days of creation took only one day. Sometimes a day is made to represent a year (Numbers 14:34, Ezekiel 4:6 and Luke 13:32). Sometimes a day represents a thousand years. 'With the Lord one day is as a thousand years' (2 Peter 3:8). Moses himself, when commenting upon the vastness of time in creation, in Psalm 90:4 says that a thousand years is like but a few hours in the night for the one who formed the earth.

A 360-Million-Year Day?

The recent mapping of our Galaxy by the radio telescopes of the world, places our solar system on an outer arm of the Milky Way called the Orion arm. It also reveals that, about every 360 million years, our revolving Galaxy passes through a dust cloud lying across its axis. This would bring darkness and then light each time. It could be significant therefore that the time periods in Genesis chapter 1, are marked off by the Hebrew expression, 'evening came and morning came'. Thus it is the dark–light experience which is emphasised rather than the length of a day which in that case would be measured from morning to evening, not 'it was evening, it was morning'.

They support this possibility by noting that if we correlate what God did on the fifth day with the geological fossil scale from the Cambrian to the Permian which records the same happenings, we find that the time calculated by science is the same – 360 million years.

Arnold Wolfendale, Professor of Physics, says that the rotation of the Galaxy takes about 250 million years, but what is less well known is the fact that the solar system has its own velocity which would lengthen the time.

Nigel Calder, a Cambridge physicist, says that parts of the Galaxy revolve at various speeds. The outer arms formed by trailing behind

Figure 3.1. The Milky Way Galaxy. Idealised plan of our Galaxy, the Milky Way, based on radio observations of hydrogen gas lying along the spiral arms. S marks the position of the Sun. Note the expanding cloud of gas emanating from the centre. The combined results of work in various countries have revealed convincingly the double spiral shape of our Galaxy. We can now state our whereabouts more precisely: we are in a spiral arm of the Galaxy that runs in the general direction of the constellation of Orion and is therefore known as the Orion Arm.

Courtesy: Nigel Calder 'Violent Universe' BBC Publications

taking longer to complete their orbit. A superficial look at a map of the Galaxy and by counting the number of arms gives the impression that it has revolved six times; this could be misleading, but could it represent six galaxy-days of creation?

The galaxy-days would begin many million years before the sun and the earth and planets were formed and that may be why the solar system is not mentioned until the fourth day in Genesis. The Hebrew tense of completedness would mean that God had made the sun some time earlier, but obviously makes the days of Genesis independent of the sun. This, contend age-day believers, gives strong support to their suggestion that they were galaxy-day/ages, dependent upon the Galaxy rotation.

In this case, God's Sabbath rest of Hebrews 3 and 4 refers only to resting from creating new orders. This Sabbath would last until the time comes to fulfil the words, 'I will create new heavens and a new earth'.

Biblical Arguments for the Age-Day View

The arguments from the Bible for an age-day view are here taken from an article by Robert M. Bowman, Jr., who stated in a lecture at the Baptist College, Pretoria, S. A. in 1989:

> There are essentially three positive lines of evidence which may be used to demonstrate that the scriptures indicate that the 'days' of Genesis 1 are far longer than 24 hours each . . . that in fact each day of creation in Genesis 1 stands for an age of undetermined length. These arguments are as follows:
>
> 1. The sixth day of creation is clearly longer than 24 hours, since on that day God does a number of works which are described as taking considerable time, and since Eve's creation is welcomed by Adam as having come 'at last'.
> 2. The seventh day has not ended yet, since it is not closed out by 'And there was evening . . .' as were the first six days; no new creation week has begun since man was created; Christ argued that doing works of mercy on the Sabbath was appropriate, since God was doing so on his Sabbath; and the epistle of Hebrews explicitly says that God's Sabbath rest is still continuing.
> 3. Comparing God's eternal pre-existence to the age of the mountains and the earth (Psalm 90:2) makes little sense if, as the young-earth view requires, the earth was created only five days (120 hours) prior to mankind, and the mountains only three days (72 hours) before mankind.'
>
> A careful study of Genesis 1–2 reveals that the following events took place on the 'sixth day'.

1. God made the land animals (1:24,25).
2. God created Adam (1:26,27; 2:7).
3. God planted the Garden of Eden (2:8).
4. God placed Adam in the Garden (2:8,15).
5. God told Adam not to eat of the forbidden tree (2:16,17).
6. God brought the animals to Adam to be named (2:19,20).
7. God put Adam into a deep sleep and removed a rib (2:21).
8. God built the rib into a woman (2:22).
9. God brought the woman to Adam, who named her Woman (2:23).
10. God told Adam and Eve to populate the earth and subdue it (1:28).

The language used to describe many of these events implies that they were processes involving the passage of time ('formed', 'planted', 'named', 'built', etc.). The fact that Adam was placed in a 'deep sleep' necessarily means that the operation of removing the rib took some time, probably several hours at least.

The naming of the animals, however, is the major obstacle to the 24-hour view of the sixth day of creation. Even assuming that Adam had to name, not every individual species of animal, but only major kinds, these alone would run into the hundreds. Assuming that Adam worked during the daylight hours only, and that he only had to name 300 different animal kinds, he still would have had only about two minutes with each animal. If, as is more likely, the number was three or four times that, Adam would have had half a minute or less with each animal kind.

Such a hasty procedure is ruled out by the significance of the naming process. The point of Adam's giving the animals names is that he had become familiar enough with them to know their characteristics, that he had developed a relationship with them and established his position as master (compare 1:28). In each case, he would come to the realization that the animal he had come to know and name was not his equal, but that he was the master and they the underling; and this realization would create within him the desire for a mate, someone his equal with whom he could share his life. Such a process obviously required time – far more than a few hours.

That this process required a great deal of time is confirmed by Adam's emotional cry of 'at last' (2:23) upon seeing Eve. A check of the concordance will confirm that this term regularly was used to denote an occurrence which came after a long wait or at the end of a long process.

The best response young-earth creationists have given to this argument, so far as I have been able to find, is that what would have taken us a long time to accomplish might not have taken Adam much time at all. Perhaps Adam, because he was not yet fallen into sin, had a higher sensitivity and self-awareness, and so knew immediately of his need for a mate. Perhaps he was endowed with far greater intelligence and perception, so that he was able to become well enough acquainted with the animals to name them in only a few seconds each. Perhaps; but there is no evidence from scripture to support such assumptions. In light of Adam's 'at last', it seems more probable that the events of the sixth day did indeed take place over a period greater than 24 hours.

Each of the first six days of the creation week end with the statement, 'And there was evening and there was morning, the first (second, third, etc.) day'. The seventh day, however, does not end with this statement, nor any other indication that it has ended. Since God's work of creating this world was not resumed on an 'eighth day', the open-ended nature of the seventh day makes it almost certain that we are to understand it as still continuing.

This understanding of the seventh day is confirmed by two passages in the New Testament. In John 5:16,17 we read, 'And for this reason the Jews were persecuting Jesus, because he was doing these things on the Sabbath. But he answered them, "My Father is working until now, and I myself am working".'

The evangelical biblical scholar, F. F. Bruce, explains Jesus' words as follows: 'The point of this reply to the charge that Jesus had broken the Sabbath by performing an act of healing on that day is this, "You charge me with breaking the Sabbath by working on it". But although God's Sabbath began after the work of creation was finished, and is still going on, he continues to work, ". . . and therefore so do I".'

That God's Sabbath rest has not ended is explicitly stated in Hebrews 4, where the statement, 'And God rested on the seventh day from all his works' (Genesis 2:2), is cited as proof that God has rested and is resting, and so those who believe can also have rest: 'For the one who has entered his rest has himself also rested from his works, as God did from his (4:4,10). For God, to 'rest' is not to be inactive, but to cease from creative work and instead interact with and enjoy his creation; by responding to God in obedient faith, we can be on the 'receiving end' of God's rest. The final result for the believer will be that, having persevered in faith as proved by good works, he will be able to cease from his works and enjoy the fruits of his perseverance in unending fellowship in God's rest (Hebrews 6:10–12; 10:24,25,36–39; compare Rev 14:12,13).

Young-earth creationists generally argue that the rest day of Genesis 2:1–3 was a literal 24-hour day, marked by God as a type or picture of his eternal rest in which Christians will enter according to Hebrews 4. This view does not take John 5:16,17 into account, however, and also makes a distinction between the rest of Genesis 2 and that of Hebrews 4 which neither text makes.

According to the young-earth view, the earth was created on the first day, the mountains on the third day, and mankind on the sixth day, so that all of these were created within a six-day span or 144 hours (roughly). This means that mankind was created about 72 hours after the mountains and about 120 hours after the earth.

Psalm 90:2, however, seems to imply that the mountains are far older than mankind, since God's antiquity is compared to that of the mountains (as well as the earth). This suggests, on the face of it, that the ages of the mountains and the earth are somewhat comparable, and very long in comparison to the age of humanity. Of course, that is precisely what the age-day view holds, according to which the earth is about 4.5 billion years old and the mountains about 4.0 billion years old, whereas man is about 8–25 thousand years old.

It may be objected that none of the above arguments are absolute proofs for the age-day view. That is probably true. However, they do give the age-day view a certain probability; they would appear, in fact, to make the age-day view the more probable. At the very least, these arguments should show that the age-day view is not the compromise position which many young-earth creationists have condemned it as being.

Conclusion

The age of the earth is a hotly debated subject among Biblical scientists. Nevertheless, we can be sure that God will, one day, reveal these things to our understanding, as we are assured by the apostle Paul in 1 Corinthians 13:9–12.

There are two important points you need to remember. **First**, the events of Genesis correlate with the findings of science; the timing is a different matter. **Second**, the mark of a true Biblical scientist is not whether he believes the particular view you subscribe to, but whether he believes the Bible to be the unerring Word of God.

SUMMARY

GOD'S TIMING AND HUMAN ASSUMPTIONS

Order of creation is more important than the length of time. Don't insist on voicing your pet time schedule!

Five Fashions of Biblical Scientists

1. Age-day theory for creation days
In the 19th century most Biblical scientists accepted age days. Founders of Creation Science Movement accepted this theory, as Dr David Rosevear said (but many in it now press for 24-hr days of creation). Founders were Dr M. Davies, D. Dewar, Prof. Ambrose Fleming, Prof. F. A. Filby, Dr R. E. D. Clark, W. Beasley, Prof. Rendle-Short.

2. 1,000-year days then became popular;
Adam lived nearly a thousand-year day. Cf. Gen 2:17. According to Usshur, six millennial days have passed. Seventh millennial day of rest and Christ's reign is near (2 Pet 3:8).

3. Revelation to Moses took six days
Advocated by Prof. D. Wiseman, Assyriologist (London University)
Accords with ancient Middle East methods.
Prof. Van der Spuy similar 'six-day blueprint of billion-year programme'.

4. Galaxy-days 360 million years long
Milky Way Galaxy takes 360 million years to revolve. Dust across axis makes it go dark every revolution. Genesis 'It was dark. It was light, the second day' (light before the sun) agrees.

5. 24-hour days based on Exodus 20:11
Prof. Enoch says sun created after the earth. This misinterprets Hebrew historic tense on fourth day: 'God had made sun.' Difficult sixth day afternoon, when ten major events took place. Note that seventh day did not end (Gen 2:1-3). Heb 4 says God still rests (from further acts of creation).

Essentials: Believe God's words to be true, but don't cause divisions over creation timing (1 Cor 13:2).

4 MOSES IN THE TIME MACHINE
AN IMAGINARY SPACE-TIME JOURNEY

Truth can be entertaining! Permit me now to sum up what we have learnt so far using a bit of space-fiction or science-fiction and adding more details as we do so. I have the following script dramatised on cassette (see p 97), it is something which could arouse interest amongst your friends!But let me tell you how I got this idea for our space-time journey.

Two scientists suggested that the 'days' of creation in Genesis chapter 1 were the days in which God told Moses how he had created everything. Those days of creation, they said, were not the length of time God took to create, but the length of time he took to tell Moses all about it. You may remember that the Bible says that God spoke to Moses face to face as a man speaks to his friend, and that Moses wrote down everything God told him. Professor Donald Wiseman is one scientist I have mentioned. He is a great expert on archaeology of the Middle East and he declares that the methods of the ancients would confirm his suggestion. It is that the six days were the days during which God revealed his creation to Moses; *not* how long he took over creation itself.

The other scholar is Professor van der Spuy of South Africa. He wrote to me to suggest that God worked out, in six days, a billion-year plan of creation. This suggestion is rather similar to Professor Wiseman's six days of planning, but billions of years to implement. He calls it, 'A Six Day Programme for a Billion Year Future'. If this were so, it would be this six-day blueprint which he would reveal to Moses.

Whether you agree with this or not, carry on reading, because, although the idea may seem unusual, I am merely using it to illustrate the discoveries which science has brought to highlight the wonders of Creation in Genesis 1 and 2. This drama allows us to visit Moses in a time machine.

Time in Space

Dr Michael Shallis, the scientist, imagines an amusing situation to illustrate the relativity of time. A 50-year-old man leaves his daughter aged 25 to go on a spaceship journey. He has with him an atomic clock to check how long he will be away. His space capsule rockets away at

90% of the speed of light and returns to earth four months later according to his atomic clock. To his surprise, an old lady awaits his arrival. She is aged 60. It is his daughter who cries, 'Where have you been all these 35 years!' The daughter is now ten years older than her father! She had kept careful time by her atomic clock on earth.

This scientist declares that this possible effect of time–space flight has been verified by astronauts using very precise atomic clocks. This includes those who went to the moon in 1969.

The radio telescopes and satellite probes can look out to the margins of the universe. By this they see what the universe was like near the beginning of creation. This has prompted me to join Moses 3,500 years ago in a time–space capsule and, in imagination, watch him writing the first chapters of the Bible and see the exciting happenings many ages ago.

So I hope you will join me in this time–space capsule!

ALL ABOARD THE TIME MACHINE!

Here is our time capsule. Step inside. The door shuts automatically. There is a row of buttons with flashing lights. Press the button for 3,500 years back to Moses. Phew!

Here we are looking at Moses on the Mount. But which Mount is this? The Mount of Transfiguration, 2,000 years ago? No, it is Mount Sinai, 3,500 years ago. Take off your shoes! You are treading on holy ground! O Lord have mercy! I am a man with unclean lips.

Quick, press the time-speed button! That's too fast! You've made time stand still – listen! What's that voice now time has stood still?

'I am that I am! I am the eternal present! This is where I plan the future as if it were present.'

Oh! press the emerald button. An emerald rainbow surrounds the throne of God. That button makes all universe history pass by in six days.

Ah! Moses has already done it! Here we are back to the first day of creation, back in time with Moses. He is busy, jotting it all down in his notebook. That's a habit with Moses – he was taught it in the wisdom of Egypt. On the walls of the tombs there are paintings of scribes writing down everything – the operations of the workers, how long they are taking, everything is written down.

Oh Moses – not so fast please. Your notes are so concise and so correct. You are writing down the whole creation on one page! We have it at the beginning of our Bibles.

Here we go, back to the beginning.

'In the beginning, God.'

Look we have sped up to the NASA space probe sent up by America. That is also filming back into the beginning. Now we have passed NASA, the space probe. The ripples – look! Can you see all those ripples forming in the dark dust of newly-created matter? The primary particles. There are the ripples – the ripples of gravity – forming. That's not quite back to the beginning of creation. The scientists called it the 'lumps in the primordial soup'.

Let's see, what is Moses writing?

'Without form and void and darkness was upon the face of the deep and God's Spirit moved upon the surface of the waters' – that's where you got your ripples.

But Moses, please take us back to the beginning.

'In the beginning'. Yes, that's it. It's as far as the scientists got with the NASA space probe. But what's before the beginning, Moses?

'God! In the beginning God!'

Ah, the scientists have not got there yet. They have not gone back far enough. They have not got back to the first cause. Here is the first cause – God. In the beginning God created the heavens and the earth. Look! There is the great white throne from whose presence heaven and earth is flying away. How awesome, how fearsome! Moses, why are you writing the holy name of God in the plural – the triple plural, meaning three – when you are writing the verb 'created' in the singular?

'Because God is Trinity, yet he is one.'

Let's get to your next word, 'created'. You write the Hebrew word '*bara*'. That means 'create from nothing'.

'Yes, I shall write that word only *three* times on this tablet. Three times God created from nothing – matter, life and the soul of man. From matter, animal cells and then soul, God made everything else. He formed, moulded and brought forth all things from those three basic creations.'

Oh Moses, you are going too quick. Back to the first day's recording.

'Let there be light!'

Oh look, our scientists agree with that. They agree with Dr Geo Gamov and the famous physicist, Le Maitre. Le Maitre said, 'The Divine command, "Let there be light" is entirely consistent with the intense radiation at the beginning of creation!'

'How very condescending of them to agree with what is true! Don't bring your limited scientists into my record Victor. Some of their findings are darkened by unbelief.'

Oh, but Moses, our earthlings have limited earth-minds. $E = mc^2$ is as far as they can get and quantum mechanics. Have patience with them Moses, they are not in touch with the Creator as you are. Besides, be fair to Gamov and to Le Maitre. Some have criticised their findings; they have accused them of making a theory so that they can account for creation without a Creator. But that's not true. Definitely not true! Both these scientists are believing Christians. They both say that it was God who said, 'Let there be light!' They actually exposed a rival theory which tried to do without a Creator. It was a theory which said there never was a beginning. Now, all scientists accept the evidence that there was a beginning. They support the first words which God gave you to write, Moses.

Relative Time

From our time machine which took us back to Moses, Moses looks startled as we stare at him from the future.

Moses, I explain, I'm watching you take down in six days God's blueprint plan of creation. Why do our scientists think it took God ages to implement it?

'All time is relative,' says Moses. 'In eternity nothing is either long or short. Don't you remember what I wrote in Psalm 90 about the God of the ages. Look at it!'

Oh yes. At the top of the Psalm, it's got your name! It says, 'A prayer of Moses, the Man of God.'

'What did I say about creation and time? Read it Victor.'

'Before the mountains were brought forth and before you ever formed the earth and the world, from everlasting to everlasting, you are God . . . For a thousand years in your sight are but like yesterday when it has passed, or as a watch in the night.'

'And what did Peter write 1,500 years later? You know, dozy-headed Peter. I saw him dozing on the Mount of Transfiguration!'

Oh, he wrote in his second letter, 'We were eyewitnesses of the glory of the Lord Jesus Christ when we were with him on the holy mountain . . .'

'Yes, yes, I know,' interjects Moses. 'But what did he say about time?'

'With the Lord one day is as a thousand years and a thousand years is as one day.'

'That's right – he was referring to my Psalm 90 and relative time. Even Satan knew that. He tempted Jesus by showing him all the kingdoms of the world in a fraction of time. God could show me the long ages of creation in just 24 hours.'

By searching the outer edges of the universe, they claim to have gone back 14 billion years.

'But God did not tell me to write in any time-length. He only said, 'In the beginning'. The first day has not even begun yet. However long it took, it only took me six days to record it on God's worksheet. You must remember that space-time itself is created.'

Yes, even our scientists say that, before the universe began, space and time did not exist.

'Correct! Remember what God said to me at the burning bush, My name is, 'I am that I am'. In other words, he is the eternal present.'

Moses, it's amazing how up-to-date that is. Our scientists have found that even shortness of time is relative. We have atom-smashing machines to see what they are made of. They've found that a tiny particle called a 'charm' has a very short life. It only exists for a million millionth of a second. I can't imagine that, can you? It means that by the time you've counted up to one, a million million charms could have succeeded each other in time!

'What's a charm?' asks Moses.

It's one of those elements which holds the atom together. It confirms Colossians 1:16, 'By him all things were created – all things in the universe and on earth . . . and by him all things hold together.'

Blue Hot Stars

Moses, how did you get this information so long ago, before our scientific discoveries? Your words are so accurate.

'They are not my words, they're God's words. Don't you remember, God talked with me face to face as a man speaks to his friend. I was curious, so I asked him how he created the universe.'

Well, Moses, we've had a picture sent back to us by a NASA space probe of that early time. It scanned the outer edges of the universe. This shows us what the beginning was like. It was without form and void. Then soon, ripples began to appear. The scientists got very excited about that.

'Why. What was so exciting, Victor?'

It was because those ripples must have been made by gravity. Without gravity all the matter which had been created would be void. It would not form into anything, but those ripples proved that the primary elements of matter were being drawn together into lumps. These lumps would form the stars of the heavens and other lumps. One lump would become our planet earth.

Moses looks at me and says, 'But your scientists have left out an essential factor. It was the Spirit of God who moved upon the face of that shapeless mass. Here are the words I wrote . . .'

Moses, Moses, look! I shout excitedly. That space probe has just whizzed past us. Hold tight while my time capsule catches up with it. We'll tune in to its picture of the past.

We are not conscious of the terrific speed of our capsule except the stars and Galaxies seem to pass us with a rush, registered only by our sight as we peer through the capsule perspex panel.

Look! a great arch of blue hot matter is breaking up into lumps and galaxies. The Galaxies are beginning to turn like a huge Catherine wheel. Huge bits are condensing into blue hot stars – huge stars – much larger than that which our sun became.

Moses looks puzzled. 'Why were large stars necessary to manufacture the elements for our earth when we needed only a small sun to sustain life?'

Ah, our scientists have discovered that it needed large stars and supernovae to make our earth. The heavier atoms and material and iron core of planet earth could only be realised in a big star. The big star was like a huge pressure cooker, that is what Dr Nigel Calder reports, a pressure cooker to stew the heavier elements for planet earth.

Look the star is exploding! Those heavier elements are being shot into space to make our earth. And eventually to make man of the dust of the earth. Cosmic dust is being shot out everywhere . . .

'God made man of the dust of the ground,' says Moses. 'Did I not write that? You see, God told me that he had man in mind when he made the dust.'

Just what our scientists are saying – The Anthropic Principle – earth and man from cosmic elements.

Elemental for a Fisherman

Moses, when you joined the Lord Jesus Christ on the Mount of Transfiguration, you spoke of Peter and John who were there as well. The question I'm eager to ask is, how did Peter get his scientific knowledge?

'What knowledge?'

Well, he used a very scientific word when he described the end of the universe, after all he was only a fisherman.

'What word was that?'

The Greek word *stoicheia*, meaning elements. You see, in Peter's day, the Greeks thought that nothing could get smaller than the atoms. They thought that the atom was the smallest building block in matter. But Peter referred to elements. Through our experiments in bubble chambers and accelerators, we now know that atoms are made up of 36 different particles called quarks. They are all different kinds. They have to balance one another. For example, if you have an up quark, you have to have a down quark, and each quark had to have an anti-quark, and all these are held together by another force in threes. In fact all the universal material is held together in trinities. Now I ask you this, Moses, where did Peter get the word 'elements' from and how did he know that when these particles were not held together, the universe would disintegrate?

'He got it from Jesus, obviously.' Moses then lowers his voice, 'Don't you remember how Jesus said, "The forces that are within uranium would be loosed?" '

Uranium?

'Yes, your translators have translated the word as heavens.'

Amazing! When you were on the Mount of Transfiguration, you discussed the future with Jesus, so perhaps you know that our scientists would separate the two uraniums and make nuclear fission. They've separated elements U.235 from 238 and that's made them unstable. Nuclear fission now threatens mankind.

Moses replies, 'My account was concise and correct, but I had to keep it simple, within the scope of my contemporaries, so what's this about uranium?'

Uranium was the heaviest atom. It took a lot of balancing to keep it together. Jesus must have told Peter and so Peter was able to write (2 Peter 3:12) 'The elements will melt with fervent heat and the universe being on fire will disintegrate'. In spite of that, we believers, according to God's promise, expect a new universe and a new earth where everything will go right and in which dwells goodness.

Moses' face shines out as he says, 'Did I not write: Known unto God are all his works from beginning to end?'

The Mysterious Three-in-One

Moses, in your books you described a mysterious experience with God. In Exodus 34, when you were on Mount Sinai, there seemed to be three Lords, one standing with you, one passing by in the wind, and the one in the divine voice. Here is your own writing, 'The Lord descended in the cloud and stood with me, Moses, and proclaimed the name of the Lord; the Lord passed by and proclaimed the Lord, the Lord – merciful and gracious.'

'Yes, that was the Holy Trinity, yet they are one. It is the Holy Trinity who created all things including man. Look again when I was writing Genesis 1:26.'

I look and watch Moses write: 'And God said, "Let *us* make man in *our* image, after *our* likeness.'

I am excited as a deeper insight thrills me. I see! Again you are writing God's holy name as a *triple plural*. You've also coupled it to the pronoun 'our' which is plural, and yet you write the verb make – 'let us make' – in the singular! Does this mean that the Creator is a trinity and yet one, and so created man to be like him, to be a trinity, body, soul and spirit, and yet we are one person?'

Moses' face shines with reflected glory, as he says, 'Flesh and blood has not revealed this to you, but the Holy Trinity.'

I see! I see! I shout in excitement, and is that why the universe is constructed by units of threes? Our scientists discovered that the atomic particles are constructed in units of threes. Dr Nigel Calder, who has been on BBC television, writes, 'Families of particles are made from three types of quark and their anti-quarks, and groups of three quarks.'

'Very clever!' remarks Moses, 'and what other evidence have your scientists found that the universe was created by a Trinitarian God?'

We have a Dr Nathan Wood who says that time is a trinity – past, present and future.

'How do you know that time was created like that?'

Because Revelation 10:6 says that one day, time will be no more. So that confirms Einstein's relativity with space. Space is also three-dimensional, height, length and breadth. But there is a time that every human being should understand. It is the present dimension that is important. It is written in 2 Corinthians 6, 'Look, now is the accepted time, look, now is the day for your salvation'. There is no time like the present for accepting God's salvation through Christ.'

Charming Stars

Moses, my time machine has just homed in on you writing again. Now you are writing God made the stars also. I'm surprised that you did not write that earlier!

Moses looks up from his script and gives me a penetrating look. 'Now you know very well, Victor, that this part is written in the Hebrew historic tense. It means that God had done it earlier.'

Well, that clears up that point, but that leads me to another question. Did God tell you that he had mankind in mind when he made the stars?

'Of course he had mankind in mind! The whole account leads up to the creation of man. And when he had done that, his job was finished and he rested from all works of creation.'

Well now, that is interesting, Moses, because at long last many of our scientists now say that even the great stars had man in mind – scientists like Carter and Wheeler, Templeton and Herrium.

Moses interrupts impatiently. 'Why bother me with man's opinions when it's God's which matters!'

Oh, I know, Moses, but have patience. You see it's impressive to unbelievers to demonstrate that even worldly science is coming round to the Bible's viewpoint. Dr Calder, for example, refers to Charming Stars!

'Well, of course they're charming! What's he mean by charming?'

Well, it is because those great stars contained that atomic particle called 'charm' and he says that 'charm' in the stars guaranteed human existence. It meant that exploding stars spewed out the right substances for living creatures and for man and especially the nucleic acids that God would use to record his DNA instructions for man.

'Why do you keep having to use long words? My words in Genesis were all short, single syllable words.'

These instructions meant also that God would not have to continually make each individual. By those genetics, men and women could have children and perpetuate the human race. Scientists have now found that all the mechanism for reproduction is very complicated – a mechanical device more complicated than any factory man has made.

'That's right, Victor. See God told me to write "God created man in his own image, male and female created he them, and God blessed them and God said to them, be fruitful and multiply and fill the earth." God's speech and instructions are now recorded on nucleic acid tapes, the ingredients of which the stars spewed out. They're recorded even in your own body. God had you Victor, and others, in mind when he made those charming stars.'

The Anthropic Principle

As I peer down at Moses in my time machine, Moses suddenly looks up from his script. The scratching of his pen on leather stops. He wipes his reed pen to clean it from the ink. The ink is made from the black carbon of burnt wood and mixed with water. Moses is sitting upon a low wool sack. He is not using a table to support his manuscript, for tables were not used by scribes until much later. The white sheepskin scroll spreads over his knees and trails down to the floor.

He startles me as he speaks, 'You modern scientists think you're pretty clever with your space-time capsule, don't you! Why is it you need all this proof when God has spoken? Isn't it sufficient that the order of creation he's given to me harmonises with what you scientists have found out?'

Well, it should be, Moses, but you see, several of our generations have been brainwashed with unbelief. They thought that mankind and the earth were so small in this vast universe that man was not central to the Creator's plans.

'So are their theories changing?'

Yes, evidence is flooding back and making even unbelievers see that man is back in the centre. They call it the 'Anthropic Principle'.

'The what? You used that word before!'

Anthropic is from the Greek word *anthropos*, and it means that mankind is the centre of the universal plan.

'How is it that your scientists can't believe anything without giving it a long name? What is this anthropic principle?'

It's based upon the strength of gravity and relative size. You see, the electron microscope has revealed the smallness of things. The minute mechanisms of life and particles have shown that man is halfway in size between the huge universe and infinite smallness.

'And what's that about gravity?'

The strength was just right for man, just right for man to walk upright with 12,000 kilometres of earth beneath his feet. Just right for those gravity balancers God has put in man's head for a balanced walk. On a larger planet, gravity would crush us like a super magnet. The strength of gravity was also just right to capture the air around the earth!

'I've written about the air in the second day that God told me about creation,' said Moses.

So gravity attracts things vital for life. It's like Jesus who attracts us to gain eternal life.

The Second Day of Creation

Moses, I'm looking over your shoulder to see the next words you're writing. It's the second day you've got down to. What's this you're writing?

'And God said, let there be a firmament in the middle of the waters . . .

That's a funny old word, 'firmament'. What on earth does it mean?

'In my time, we had no word to use like your "atmosphere". It was the atmosphere which made evaporation possible to separate the waters from the waters.'

Splendid! Our humans will be helped to read what our British Museum has said about this. In their book on the order of things, it says, at this point, 'The earth was surrounded by a thick, steamy atmosphere. As soon as the surface of the earth became cool enough, the water vapour condensed as rain, producing rivers and seas.'

A faint smile flits across the bearded face of Moses as he says, 'So your scientists have got it right at last!'

Yes, Moses, but I see you've missed out something in your notes on the second day. You have not given the usual ending. Your usual ending was, 'And God saw that it was good'. Have the words got lost in our copies?

'You know very well, Victor, that the Dead Sea scrolls reveal that all copies were very accurately and carefully written. No! God did not tell me to write the phrase for the second day. Have you not heard that Satan is the Prince and Power of the air! Satan took up his refuge in it. That is the time he rebelled against the Creator, lifting himself up with pride.'

How right you are Moses! Yes, and God told the prophet Ezekiel in chapter 28 that it was in the mineralogical era that Lucifer fell and became Satan. 'Every precious stone was your covering – topaz, jasper, chrysolite, beryl and onyx . . . you walk amidst the stones of fire.' We geologists know that it was then that crystallisation was forming in volcanic pipes.

'Yes,' says Moses, 'God created all things good but Satan fell and wrecked it – then I had to write in the third chapter of Genesis how he caused your race also to rebel.'

That's terribly sad. Paul wrote in Ephesians 2, 'You followed Satan, the Prince and power of the air, the spirit which now works in the sons of disobedience.' He then urges us to be re-created by Christ's changing power.

The Third Day

Let us come back with Moses in our time machine to the third day. We look and see the barren earth, the sticky clay, the sialic rock layers emerging from the waters, pushed up by the heavier sima layers of the earth's crust. 'Come back later,' God tells Moses. We go back and what do we see? A strange formation. The earth is green. Sloping hills and dales are refreshed with the first plant life. Everybody's worried about the green earth today, and so they should be. All life started with greenness. 'Let the earth bring forth grass!' I said, quoting the Old English.

Moses interrupts, 'Your translators are not accurate. I think you'll agree that I should know Hebrew – my own language. It's not grass. It means greenness.'

Thanks Moses, that explains a lot, because the fossil evidence is that green algae came first, then plants and green-leafed trees. That's all set out as starting in the third-day programme of work for God. It's the chlorophyll which gives greenness. Green chlorophyll is very important. It captures the light and turns it into oxygen. It was no use God creating air-breathing animals until the chloroplasts had put enough oxygen into the air.

'That must be why God told me to write "greenness".'

Yes, Moses, Dr Croft said the making of oxygen is extremely complicated. 'Could such a complex arrangement have arisen by blind chance?' he asks, 'Any reasonable scientist is forced to express doubts about this' – and this so early in the history of creation!

'So your scientists are beginning to believe, are they?'

Oh yes, Moses. There have always been a lot of believing scientists. It is the unbelieving ones who are beginning to think again. By the way, Moses, you state the next big miracle very briefly. It's that miracle of reproduction. All these plants must reproduce themselves by seeds. Every seed contains the full DNA code instructions and a very complicated mechanism of cell division.

'My creation tablet soon settles that scientific problem. It was *God* who spoke!'

Absolutely, Moses. Our scientists find that his words were recorded in every living plant cell. The alphabet of the DNA code came from Jesus. 'I am the Alpha and Omega. In him, the Word was life,' declared St John.

Moses raises his bushy eyebrows. St John was fond of bringing out double meanings in his reference to creation. He's using physical life to illustrate that Jesus the Word can bring spiritual life to those who believe his word.

'Yes, indeed,' agrees Moses, 'Don't forget he was with me on the Mount of Transfiguration with Jesus and Peter!'

Ah, Moses, that reminds me of a question I wanted to ask. Jesus said, 'As Moses lifted up the snake in the wilderness, even so must the Son of Man be lifted up'. Did you realise the significance of what you were saying?

'Not until that long talk with Jesus on the Mount of Transfiguration. It's Luke who tells you what we were talking about. We were talking about his exodus – yes, his exodus, not mine. The Lord Jesus told me (Moses' voice lowers to a whisper), that the Exodus Lamb depicted himself as the Lamb of God whose blood saves a believer from death. His exodus on the cross would fulfil all that – and my lifting up the snake on the pole. Elijah and I wept to think of it! Peter himself was unwilling to think it. He was shocked. "No! No!" he said. It was a shock to me as well. It was a long discussion we had on the Mount of Transfiguration about the connection of **his** exodus as a fulfilment of mine. That green mountain top suddenly seemed to turn grey with grief, that God's good earth would one day receive pools of blood from its loving Creator.'

The Fourth Day

I got back into my time-space probe and soon whizzd back again to 3,500 years ago. I was just in time to join Moses on the fourth day of creation. It was to see what God was revealing to him on that fourth day.

I was surprised at how dim it seemed. The clouds were quite opaque, and although daylight filtered through, I could not see any sky or the sun or the stars. Then a great voice shook me until I trembled right down to my toes.

'Let lights appear in the heavens to divide the day from the night – the sun, the moon and the stars!'

I turned pale-faced to Moses and said, Moses, surely God did not wait until the fourth day to create the sun!

'Did I not tell you to read my Hebrew more carefully? Did I not use the historic tense? That is a kind of "fact-accomplished" tense. It means that the sun, moon and stars are already there, but you cannot see them. They are obscured from our view.'

Oh, yes, I chirped in, God told Job that when this planet earth was a baby, he wrapped it up in swaddling clothes. That was a poetic way of referring to the bands of steam and cloud and vapour enwrapping the earth in its babyhood.

'Look!' said Moses, 'It's gradually clearing. The vapours are evaporating away. See! The glorious sun has burst through with golden rays. On this fourth day, God is taking us back in time to see it actually happening way back in time! All the stars of heaven are singing with joy as the swaddling clothes of baby earth are unwrapped!'

Ah, that explains another problem, Moses. Dr Hugh Ross says that the first baby plant life needed protection by opaque light. And even our British Museum handbook says, 'For long ages the earth was surrounded by a thick steamy atmosphere.'

'Good description! It's certainly steamy!'

But in that case, Moses, where did this light come from earlier in the universe?

'That was cosmic light! That was the light which burst from the great white throne when heaven and earth fled away from his presence. God is light and in him there is no darkness at all. Why, when I was on Mount Sinai, God had to shield me with three filters before I even looked on his back.'

I was suddenly inspired as I exclaimed that God filtered down the light still further so that we could see him. He filtered it down by the incarnation – I mean by Jesus becoming man! 'I am the light of the world,' said Jesus, 'He who believes in me will not walk in darkness, but have the light of life'.

The Fifth Day of Creation

I was a bit late joining Moses again on the fifth day of creation. God was already showing Moses the next stage in his creation. There was hardly enough time to run back the time records to enumerate all the marine life which suddenly appeared in the waters. It would take more than the morning of the fifth day to show Moses all this.

I knew from my field work with other geologists that the fossils showed a sudden appearance of more than 11 different forms of life in the waters all over the world. I had intended complimenting Moses on using such accurate language. His Hebrew said that God created swarms and swarms of living creatures.

But I was too late to make such condescending remarks. Even as my time capsule landed by Moses' side, he was gazing out into the vast blue ocean. The seas were dancing with white waves of expectancy as if rejoicing in a greatly important event about to happen. The sunny, green, translucent waves held Moses' gaze as he seemed to see in a moment of time all the oceans of the world.

Suddenly I heard the voice, 'Let the waters bring forth swarms of living creatures which move.'

Moses had pen in hand and wrote speedily, 'And the waters brought forth abundantly after their kind . . . and God blessed them saying, "Be fruitful and multiply and fill the waters in the seas!" '

Moses, that's just what our geologists have found. All those 11 phyla of marine creatures have left their fossils so thick together. They're all in one layer called the Cambrian strata; and there are no fossils before them. Our scientists are admitting that it looks like a sudden creation.

'All these creatures had to multiply and spread themselves wide, just as I have written.'

Yes, I know, Moses, but what I mean is the earlier rocks do not contain any evolutionary creatures leading up to them. It's puzzled even our unbelieving scientists. One name, Levi-Setti, said, how all these creatures with advanced mechanism suddenly arrived is a mystery. Perhaps they came from outer space.

'They did!' said Moses, 'They came from God when he said, "Let the waters bring forth swarms of living creatures which can move".'

The Sixth Day

What a busy day the sixth day was! Moses hardly had time to be shown on the sixth day of creation all that God had created in this last work schedule.

Dawn had hardly broken as I landed my time-space capsule alongside Moses, 3,500 years ago. It started with God telling Moses how he had created land animals. Well, I had expected that, because our scientists had found that land animals did arrive next on the scenario.

Well God had not time to describe every land animal on that morning of the sixth day, because in the afternoon he would have to tell Moses all about how he had created man and woman.

But I'm running ahead of myself. As soon as I had landed my time-space capsule beside Moses on that sixth day morning, I asked Moses what had God revealed so far?

He replied, 'God said, "Let the land bring forth the living creature after his particular category, cattle after their species, and everything that creeps upon the ground after its kind." And it was so!' added Moses, 'God showed me how he had made the land animals after their kind and the cows and bulls after their kind and all the creepy crawlies.'

The creepy crawlies! Why on earth did he make them? I could well do without some of them!

'They all had a job to do in the carbon cycle. Think of the earthworms . . .'

Oh yes, of course, without their fertilising action, the gardener and farmer would have a very barren plot. Incidentally, Moses, you'll be pleased to know that our scientists find that you're right after all. The land animals did come next in the fossil record – and the mammals!

'How very condescending of them to agree with what the Creator has told me. If they humbled themselves a bit more, they'd get more things right. They would not have to be constantly corrected by facts.'

The Sixth Day Afternoon

What, only an afternoon given over to God's most important project! Only six hours daylight in which to describe to Moses all about man and woman and zoology and hunter gathering and farming and . . .

'Hold on a minute!' said Moses as I landed my time-space machine beside him. 'Can't you see we're busy! It'll take all afternoon to record it, let alone put it into operation.'

Operation! Oh yes, you record two very interesting operations that God did – one to create man and then one to make a woman. I see that you have written, 'God created man, male and female' as if he did the two together, but it is not until you inscribe your second tablet that you show that a lot happened between when God created man and when he made a woman from Adam's cells. You show that between those two operations, Adam had to name all the animals God brought to him.

'Yes,' replied Moses, 'Look, I've written that the Lord God brought every animal and every bird to Adam to see what name he would give them, and whatever the man called every living creature, that was its name. Furthermore,' persisted Moses, 'I wrote, the man gave names to all the cattle, and to all the birds which flew, and to every animal roaming the fields.'

Quite, I said. You see the point is this, Moses: it took our pioneer zoologist years and years to classify all the animals and birds and to give them names. Yet, with Adam on the sixth day afternoon, all this was to happen between those two operations – one operation to create the first man and the second operation to make a woman.

'Ah, you don't get the point Victor. It was only God's schedule of work I was writing down, not how long it took him to work it out! It took me all the time to get all those notes down in the brief hours of afternoon daylight.'

Oh, brilliant, Moses, that's just what our Professor Donald Wiseman says, and also Professor van der Spuy. Van der Spuy calls your notes, 'A six-day programme for a billion year future'.

'Now don't bring me into your controversy that some of you Christians love to argue about instead of witnessing to the world. My own commitment is in Psalm 90 which I advise you to read carefully. Meanwhile, let me get on with the few hours of daytime left.'

Well, I left busy Moses that late sixth afternoon to complete his recording. I returned to my time-space capsule.

Operation Hominid

Then I looked out of my time-space capsule and saw Moses 3,500 years back, all excited. The supreme moment of God's plan was being worked out. All creation was leading up to the creation of man, 'The Anthropic Principle' as our scientists had called it; renowned scientists like Dr Nigel Calder, an astro-theorist of Cambridge University, Brandon-Carter, and Dr John Wheeler of Princeton University, and others, saw the whole universe as having man as its object.

I landed my time capsule alongside Moses again. Moses! I shouted, what are you so excited about?

'Look!' he said, 'God is showing me how he formed man from the dust of the ground!'

Yes, Moses was seeing something similar to what our NASA space probe had revealed. I expected to be looking at the Garden of Eden, but no, the process went further back than that. I was seeing huge stars exploding. It was very frightening. Huge supernovae were spewing out matter in all directions into space.

'That's the dust,' shouted Moses, 'from which God made man later. It had to be manufactured in big hot stars. The stars had to be made big enough for the heat and pressure to be great enough to make dust for man. Don't you remember, I wrote, "God made the stars also"?'

Oh yes, I remember now. Our Dr Nigel Calder says those stars were like a huge pressure-cooker, forcing the atomic particles together.

'Now what's in that dust?' asked Moses, 'In my vision of the universe, I see the Horsehead Nebula in the Orion constellation.'

That's all cosmic dust, I shouted.

'No wonder God asked my contemporary, Job – you know Job, who descended from Esau. God asked bighead Job, "Can you loose the pressures of Orion!" '

The Horsehead Nebula is dust. It is an example of star-pressured dust shot out into the universe.

'Do you know the ordinances of the heavens, then?' asked Moses, using God's words to Job.

Well, we claim to know. You see, that dust contains hydrogen, helium, carbon, oxygen, sulphur, silicon, iron . . . I was interrupted by more big flashes and explosions. The pulsars were flashing like police beacons, each marking the scene of a cosmic accident. But it was a planned accident. God was making dust from charms and quarks, to make man.

Just then I caught sight of Moses writing down hurriedly 'Then the Lord God formed man of the dust of the ground.'

Enzymes Piece Man Together

I was back on planet earth after watching the stars like pressure-cookers making the elements for man's body. A great voice echoed round the universe, 'I need a farmer to cultivate the garden!'

From my time-space capsule, I watched Moses writing 3,500 years ago, 'Then the Lord God formed man of the dust of the ground and breathed into his nostrils the breath of life, and man became a living soul.'

Moses, I said, this is clearly an operation.

'Yes,' he replied, 'My Hebrew word for 'formed', means a process. Already the operation is far advanced.'

I agreed. With our modern knowledge of genetics, I see dictated all the mechanical instructions on to a DNA tape, the Lord God is using the enzymes of genetic engineering to put all the parts of Adam's body together. The enzymes God has made are amazing machines! They clipped and joined and edited each bit of God's instructions and applied it to the appropriate parts of Adam's body which I can see coming together. First the framework – the bones cleverly engineered with joints for leverage or universal joint action. Then the build-up of muscles. Those enzymes looked amazing. Every one knew its particular job. They directed thousands of ribosomes to produce protein chains for liver, kidney, intestine, heart and brain. There were thousands of them. It looked more like a military parade ground. They even looked as if they were carrying guns.

Space and size were also relative and suddenly we were shocked to find that the capsule was shrinking us down to the size of minute molecules. We were peering deep down into infinite smallness to see these minute miracles happening. But suddenly my view was blocked. I could not see everything. White figures like assistant surgeons were gathered around the developing body to assist the chief surgeon. They must have been angels in white. We had come up back into normal size.

At last the body was ready. There it was, a beautiful, strong, muscular man. But it was lying out flat but lifeless. 'Get the circulation going!' came the order. A shock of power was administered to the heart. The heart began to beat.

A voice came in vibrant loving tones, 'I, myself,' saith the Lord, 'will give the kiss of life – mouth-to-mouth resuscitation by me, the Lord God, is what is worthy; for this peak of creation is after my own image and after my likeness. I myself will breathe into his nostrils the breath of life, and I will bless him with my father-like love.' There was a pause, 'But I cannot say yet, be fruitful and multiply. Why? Because another operation will be necessary first and that won't be yet.'

Yes, the farmer wants a wife!

Adam Speaks in Day Six

The surgeon angels had withdrawn. Shock power had started Adam's heart. God breathed into Adam's lungs. Adam's chest rose and fell. One, two, three, pause. One, two, pause. One, two, three, pause. One, two.

Adam sat up! All the angels sang! Adam sprang to his feet! All the angels praised! But Adam could not put words together yet. He needed speech therapy. Speech therapy started as it did with the deaf and dumb. It started with names.

'Come my love,' said the Lord God, looking with pride and joy at the son of his creation, 'I will bring animals to you. Your language learning will start with names. *Name* each one. *Remember* that name, then what it looked like, then the action with which the animal walked up to you. That is the way to put a sentence together.'

An animal jogged happily to Adam. Adam said, 'I name this animal 'dog'. He shall be man's first friend.'

All this remarkable experience I was observing from my time-space capsule and I said to Moses, that's just what we anthropologists have found. The dog was man's first friend to round up the sheep.

'Hush!' said Moses, 'and watch!' The dog bounded around, licked Adam's face and rushed off and rounded up a white woolly animal to bring to Adam.

'I name this animal, "sheep".' pronounced Adam in solemn tones.

'That then shall be the name of that animal I created – sheep!' said God.

So I watched as the names of animals and their actions were added to Adam's vocabulary. I watched Moses hurriedly writing them all down.

You know, I said to him, evolutionists think that human language started with grunts and growls and developed later into a language. But the evidence is opposite to this. The further back you go, the more complex the grammar structure is.

Yes, and what were regarded as primitive tribes, usually have the most complicated language. It is later that verbs and declensions get slack and careless.

Also, brain specialists find that the brain has a built-in package area for language. It is an outstanding fact that only human beings speak and write in languages. Such a contrast with other animals must be because God was to reveal himself by his written Word and speak to us through his Son.

What a long afternoon this is. Yet God still plans the planting of the garden. He still has to set out the plants. He still has on the genetic drawing board the making of a wife for the farmer.

Think I know how he did it, I said to Moses.

He looked very shocked. 'Indeed,' he said, 'You modern scientists are becoming too "know-all". That sounds an insolent claim to me!'

Too true, Moses! Did you know that it is claimed that a scientist has cloned a man?

'Horrors! really!'

And that he is walking around today. He would be a teenager by now. That is a claim made by David Rorvic.

'Well who is it?'

That is a closely guarded secret, says David Rorvic, to protect the cloned individual. That individual himself does not even know that he was cloned. He had no mother. He was just cloned from a man's tissue

'But is this true, and what if it got into the wrong hands?'

I will answer that, but first consider something we do know to be true. It is this. You and I, Moses, are descended from a cloned woman. All the races on earth are descended from a cloned woman. Your own account makes it quite clear in Genesis chapter 2:21–23. The genetics were taken from Adam's side. You recorded how God did it in some detail. Today we would call it cloning.

Moses looked shocked.

Don't worry Moses. Your account is fully scientific and even science is now agreeing that all the human race is descended from one woman – 'The Great Mama'. Only the mother passes on the mitochondrial DNA to following generations, I added, ventilating my science proudly.

'Wait a minute, Victor. You're going too fast! What about that claim that a scientist has cloned a man.'

The account is written by David Rorvic in his book entitled *In His Image*. It claims to be factual.

'This is going too far. This certainly is playing God! Did he get his idea from Genesis? Why did this scientist clone a man?'

He was asked by a millionaire to do it. This millionaire was not married but wanted someone to inherit his wealth and business. That heir must be from his own body but with no mother. The scientist claimed he could produce such a person from a tissue cell of this millionaire. The resultant human being would be an exact replica of the millionaire himself, 'In his own image'. Why? Because it would have no mixture of genes and chromosomes from any woman mother.

Now I had shown in 1969 from my book, *Who was Adam?* that this was possible. I knew the experiments which were taking place when I was at Oxford at the time by Dr John Guerdon. It is made possible because every cell of your body is capable of producing a whole complete human being – even from your tissue cells.

'How is this?' asked Moses.

It is set out in what you've written in Genesis. God told you that he gave the full instructions into the cell 'whose seed is in itself'. The human seed is now called the DNA code. It is called by the scientist, The Book of Man. Why? Because its instructions are on how to make a human and the scientists are now producing these instructions page by page. I have a slide of one of those pages. This book of man is spoken of in Psalm 139, 'In your book (O Lord) all my body parts are written'. That is why David Rorvic calls his book, *In His Image*. I think he must have got the thought from Genesis 1:26, 'Let us make man in our image'. 'Male and female created he them.'

'So then,' gasped Moses, 'this scientist, so you say, took the instructions – the seed's instructions and activated them in the machinery of another seed?'

Yes, a simple illustration is, it is like taking the embryo out of a chicken's egg and putting it into a crow's egg so that the crow hatches out a chicken! Nothing to crow about however! I chuckled, Why? Because it is actually simpler to reproduce a whole human being than to do some of the genetic engineering experiments done today. Why is that? It is because the whole human instructions were used without clipping out bits of it. It was not interfered with in any way – only copied. The whole of it! Today our scientists do not use the *whole* code but only bits of it and have produced for us our biological washing powder; suntan or sunscreen lotion; insulin for diabetics; genetically-modified apples, bananas, cabbages, carrots, peas and pears; and the short-stalk wheat now growing in fields.

'How?'

By clipping out short sentences from those instructions God put in the DNA code and adding them to the instructions already in those cabbages and carrots. This editing and re-editing of God's instructions in our cabbages and carrots is a recent advance in technology because man is discovering some of God's secrets. This clever machinery of life is in every living thing. These editors are called enzymes.

Moses looked even more shocked. 'Have they asked God's permission to do this?,' he gasped.

Scientists are only using what God has provided. They use these enzymes to clip out a section of instruction which they can use. It is an enzyme which breaks down fat which is added to our washing powder, making it biological. It is an enzyme which clips out God's recipe for insulin for diabetics. It is another kind of enzyme which produces vaccines against diseases. They are only using the tools provided by God. They have not created anything from nothing.

'And yet, Victor, did you tell me that some think that chance could account for all these very technical instructions? If it has taken your cleverest brains, with remarkable instruments to make these discoveries, how can they say that it's all the result of no brains and no divine technology! I hope your scientists are not blaming me for putting the idea into their heads!'

Not blaming you, Moses. It's only man's misuse that is to be blamed. The logic that life resulted from our Creator God, is substantiated by your description of how God did it. For example, God told you, Moses, how he cloned a woman from Adam's tissues and so started the human race. Your description of how Adam was put into deep sleep for the operation, and the genetic result that Eve was flesh of Adam's flesh and tissue of Adam's tissue, is very advanced science. Psalm 139 develops your insight. It is that all the genetic instructions are like a book. The scientific book of man. It is being copied page by page today.

God told you also, Moses, that all life is the result of seed; the seed of plants; the seed of fishes; the seed of animals; the seed of man. How did you know that the seed in a plant works on the same principle as the seed of man. We now know that the basic DNA code underlies the production of all life with its genes and chromosomes, with its machinery for copying the master tape, and editing and sub-editing, its cutting and its rejoining of instruction tapes to feed into machinery in your body to produce heart, liver, muscle and brain; or the same language to feed into a plant's machinery to produce carrots, cabbages, conkers and coconuts; or the same language to produce a Welshman or a daffodil. The same genetic language to produce a Scotsman or a thistle, or an Englishman or a rose; or the same genetic language to produce an Irishman or a shamrock.

'You scientists are clearly getting puffed up with knowledge. Did I not write in Genesis chapter 1, God spoke eight times this same genetic language to plant, fish, animal and man?'

Yes, you were right. God spoke eight times. Only recently have we discovered how God's words were recorded in the DNA code, and copied and edited and sub-edited, and recombined, by the most complex and clever machinery so small that only the most powerful microscope lets us see the machinery working. It takes an atomic microscope to blow up the size so that we can see God's computer machinery working furiously to his coded instructions.

Moses looked worried as he declared, 'Your generation is getting too big for its boots; too clever. Did I not also write of the Tower of Babel when godless men left the Creator out of their clever schemes?'

Moses, you're the clever one! Did you know that all modern surgery comes from the cloning of Eve in your record of Genesis chapter 2:21? To obtain a cell from Adam's side, anaesthetics start there too, because, as you know, Dr James Simpson who started it with the use of chloroform, got his idea of sleep for operations from the words, 'And God caused a deep sleep to fall upon Adam'. In fact he called it 'deep sleep' for operations.

By the way, Moses, your word for rib is a very ancient Sumerian word much older than your Hebrew. Its meaning is obscure and could mean 'round' or 'bowed'. Translators therefore translated it as rib, but it could mean cell. Did you get this from an older tablet handed down from Abraham? Whichever, it is does not matter, because the rib contains and makes blood cells anyway. Cloning for better products or corrective genetic engineering is done through the cell today, because in the cell is the wonderful world of engineering machinery. We know so much about it now, how DNA produces all the body parts by the machinery in the cells of your body and mine.

Watching God Make a Woman

Moses, why don't you join me in my time capsule? We'll whiz back in time to when God showed you how he made the first woman. Genesis 2:21–23 does describe an operation. Let us watch how God probably did this marvellously successful operation. Moses, step into my time capsule. It'll take us back thousands of years to Adam's time. Angels were present at the birth of Jesus and so I expect they were there as assistants at Eve's cloning, so let us join the master surgeon of Eden.

There he is! Surrounded by angel assistants, clothed appropriately in white. They hide the Lord God from view!

Look! Adam is anaesthetised into deep sleep and sustained. Now comes the perfect loving touch of God. He carefully removes the rib from Adam's side, making sure that the pleural cavity is not punctured, otherwise the lung would collapse. Angelic life support machines are at the ready by those in white standing around. The rib is carefully conveyed to another seclusion, while the Lord God closes up the place where the rib had been. No stitches are needed because God used the enzyme 'ligase' which has as its function the job of gluing ends of flesh together.

Now God goes to the other seclusion, leaving the angel nurses to care for Adam as he slowly comes round.

Moses said, 'And the rib which the Lord God had taken from the man, he built up into a woman.'

Moses, he must have done this away from Adam, because when the cloning was complete, he brought her from there to Adam.

Our latest knowledge of cloning helps us to understand how the divine surgeon operated. That cell would be a body cell, a somatic cell, not a sex cell. (This means that the multiplication of cells would be by mitosis and not by meiosis.) It would mean that Eve had no father or mother. Genetically, she would be the twin sister of Adam because the genes and chromosomes would be Adam's and not an assorted meiosis from any other donor.

Moses interrupted me and said, 'Would you kindly stop your technical clap-trap. The Lord God is now hidden from our view by his white-clothed angels. So, from your knowledge, what would be going on now?'

Think of the process of cloning that this Chief Engineer is doing. He uses the eight enzymes God placed in Adam's cells which have as their job the cutting out of lengths of DNA instruction registered by Messenger RNA.

'What did God have to cut out then and why would it be necessary?'

It's because Adam was made a male by the 'Y' chromosome, so this 'Y' chromosome would need removing, and then Eve's 'X' chromosome would be doubled to make her a woman with XX, like two kisses. (Nothing to do with love and kisses, though that was to come later!)

Moses shrugged his shoulders impatiently. 'I think the description which the Lord God gave me is simpler. "He built up Adam's cell into a woman".'

All right then, as the Lord God 'built up' the parts (to use your Hebrew expression), he would use his single strand Messenger RNA to put in the X chromosome copied and transferred by Transfer RNA. The appropriate enzyme 'Terminal Transferase', used for repairing tissues, is now placed in the new copy.

'Victor, will you be more simple!'

Yes, Moses; and I pressed on, describing what must be happening. Adam's edited flesh cells are now ready for multiplication. They are now being nurtured in the cytoplasm of other cells in Adam's rib. Cell multiplication starts at a terrific rate, even quicker than normal gestation. As cells multiply, they are specialised by chapters from the DNA code to manufacture different parts of Eve's wonderful body. Even in normal gestation, each cell would have 20,000 ribosomes shooting out molecules for Eve's heart or liver at a rate of half a million per minute. This 'build up' is even faster.

Then Moses asked a funny question. 'Does Eve have an umbilical cord?'

Probably, because the genes in the code are there for one. Perhaps the necessary sustenance is fed by God through it.

The Second Person of the Holy Trinity is most interested in this because, later in history, he, himself, is incarnated by a similar process, but at the natural gestation rate of nine months as recorded by St Luke. In his case, the 'Y' chromosome for males would be added, not removed, as for Eve.

'Look!' said Moses, 'Adam is recovering consciousness. He will be waiting to see if the operation was successful.'

'What has happened?' asks Adam, shaking off the artificial sleep treatment.

As the Lord God was busy with building up Eve's cells from Adam's, the angel explains the mechanics of the cloning operation. This is evidenced by Adam's delighted exclamation later. 'At last! She is bone of my bones and flesh of my flesh, body cells of my body cells!'

The angel knew that once Adam had set eyes upon Eve, he would be too excited to wait for details after the introduction. He would be in too much of a rush. He was right.

Look! God is bringing this beautiful young woman to meet Adam. Her lovely hair flows in tresses down over her shoulders. She walks with graceful balanced tread. She is slightly nervous as she passes a bush full of blossom into Adam's sight.

Adam exclaims, 'At last! She is bone of my bone and flesh of my flesh!'

'Yes,' said Moses, 'His exclamation was a terrifically excited one. That is what I tried to convey in my Hebrew. Rather like – how would you say, Victor?'

I'd say, Wow-ee! Thanks God! What a marvellous and beautiful job you've done – all from my cells!

An awesome silence came, until I said that Adam was also given other details which genetic engineers have only recently found the truth about. It is that all the human race is descended from one woman. This is because (and I'll explain the word in a minute) we all have mitochondrial descent. This only comes from the mother. So that is why Eve was called Eve. That is why Genesis 3:20 says, 'Adam called his wife's name Eve because she was the mother of all living.'

The Busy Afternoon Continued

I looked at Moses from my time capsule. We were still at that sixth day afternoon. Moses was still trying to get down all the events of that afternoon. Already he had recorded the creation of Adam, the planting of the garden, the naming of all the animals. Everyone of them.

Moses nodded, 'It was a busy time. That's why Adam exclaimed, "At long last!" when he saw Eve after their operation. Y'see, he'd named all the birds; he'd named all the wild animals; he'd named all the mammals – the cattle and, of course, the dog, who rounded up his sheep.'

Whom did he name next, Moses?

'His wife, of course! He named her Eve, because she would be the mother of all living. Her name means "life".'

I was excited. You made a great scientific statement there. Did you know, then, that scientists have now discovered that all the human race is descended from one woman?

'There you go again!' Moses looked up from his scroll, 'Looking for scientists to agree with what God has revealed to me. Of course they'll agree when they get their facts right.'

That's all very well for believers, Moses; but it's impressed the world, and that helps us to lead them into spiritual truth.

'What made you scientists agree that everybody was descended from one mother?'

It was that only the mother passed on the mitochondrion.

'The mito . . . what?'

. . . chondrion. That's what makes all the machinery in our bodies work. It supplies the fuel to make the machinery in our bodies work.

Moses raised his bushy eyebrows in surprise, but I continued, trying to impress with my expert knowledge. As I have said, the mitochondrion is only passed through the mothers. Without this, none of the cell machinery would work.

'Why?'

Because the mitochondrion is the power station. It supplies fuel to work all the machines of the cells of your bodies. Without it, it would be like cars without petrol. Now, the astonishing thing is this. The secret code for manufacturing this important power station is entirely the woman's prerogative. She has all the copyrights to the fuel.

Moses turned abruptly to me, 'How have your genetic engineers discovered this?'

They found that in conception, as a sperm (that's the seed) enters the egg (that's the woman's seed), the wiggling flagellum tail breaks off outside the egg and is lost. That tail contained the mitochondrion which supplied fuel to that tail in order to empower it forward, but the moment that the male sperm enters the egg, it is lost and so it will be empowered by the female's power station and so all the machinery of the embryo will be empowered and copied from her mitochondria.

Moses stood up in horror. 'Wait! wait! not so fast. Are you talking about the seed of the woman, God spoke of?'

Yes, I said, the mother holds the copyright. Why? Because this power station has its own coded instructions independent even from the cell's code of instructions. That is why it is called the mitochondrial DNA, to distinguish it from the cell's DNA. It is a private company which has the monopoly, with a woman company director. And what a factory she controls! Scientists describe it as more complicated than any man-made factory. Dr Malcolm Dixon of Cambridge, who was head of the enzyme biology department, said that there are six processes through which the raw materials have to go before fuel becomes available. Each process is complex and called Creb's cycle, after Professor Creb of Oxford. But the problem is that this power station needs the fuel which it manufactures to start up all its own machinery! So who supplied the first can of fuel for the mitochondria to produce fuel to start its factory to produce the fuel?

'Are you asking me?' said Moses, 'Well obviously, you saw him empower her with life – Life! Yes that's her name!'

For clarification I added, Yes, God did, when he built up the first woman and started her machinery going. He poured in the first can of fuel, so to speak. So then, this power station is a private monopoly. It has its own secret code to construct the factory itself, and the copyright is passed on down through the mothers.

Now here is the next mysterious fact. Genesis 3:15 implies that the Saviour of the world would descend through the woman's seed (DNA) to defeat that snake, Satan. Sure enough, it was through the virgin Mary that Jesus was born, without any human father, yet from King David's lineage – the woman's seed supplying fuel supply at each conception. This highlights another mysterious fact which no one else seems to have noticed. It is this. Whenever the heir to the throne of David's lineage is given in the Old Testament, the mother's name is *always* supplied, because it was through the royal women of the southern tribes of Israel that Jesus descended. This is a contrast to the northern kings of Israel. Their mother's name is *never* mentioned.

This explains Matthew's table of Christ's lineage where, contrary to custom, the names of several women appear in it. Yes, as Paul wrote, 'In the fullness of time, God sent his Son, born of a woman'. From Eve through to Mary!

I selected the button for the present time on the control panel of my time–space capsule. The years whizzed by. Then I bowed my head to thank God for the wonderful insight he had given me with Moses.

SUMMARY

MOSES IN THE TIME MACHINE

In an imaginary six-day space-time journey, we see how God created the universe and man, male and female. If space and time are relative, it avoids conceptual difficulties; so we speed back with NASA probe to see God actually creating the universe and how it all accords with Genesis and we converse with Moses as he writes it down!

The Sixth Day has the longest programme
In it Moses sets down the blueprint for the following busy schedule:

1. God made the land animals from the ground.
2. God created Adam from the dust and nuclear acids left by super novae.
3. God planted the Garden of Eden and made trees and plants to grow.
4. God placed Adam in the garden to cultivate it.
5. God told Adam not to eat the forbidden fruit.
6. God brought all the animals and birds to Adam to be named.
7. God put Adam into a deep sleep and removed a rib.
8. From a cell in his rib, by genetic engineering, he built the cell into a woman.
9. Introduces Adam to her who exclaims '*At long last* one made flesh from my flesh!' (cells from my cells).
10. They were joined as husband and wife and became 'one flesh'.
11. God told Adam and Eve to populate the earth and subdue it.

It is exciting to watch the operations with the knowledge we now have of the eight enzymes for genetic engineering.

An audio tape of 'Moses in the Time Machine' is available, made by the author (with entrancing sound effects by technician Tony Newnham). It will thrill youngsters of all ages and uses language of contemporary science such as 'lumps forming in the thin gruel of space at the appearance of ripples'. Price £5 from UCB.

5 GOD'S AMAZING WORD PROCESSOR
THE GENETIC BOOK OF MAN

To illustrate the miracle of the DNA code of instructions, I will describe to you how wonderful those instructions are in the 'Book of Man'. 'The Book of Man' is what scientists are calling those instructions. Where is that book? It is contained in the middle of every cell of your body and also in the cells of animals and plants.

Scientists (molecular biologists) are now able to read the message of the genes. Yes, and what is more, they are printing out that message page by page, part of which is shown in Figure 5.1.

Q 'The message of the genes'. What message is that?

They are the instructions in your body on how to manufacture and reproduce the parts of your body. They are set out in sentences, paragraphs and chapters.

GCTGTTCAACCACTAATAGGTAAGAAATCAT
TCCAGACCGCTTTGGCCTCTATTAAGCTCAT
AAGATGATTTCGATTTTCTGACGAGTAACAA
CTCGTCGCTGCGTTGAGGCTTGCGTTTATG
TTCCTGCTCCTGTTGAGTTTATTGCTGCCGT
TTCAAACGGCCTGTCTCATCATGGAAGGCG
TCGAGCGTCCGGTTAAAGCCGCTGAATTGT
ACACTGACGTTCTTACTGACGCAGAAGAAA
TGATGTAATGTCTAAAAGGTAAAAAACGTTC
GCGAGGTACTAAAGGCAAGCGTAAAGGCG

Figure 5.1. Human genome
This is a quarter of a 'page' from 'The Book of Man' or the human genome. From a slide given to the author by Dr C. Berry, the geneticist.

The genes themselves are like sentences. Several genes together make a paragraph and many paragraphs of gene clusters make a chapter and many chapters make a book, called a chromosome. There are 23 chromosome books to make the whole encyclopaedia of instructions. An encyclopaedia specifies a man. This is duplicated to make an identical copy so that the body has two encyclopaedias – in other words, 46 books or chromosomes in each human cell. These books have so many words that the human encyclopaedia is over ten times as long as *Encyclopaedia Britannica.*

These are instructions, so what do they instruct? They instruct complicated machines, called the ribosomes, to make the proteins which construct the shape of your heart, blood cells, intestines, stomach, liver, kidneys, glands, eyes, brain, bones, muscles, etc. and to put them all in the right place for a human being.

There are other machines in your body cells to help all this to be done. They are called organelles. Without them, there would be no cellular production.

In the central office of the cell, the master copy is kept – that is the complete book of man. This master copy is never let out of the office, so it has to be copied. The machine which copies it is an enzyme, which works rather like a fax copier. The copy is called RNA. This in turn has to be edited in sections so that only the sentence and paragraphs are sent to those ribosome machines which are going to produce that particular body part.

Genetic Sub-editors

These are called Messenger RNA. To edit and copy these sections, there are eight main enzymes. These are like sub-editors of a newspaper. One recognises the beginning of a sentence and so cuts the copy at that point. Another recognises the end of the sentence or paragraph needed and so cuts it there. Another office assistant, or enzyme, has the job of 'gluing' together the loose ends to other sections that sub-editors have selected and which need joining up.

This edited copy (Transfer RNA) is then taken by workers and co-workers on the 'shop floor' of the cell to feed into the translating machine. There are over 200 different workers, each a member of a different 'trade union', because each has his own special key to start up his machine. No one else has a copy of that particular key. Each worker has an assistant called a co-enzyme.

There are over 15,000 translating and production machines in the simplest cell, such as E coli, so there must be some 30,000 workers and they never go on strike and they work at a furious speed, handling thousands of molecules a minute during gestation. They are placed on a mass production assembly line with enzymes as machine tools.

Why does the message need translating? It is because it is in code – the DNA code. Think of the Morse code of dots and dashes. You would not be able to obey the instructions unless it was translated into your language.

Female Copyright

Now the scientists have discovered an intriguing thing. It is that the DNA code for its own fuel production is passed on from generation to generation only through the mothers.

For this reason, the scientists have pronounced that we are all descended from one mother (nicknamed 'The Big Mama'). This is exactly what Adam said in Genesis 3:20. He 'called his wife, Eve, because she was the mother of all living'.

The obvious question is, of course, who made Eve? There is a problem, too, about the mitochondrion fuel producer for one who does not believe in a Creator. It is this. It needs the fuel it produces to drive its own machinery, so who provided the fuel to start it up in the first place?

Moreover, the programme to produce energy is very complicated. Professor Malcolm Dixon was head of the Enzyme-Biology Department of Cambridge. He says, 'There are six processes through which the raw materials have to go before fuel becomes available. All of these processes are very complex.

The mitochondrion, itself, has been described as being as complicated as a fully-automated factory. But how could it go through six stages of manufacture without fuel before it can produce fuel to make the six stages work? He says, 'It is like trying to build a machine-tool factory without machine tools to build it'. That is unless there was a Creator.

But now listen to this. There is a similar problem with every organelle machinery in the cell that I have mentioned, if you try to account for them without a Creator. The enzyme which copied the Messenger RNA is created by that copy. It would not exist to copy unless there was an original Creator. All the editor and sub-editor enzymes exist as a result of the editing. They would not be there to edit unless there was an original Creator. The 200 specialist workers are all made by the machinery they feed. To try and account for their existence, Dr F. Crick asks for 200 frozen miracles.

Then there is the mystery of the translator. Surely the one who knew the translation to put into the code-breaker, must be the same one who composed the DNA code, the Book of Man!

So even if you thought that such clever technical instructions to make that marvellous engineering feat, the human being, fell together by a series of accidents selected by environment, you still have to explain how the translator knew the code and how such an intricate manufacturing machine became available to make the goods – including making man's brain.

Professor Catchside, giving the Oxford University lecture before the Chancellor and Senate, when I was present, said that we must take the cell as one complete working unit. Only the whole factory could provide the full processes. The old idea that a cell could have developed from a simpler virus is untenable. Why? Because without the cell mechanism, the virus cannot reproduce itself. It has no machinery to reproduce viruses, so it invades and takes over the cell's machinery. It is indeed a parasite and, as such, appeared *after* the cell.

TRANSLATING THE DNA CODE

Sometimes you see in the newspapers' personal column a secret message which may read: GO ROUND THE GREEN FOR EDWIN.

The secret agent will have a key to decode it. His key may be: 2, 3, 7, 10, 12, 15, 17, 21. By using those key numbers to pick out the 2nd, 3rd, 7th, 10th . . . letters, he gets the message: ORDER NOW.

The translating section of the ribosome changes the code into an alphabet of 64 letters or codons (code sections) by a 3 on 4 method in which the ribosome marks off in threes the four nucleic acids on the Transfer DNA tape. See Figure 5.2.

The production ribosome obeys the instructions by selecting from 20 amino acids, a string in a pattern to make its particular body part. It is like a string of different coloured beads, to make a protein. The protein can be a thousand beads. Several proteins wrapped together make a polymer for a tissue, or blood cell, or liver cell, etc. The product is then conveyed to the export canals opening out at the cell's outer membrane.

But there is still another very important department in the cell. The cell factory needs fuel or energy to run its machinery, like a man-made factory. This department is a power station with an efficiency better than our most up-to-date power station. It is a very complicated factory in itself. It is called the Mitochondrion and it produces fuel (ATP) in three grades – one star, two star and three star – or ordinary, medium and super grade. (Some of the ribosome production machines would burn out on too high a grade.)

Now the Mitochondrion fuel producer is very independent. Whereas all the other machines in the cell factory are manufactured by instructions from the master copy in the cell's central office, the mitochondrion has its own independent DNA instructions called Mitochondrial DNA (Mt DNA).

The Book of Man

Now that we have looked at the biological factory which carries out the instructions of the DNA code, the Book of Man, it is natural to ask, 'Why do scientists want to spend three billion dollars on putting the whole human genome (genetic content and order) into a printed book?'

The reason is mainly medical. It is to have a tool to correct genetic faults which have arisen. Some genetic diseases are the result of only one faulty gene. That sad children's fatal complaint, cystic fibrosis, is the result of only one gene sentence fault. It is in chromosome book 7, Chapter 5, paragraph 3, sentence 9.

Huntington's disease is at the top of chromosome book 4, but Down's Syndrome has three chromosomes instead of two in book 21. So the extra chromosome needs snipping out, just as God must have snipped out Adam's 'Y' chromosome to make Eve.

So, if the Book of Man is completed, the genetic engineers can in future use God's search enzyme which searches out the named sentence gene and marks it for treatment. But of course the question is, what happens if genetic engineering gets into the wrong hands?

So the words which God spoke in Genesis 1, created all life and are contained in the cells, in the DNA books and chapters. It is the same code in plants or animals or humans, only the instructions are different. All the cell machinery is the same, except that plants have the additional chloroplasts. (Did you know that donkeys have more chromosomes than humans?!)

The Cell

So now let's look at the cell. I will make it simple because, even if you can tell someone only one or two simple points, you will give them powerful evidence for creation.

The reason is that evidence from the cell is very convincing. On the following pages you will see I have outlined (in a diagram and a summary) seven big problems, A to G, about the cell which modern knowledge presents to one who does not believe in the Creator.

Even if you master only the first two points, they can confound an unbeliever unless he just won't face up to the implications. So don't think you have to digest all the points at first.

More and more books by scientists are questioning Darwin's evolution theory and what others deduced from it. One scientist calls molecular biology 'Darwin's Black Box' because it reveals why his theory has crashed like an ill-fated aeroplane. The black box in this case is the cell's intricate mechanism – more intricate than any computer factory.

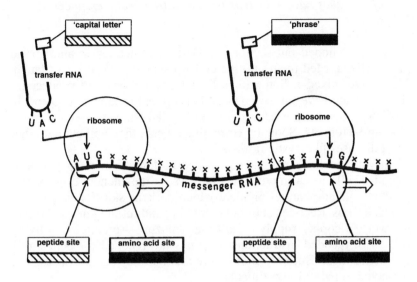

Figure 5.2. Machinery in our cells: Ribosomes and an RNA assembly line
Both the 'capital letter' and the 'phrase' (methionine) are carried by a transfer-RNA that can plug into the code section (codon) AUG. However, the capital letter transfer-RNA can only fit into the peptide start point, while the phrase transfer-RNA can only fit into the amino acid site. When AUG occurs at the beginning of the messenger-RNA it first appears in the peptide start point, so the capital letter slots in. When the AUG code section occurs in the middle of the messenger, it first appears in the amino acid site, so that the phrase fits in.   *Courtesy: C. Cheold 'What's Life?' BBC Publications*

Can Man Create Life?

The following is typical of the kind of questions which can arise in everyday life, and I am trying to provide you with the kind of answers you can give.

Q I hear the scientists have made bigger vegetables by genetic engineering! But are scientists able to create life and, if they are, does that mean that there was no Creator in the first place?

I get letters from those who are upset by press reports. With typical journalism, the reporters claim that scientists can now create life. They point to the cloning of a different type of animal, or the cloning of insulin by genetic engineering. But man has not created life. He is only using the tools already made by God.

Q So what have scientists produced by genetic engineering so far?

They have clipped out sections of God's instructions in animal and plant cells and fed them into the cell's machinery. Well, don't laugh. They have mixed a lion with a tiger's instructions and produced a 'Liger'. They have mixed goats and sheep and produced a 'geep'. In medicine, they have produced insulin for diabetic vaccines and blood clotting factors etc. Soon, by correcting a gene, they will cut out killer chest diseases like cystic fibrosis.

In your kitchen, they have provided biological washing powders. Recoded cells are even producing plastics for the kitchen. Commercial products include natural pigment which darkens skin for use in sunscreen lotions. Recoded cells are extracting and refining nearly 20% of the world's copper supply – isn't that amazing – produced by living cells with recoded instructions. Animals are recoded for better milk and better meat. But how anxious we are that they are not misused or subjected to painful experiments.

Genetic modifications are producing better bread, wheat, bigger apples, better sunflowers for margarine, better rice, rye and tomatoes.

The news in 1997 that Scottish scientists had cloned Dolly the sheep from liver cells caused worldwide concern. Such techniques in the wrong hands could lead to disaster, especially if applied to human beings. The perfect example of cloning a human being is found in Genesis 2:21–23 which of course was in God's safe hands. The bone marrow of Adam's rib would have permitted what is called 'somatic cloning' for the production of Eve. In 1967, I stated in my first edition of *Who Was Adam?* (Paternoster, p 96) that Eve's creation would have been possible in the way now demonstrated by scientific achievements 30 years later.

Spare-part surgery through genetic engineering will soon become commonplace. In January 1998, a new genetic engineering development was announced, namely a replacement human breast for mastectomy patients.

The term 'genetic engineering' is usually reserved for when only a part of the DNA code is used to develop one organ or part. The term 'cloning' is used for when the whole DNA code from one body cell is used to produce a complete replica as in the case of Eve from Adam's 'spare rib'. Incidentally, a specialist bone surgeon confirmed in 1997 that the rib is the only human bone which can be made to grow again if removed!

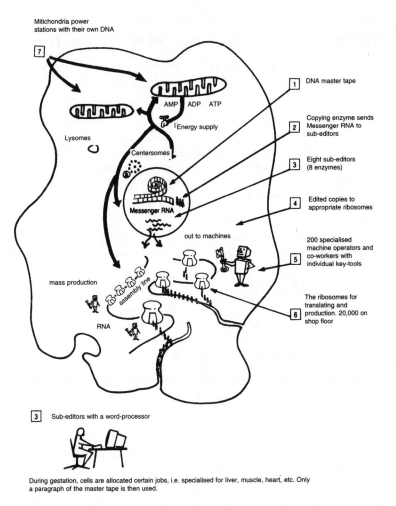

Mitichondria power stations with their own DNA

7

AMP ADP ATP
Energy supply

Lysomes

Centersomes

Messenger RNA

out to machines

mass production

assembly line

RNA

1 DNA master tape

2 Copying enzyme sends Messenger RNA to sub-editors

3 Eight sub-editors (8 enzymes)

4 Edited copies to appropriate ribosomes

5 200 specialised machine operators and co-workers with individual key-tools

6 The ribosomes for translating and production. 20,000 on shop floor

3 Sub-editors with a word-processor

During gestation, cells are allocated certain jobs, i.e. specialised for liver, muscle, heart, etc. Only a paragraph of the master tape is then used.

Figure 5.3. The Cell's Automated Factory showing the main machines (organelles)

Q But can they produce better people, kinder people, more honest people?

It is only the gospel of Jesus Christ that can change people. Only God's instructions in the Bible can do that. 1 Peter 1:23 says, 'Being born again, not by corruptible seed, but of incorruptible seed, by the Word of God'. As this cloning is done by man's intelligence, it argues for a higher intelligence in the first place. Yes, a very wonderful, divine intelligence. We are discovering more and more about the amazingly intricate mechanisms which make life possible. As an anthropologist, I had to study what is called molecular-biology. It showed how God

'BLACK BOX' EVIDENCE OF THE CREATOR FROM THE CELL

Here are the **seven big problems for an agnostic or atheist**. *Each implies a Creator not a process of evolution.* Check each reference number with that on the cell drawing, Figure 5.3.

A. The DNA code (No 1) – requiring one million pages of instruction. Gives complicated technical instructions to make a plant or an animal or man. They are more technical than any man-made computerised code to make an airliner etc. or any of the computers of the world – the brain is as complicated.
Comment: Could a series of faults in instructions (mutations) make, by accident, such a technical code?

B. This code needed someone who knew the translation and who then made a machine to translate it. This involves the ribosomes (No 6 in diagram).
Comment: Someone was needed to know the code secret and make the code breaker.

C. The ribosomes (No 6) are on an assembly line to obey the decoded instructions and to produce the parts for the body. Complicated machines like the non-stop blood-pump (the heart) and the circulatory system of pipes to and from every organ. Some cells become the nerve system of the brain.
Comment: Requires technically complex and compatible machinery to read off instructions and to manufacture accordingly.

D. Edited copies of the instructions are sent out to every ribosome (No 4). Sub-editors with word-processors specialised to make either liver, muscle, heart, etc. The right sentence of instruction is selected to send to the ribosomes. These editors are made by the cell factory.
Comment: They are made by the cell, but the cell cannot make them until they are made, because they are part of its machinery.

E. 200 different specialised workers, or enzymes (No 5), attend the production machines (ribosomes). These are all made by the cell factory.
Comment: Dr Francis Crick said that these were '200 frozen miracles'. The cell cannot make them unless they already exist to make them.

F. The Fuel and Power department, or Mitochondria (No 7), supplies fuel for every working machine (organelle) in the cell. It supplies fuel in three grades – one star, two star and three star. This power station is as complicated as any made by man.
Comment: It needs the fuel it produces to start its own fuel-producing machinery to make fuel. Who produced the first fuel?

G. When a cell itself has become specialised during gestation it becomes part of the brain, heart, or blood cell. etc. The centrosomes (No 8) multiply it into those cells and it is directed to become part of that organ in the right part of the body.
Comment: Who provided the 3-D blueprint for correct positioning?

put these instructions on to the 'ribbon' called the DNA code. This ribbon is rather like a cassette tape upon which words are recorded, but the DNA tape is a double helical tape, rather like a spiral staircase.

When you speak into a tape recorder, the words are recorded on oxide in the plastic tape. But, in the DNA tape, **God has recorded his instructions in four nucleic acids.** These instructions – God's words – were the cause of all life. For me, that argued for an originator of those instructions – a Creator. This ribbon of instructions is in the body cells of every creature.

Since my university days, much more has been discovered. In fact the scientist today can translate most of the coded instructions in the cells of any animal, even man. So the Book of Man is now being printed out page by page as in Figure 5.1, and it will take one billion pages to print all the instructions. It will be the most expensive book ever published. The scientist can take portions of these instructions and use them to make some part of the things of life for himself.

Using God's Tools

Q You said that man is only using God's tools, didn't you? He is taking those instructions to use for himself. That does not mean he has created life. All it means is that he is using what God has already created in a very clever way.

Absolutely. The more we discover, the more complicated the mechanism of life proves to be. Twenty years ago, it was thought that your body cell had only to copy the master copy of instructions and then feed these instructions into your body machinery to turn out that part of your body required. Now we find it is even more complicated. This copy of God's instructions has to be re-edited. Sections of instructions have to be cut out, selected and then rejoined together and then they have to be transferred to another tape to be fed into machines in your body which will obey the words and manufacture the required bit of the body needed.

The whole process is like a modern computerised factory where the machinery is automatically instructed to turn out living organs and parts for the body. All this argues that life's instructions were not man-made, neither did they result from a series of accidents. It helps you to believe the Bible which says that God spoke those words and made the mechanism for copying them, re-editing and self-checking them, so producing each product according to God's original instructions.

Q But this is very complicated indeed. How does God's re-editing in the cell's machinery work?

Have you been to the reference library of your local library? In a reference library, you are not allowed to take the book away. That is the same in the cells of an animal. There is a master copy of those instructions. That master copy is kept in the central office of your body cells and is never allowed out. Now, in the library there is a photocopier, so you put your blank sheets on it and get the copier to copy on to it. But there may be only certain paragraphs and sentences that you need, so you take your scissors and snip out those paragraphs.

God has provided a photocopier in the cells like that. The book of life (physical life) is opened at the right pages and the photocopier copies them. In your body this is called the messenger copy (M-RNA). This messenger copy is re-edited by a word-processor which God has also provided. The keys are called enzymes. They correct parts of the message and another key joins up the remaining instructions. This re-edited version is then checked and copied on to a transfer ribbon which takes the instructions to the machine which will read the instructions and make those living parts.

Q But surely scientists have an explanation to how this editing process first started without necessarily involving a divine engineer Creator?

Well they have a problem there! The Designer had to know what he was designing before he did the re-editing. He would programme the life machinery to take the photocopy off the copier, snip out the unwanted sentences and paragraphs and then join up the remaining pieces. Then copying that again and sending this to the manufacturing machines in your body. It is the enzymes that do the snipping. Different enzymes recognise the start and end of words and snip out the required sections. Then there is 'sticky gum' on the next sentence for joining. There are eight different kinds of enzyme to do this editing and 20,000 machines in every cell of your body to obey the instructions and manufacture the protein for each new body part. So, to go back to the illustration of the photocopier, we said that the enzyme sticks together those sentences which are wanted and then puts them on the photocopier. Again they photocopy that. That last copy they send to the right machine which understands the instructions and does the job. The instructions for re-editing must be coded in the original copy.

Q Now, if all this is going on in our body all the time, where did the original copy come from?

The Bible says it was made by God. **Many times in the Bible, you are told that God created by his words.** They are the instructions we call the DNA code. Copies of these words are being made all the time in your bodies throughout life, and then edited and re-edited and then fed to the machines in your body which God has also provided to carry out the instructions and produce your proteins, your blood cells, your tissues, your nerves, your heart, etc. Your body contains millions of these machines.

Genetic Engineering and Mutations

Q So the scientists have learnt to read those tiny instructions?

They have also learnt to use other tools provided by God, the enzymes, to cut up those instructions and stick them together in another order to make something they want themselves. This they call genetic engineering. But that doesn't mean they have created life. They have only used the tools and words of God, the Creator. They have taken a cell called E.Coli which contains over 20,000 ribosomes. They read off the instructions and make the required product.

Scientists are reading off all these instructions and are making a record of them in a book – the book I told you about which is costing a million dollars a page. They call it, The Book of Man, but really it is God's book of physical life! God has another book. That is called The Book of Spiritual Life. Jesus said to believers, 'Rejoice that your names are written in the Book of Life.'

There are many benefits as well as dangers in genetic engineering. I have already mentioned the production of insulin for diabetics. Well, by mapping out the genetic instructions, they will one day be able to identify the faulty gene which is responsible for diabetes, then they will correct it.

Q You said that genetics is God's speech in creation. Is it really possible now for man to read it and translate it?

The geneticist, Dr J. Cherfas, writes that 'It is becoming surprisingly easy to read off the genetic instructions in the human cell, and putting in markers for identification.'

Can they actually read and map out the genetic language? It sounds incredible.

Yes, but to look for a single gene is like looking for a needle in a haystack, they say. You know how computers can now search through a whole book for one word, well they can't do that yet with genes. At the moment it takes a large team of scientists to search sentence by sentence. So far, they have been able to identify chromosome 21 as the site of Down's Syndrome. Also, a gene on chromosome 7 shows up as the location responsible for cystic fibrosis which is the distressing child chest disease which used to cause death in childhood. (The chest fills up with fluid so that the poor child can't breathe.)

Q Did you say that the trouble is due to only one faulty gene?

Yes, just one gene causes this mutation. You know, we have never yet found a mutation which has advanced life in the way evolutionists hope. **All mutations are faulty copies of the original correct instructions and are detrimental.**

Q What about sickle-cell anaemia – that's a mutation. Doesn't that help the sufferer to be immune to malaria?

It does, but the patient is still anaemic and is at a disadvantage. He is not an 'improved species'. Look at Down's Syndrome which produces retarded people; usually very happy, simple people but not an improvement! Mutations retard rather than advance life. When I was looking into this at Oxford, they were hoping that a more advanced species could result from recombining extra chromosomes. Well, the Down's Syndrome argues against that and again knocks the evolution theory. It is the result of an extra chromosome which should not be there. The patient has three of chromosome 21 instead of two, but it does not improve the person, it retards function.

Q Is a chromosome much bigger than a gene?

Yes, it takes millions of genes to make up a chromosome. If we likened a gene to one sentence of the instructions, the chromosome would represent a whole book. So, if evolution was the result of extra chromosomes, it should be a major improvement, instead it retards greatly.

Q If an additional chromosome is the fault, could not genetic engineering cut it out?

That is what they are hoping to do. They are hoping to remove the extra chromosome so that the Down's Syndrome child will be born normal.

Q How would they set about cutting out a chromosome, or even a faulty gene for that matter. A gene is so small, isn't it?

Yes, a gene is invisible. It can be seen only under a very powerful electron microscope, so they use enzymes. In the cells of all living creatures there are these enzymes. They snip out sections of the instructions and join up sections of instructions. They do this under the guidance of the DNA code (Messenger RNA) – that is God's instructions in the cell. The genetic engineer uses these God-given tools. There are seven enzymes which do all this, and each has its own job to do. They are the sub-editors. (There is a list on the next page.) One sub-editor snips off a gene or two at the beginning of a sentence and prevents it being joined up. Another can add it to a chromosome and put a label on it, so that the sub-editor can trace it. Another removes a gene sentence at the end of the sentence which was labelled, and another adds to the end. Yet another sub-editor snips the tape only on which the message is conveyed and another sub-editor joins up the loose ends when a sentence is cut out. This is like editing a piece of recording tape by splicing it and then joining the parts we need.

By intervening in this process, they hope to cut out diseases, but they can do it only by using those enzyme tools God has provided in our living cells.

ENZYMES FOR ENGINEERING THE DNA INSTRUCTIONS

1. Terminal Transferase – joining for cloning.
2. DNA Polymerase 1 – provides copying material.
3. Reverse Transcriptase – for copying.
4. Nuclease S1 mapping – removes unwanted instructions.
5. Exonuclease – deletes both strands of DNA.
6. Endonase 1 – for labelling a word so it can be traced.
7. Ligase – joins (repairs) sequences. Can link selected
   sentences.

More about God's Words in the DNA Code

What a marvellous age of modern mechanics and machinery we are in! But supposing someone said to you, 'A word processor has formed itself by accident in my office accompanied by fully computerised machinery which fell together as the result of a big thunderstorm.' You would wonder what fantasies he suffered from. Yet there are clever men today who have a similar outlook. They prefer the fantasy to the facts, choosing to believe the wonderful DNA coding and processing system in all forms of life happened by chance! This does not surprise the one who reads his Bible.

The Bible prophesied that there would be a great increase in science and knowledge in the latter days soon before the second coming of the Lord Jesus Christ. Yet with this, there would be an increase in unbelief.

How does the Bible account for this paradox? Peter declared that it would be because many 'would be willingly ignorant' that God had created by his words (2 Peter 3:5). So then the increase of knowledge often makes people 'cleverer' at avoiding the truth. As Paul said, 'They will be ever learning but never coming to the knowledge of the truth' in the last days (2 Timothy 3:7).

God's Word-processor

Now Peter hit on an impressive fact when he wrote that God created by words. In my books I have shown that the discovery of the DNA code should convince anybody that God was the Creator. This code is declared by scientists to be the language of life. Dr François Jacob said, 'Life is a language and a programme.' Dr Geo Beadle, a Nobel Prize winner, said that 'this language is as old as life itself. Its words are buried deep in the cells of our bodies' (*Language of Love*, Gollancz, 1967).

Yes the life of plant, animal or man, begins and continues by the cell obeying a very complicated series of instructions. All living things are made up by a harmonious working together of cells. When Drs Crick and Watson discovered this DNA code, Salvador Dali exclaimed, 'The announcement of Watson and Crick on the DNA code is for me the real proof of the existence of God.'

Space Fiction or Creator?

Why does Dr Crick, the discoverer, quote Salvador Dali's words in his book? His book (*In Search of the Double Helix*, CUP, 1952) reports the details of the DNA code. Was he also beginning to think there might be a Creator? Whether or not, he avoids the issue in later books. In fact he resorts to space fiction to account for the origin of life. Here is his astonishing suggestion: 'Life on earth began when an unmanned spacecraft carrying primitive micro-organisms from another planet crashed into the sea billions of years ago.'

Why from another planet? Because now, even atheist scientists like Oparin of the former Soviet Union admit that the age of the earth is not long enough even to make the chance formation of life's first components feasible. Is this not being 'willingly ignorant' as Peter foretold, of the fact that God created by words?

This language of life is recorded on two ribbons which spiral in helical fashion. The message or instructions are recorded in four acids in code form in the same way that the Morse code conveys the message. The amount of instructions in a human cell would fill a library 300 times as long as all Shakespeare's plays. Surely the psalmist was right when he exclaimed, 'I am fearfully and wonderfully made . . . **in your book all my parts were written**, every one of them'. How exciting that scientists are now compiling God's Book of Man. God spoke ten times in Genesis chapter 1 and what he said is recorded in every cell of our bodies and in every cell of the animals and in every cell of the plants and they are all obeying his instructions, except where disease or drugs have interfered with the code.

Those instructions are more complicated and more technical than all the programs that are made in a fully-computerised factory. To suggest that they all come together by accident and that they accidentally reproduced millions of copies, is like attributing the whole of Shakespeare's works to an explosion in a printer's shop and that, by accident, it started turning out millions of copies of itself!

God's Code Breaker

I have shown that, even if you accounted for the code by way of evolution, you would next have to explain who knew the interpretation of the code. A message in Morse code is useless unless someone knows the interpretation. Even then, there has to be an interpreter.

In the body of living things, the machine called the ribosome translates the DNA message into instructions based upon an alphabet of 64 letters. So then, this translating machine changes the DNA code into an alphabet and then reads off the instructions and produces the parts of the body accordingly. How many are there of those translating machines in a cell? There are at least 15,000!

There are many other machines in your body cells just as complicated and marvellous which I shall not expand upon here. Now the impressive truth is that right from the beginning to the end of the Bible, God's Word has always said that God created by words. As I have said, he spoke nine times in the first chapter of the Bible. In Psalm 33:6 and 9 it says, 'By the word of the Lord were the heavens made. He spoke and it came into being. He commanded and it stood forth.'

Is it not significant that the Lord Jesus who is described as the Word in creation also declares, 'I am Alpha and Omega, the beginning and the end'? He was referring to the Greek alphabet. 'All things were made by him and without him was not anything made that was made.' Yes, Jesus is the alphabet, the code or the key of life. 'In him was life', both physical and spiritual life.

Even the sub-atomic particles have been named by the scientists by the letters of the Greek alphabet. Jesus is the alpha and omega of the material universe as well as of life. John's gospel opens with the statement, 'The Word became flesh and dwelt among us'. Hebrews 1:3 declares that Jesus upholds all the universe 'by the word of his power' or as the RSV puts it, 'by his powerful word'. And the Bible ends in Revelation 22 with those statements that the Lord Jesus Christ is the alphabet of creation.

Later on, in Volume 2: Archaeology, we shall see how these discoveries of the wonderful operation of the cell and the DNA code throw light on our scientific understanding of the virgin birth of our Lord Jesus Christ.

S U M M A R Y

GOD'S AMAZING WORD-PROCESSOR

1. Bible says God created by words.
DNA code demonstrates this, e.g. in Gen 1, God speaks nine times (see also Ps 33:6,9; Ps 139:16; Heb 1:3; Col 1:15–17; Jn 1:1–3; Rev 22:13). Each time God spoke, a new order resulted. All life consists of cells which are operated by the DNA code.

2. DNA instructions in Man
What Ps 139:16 calls God's book is now called 'Book of Man' (Human Genome). Chromosomes = volumes; Gene clusters = chapters; Genes = sentences. Cystic fibrosis is 'copy error' in book 7, Chapter 5, paragraph 3, sentence 9. Over a million pages are needed for all human instructions.

3. In all cells of living creatures.
The cell is a computerised factory. A 'fax copier' takes instructions from the master hard copy. This (Messenger RNA) is sub-edited by eight sub-editors. They use God's genetic engineering enzymes, for tracing, cutting, rejoining and gluing.
Edited copies (Transfer RNA) are used by workers (200 types) to feed into 20,000 translating machines (ribosomes). Only God could have known the translation.
Ribosomes obey instructions and produce protein chains. These make body organs and tissues.
Code uses an alphabet of 64 'letters'.

4. Mitochondrion fuel producer
To work cell's machinery. Has female copyright and monopoly DNA. Therefore scientists know that everybody is descended from one mother. 'Eve mother of all living' (Gen 3:20).

5. Seven problems face the atheist
The code's origin, code breaker, fax copier, enzyme sub-editors, machine operators, the fuel factory and meiosis cell division. Each of these are interdependent upon the other. The factory has to be complete for all the machinery of the cell to work including the supply of its own parts, fuel, design and manufacturing instructions and worker enzymes. This means that the factory could not have evolved but was created with the built-in production mechanisms 'after its kind' (Gen 1:11, 12, 21, 24, 25, 26).

6 THE MISSING MISSING LINK
THE FOSSIL EVIDENCE

We have seen already that science supports the order in which life appears in the Creation narrative of Genesis chapter 1. Both the Bible and science distinguish seven main orders of life which appear in the same sequence.

First we have small creatures in the waters, then backboned fishes, then amphibians, which can live both on land and in water, then the reptiles like those huge dinosaurs, then mammals, then apes, then man.

Where then is the difference between the Bible and evolution? Simply stated, the Bible says that God created each order, but the evolutionist says there were no separate acts of creation – they evolved from one to the other. Even Darwin said that if those link fossils were not found, then the Bible picture of separate acts of creation was the right one. That is why evolutionists are determined to produce link fossils!

The Absence of Link Fossils

Today, many scientists are having a re-think, in any case, the old Darwinian model has been greatly modified by two factors. Firstly, our knowledge of Mendel's genetics and Crick's DNA demonstrates that nothing can happen in a species which does not happen in its DNA genes. Secondly, it has become plain from fossil records that new and higher orders appear in groups comparatively suddenly. Consequently, some have called it 'explosive evolution', a seeming contradiction in terms.

It would be better to associate these appearances with each of the times that God spoke the creative words. In other words such complicated creatures were the result of re-coding of DNA, the language of life, when the dramatically advanced orders appear, e.g. vertebrates, amphibians, reptiles, birds, mammals, man. See my chart in Figure 6.1.

The new scientific approach is giving us a more Genesis-like picture. The old conception of evolutionary trees arranging fossils to develop smoothly from one branch into another is being questioned. It is seen that this is not the picture which the fossils give.

The overall picture is that of a series of jumps to major new types

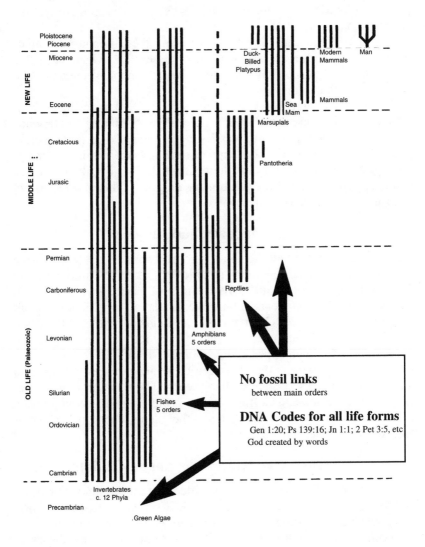

Figure 6.1. Fossil record of life, showing the sequence in which the seven main orders of life appear

Each vertical line represents a creature in the fossil record and shows the period it was/is extant.

Victor Pearce does not necessarily commit himself to the time scales usually given. The succession of fossils are those generally agreed by palaeontologists. This succession is similar to Genesis 1, but it was when God spoke that a new order came into being, not by evolution. The rocks show no link fossils between the main orders of life, so the supposed evolutionary branches have been omitted from the diagram.

of animal. It is not now sufficient to excuse ourselves by saying that we merely need to look for more fossils. That has been done, yet the picture remains the same.

This is really a death blow to Darwinism, so evolutionary scientists have come up with a succession of alternatives. There have been five new theories all succeeding each other, because none of them is satisfactory even to evolutionists.

Professor Sir Fred Hoyle and Professor C. Wickramasinghe, eminent Cambridge scientists, reflect the change: 'Contrary to Darwin's theory . . . evolution on earth was a series of leaps.' The fossil picture gives a pattern of the major groups of new advanced animals appearing together. Between them and their assumed ancestors, there is a lack of linking fossils to show evolutionary progress. This is a consistent story throughout the fossil record.

Life Appears Suddenly

The first to appear are all the non-backboned animals in the Cambrian period. Then, if science timing is followed, after 150 million years there appear, simultaneously, five kinds of backboned fish. Then another 100 million years later, five kinds of amphibian appear. Another 70 million years later appear four kinds of reptile; 200 million years later appear the mammals, then 40 million years on appear the apes, and finally, man appears after a further 10 million years.

What is important is that, between these appearances, we seem to have no fossil links or intermediary types. The position is well presented by Anderson and Coffin, who are professional palaeontologists, in *Fossils in Focus*. They maintain that the main groups have been created separately and independently.

Darwin's Own Witness Against Evolution

In his *Origin of Species*, Darwin admitted that, at the time of writing, the fossils discovered made it look like a series of acts of creation between each main order of life. But he urged people to look for links between them. He admitted that if they were not found, his theory of evolution would be wrong.

The question is, have any of those link fossils been found? Thousands of fossils have been found, but no proper link fossils. As Drs Coffin and Anderson say, it makes **the fossil records look even more like a series of creative acts than it did in Darwin's day**. They report that hundreds of thousands of fossils have been found since Darwin's day, but no link fossils. The fossils which are being found are 'not bridging the gaps between known orders', but only adding to the known orders.

Some scientists have tried to argue their way around this problem. Gordon Barnes, for instance, who is a biologist of London University, endeavours to show that it is possible to be a Christian and an evolutionist. In a review in *Faith and Thought*, 'Theistic Evolution v. Creation', he acknowledges 'the dearth of pre-Cambrian fossils, the paucity of intermediate types between major taxonomic groups' and laments, 'the speculative construction called phylogenetic trees often presented as fact in elementary textbooks'. But he claims there are some intermediate fossils and refers to the following examples.

Supposed Links

Asheaia is a fossil from the Cambrian and, although it is a member of the phylum 'Arthropoda' and class Onychophora, it resembles both the annelids and the arthropods. However, for it to be significant as a link, it would have to be in the pre-Cambrian rocks where the links should appear, but actually it is not.

Another fossil Barnes mentioned is *Seymouria* which from its appearance seems halfway between the amphibians and reptiles. If its fossil actually occurred halfway between the groups, this evidence could be convincing, but it actually occurs after the reptiles have appeared; yet it is to the reptiles that the fossil type is assumed to be ancestral. This fossil is only quoted therefore on the assumption that because its shape, or morphology, is suitable as a link, it probably has ancestors some forty million years earlier! When, however, other examples are given, and one finds that their fossils do not occur in the rocks in intermediary position, the objectiveness of the argument diminishes into philosophic presuppositions.

Living Fossils!

A similar case is the well-known **duck-billed platypus**, alive today, which is claimed as an excellent example of a 'living fossil' because it shows what an intermediary fossil should be like which would link reptiles, mammals and birds. Few realise, however, that no fossils of the duck-billed platypus are found earlier than two million years ago (to use the scientist's timing), whereas they should be found in strata 230 million years old, between the groups which they should link.

To assume that because a particular morphology must have been present in the right position merely because it was a good intermediary example (though out of sequence), indicates that a wrong methodology is being followed. Unfortunately, few students have time to check the juggling of biological examples with the actual place of occurrence in the fossil record to see how weak the argument is for the existence of intermediary fossils.

Brainwash Fiction

Barnes is understandably unhappy that Anderson and Coffin's creation model provides no theory of mechanism by which the creatures came into being. This is a relevant observation. The theory of natural selection by the environment of mutation, gene drift, etc. seemed to provide a working hypothesis which appealed to naturalists. Nevertheless, no genetic experiment so far is able to indicate how a major new creature (e.g. flying insects and birds) can be produced. Experiments demonstrate that natural selection can only give a limited range of adjustment for survival in a changing environment. Neither has evolution an adequate mechanism to suggest for the origin of the basics of matter, nor for life and spirit.

The last two, at least, are beyond empirical observation even for evolutionists. Even Crick has had to resort to space fiction for the origin of the cell as has Levi-Setti for the origin of marine animals. And as for the origin of matter, Fred Hoyle, the renowned scientist, who once believed matter created itself, now believes in a Creator and his recent book in co-authorship with C. Wickramasinghe, says that his student generation 'was brainwashed into accounting for origins without God'.

Hoyle also resorted to space fiction for origins 'by the arrival of new spores from space', but then reached the conclusion that whatever it was in space 'could only have been worked out by a superior intelligence . . . in fact, the higher intelligent Creator. The only logical answer to life is creation, and not accidental random shuffling.' As Lovell says, we go beyond these points into philosophy or theology.

Anderson and Coffin do not attempt to prove creation but are merely saying that the origins of each major group of animals cannot leave any fossil records because they were created by the invisible God.

God's Creation by Words

I am convinced the Scriptures do indeed reveal a mechanism for the origin of species, namely the provision and periodic adjustment of the DNA code, for it was between each major taxonomic group that God spoke. If we cannot accept that, then it must be difficult to explain the virgin birth (which was not by parthenogenesis – see my earlier book *Who Was Adam?* p 139) or the Christian resurrection when a change will come to the natural body in a fraction of time.

God's speech then recoded the DNA in order to supply to the next higher stage of life all the intricate mechanisms which were required to make that advance a viable one. This explains the sudden appearance of groups of new forms of life in the fossil record (see Figure 6.1).

A Recorded Absence of Missing Links

My itinerary in other countries includes many visits to universities. I show how science harmonises with the Bible. Many interesting questions are asked. One arose out of the remains discovered in the rocks. They showed the order in which life appeared on earth. Students were surprised to see it was the same as that in the Bible account of creation. But this is what arose out of it. I pointed out that there were no linking fossils between the orders of life. In other words, the theory that one type of animal developed out of an earlier type was not supported by the evidence in the rocks. Rather it showed that it was when God spoke that a new order of life came into existence.

Someone said at question time, 'Isn't this a belief in the God of the gaps?' By that they meant that, where we had not enough evidence, we put God there. This is a major misunderstanding of the evidence. This absence of linking fossils is not a lack of knowledge. It is a **recorded absence of links**. The other fossils are there, but no evolutionary links. We have a full record of all the kinds of creature. There are no gaps in the records, they merely show that missing links did not exist. The picture which the fossils show is that of a series of acts of creation at various times as new types of animal appeared.

This correlates with the statements in Genesis. Dr G. C. Simpson, the well-known scientist, admits (*Major Features of Evolution*, p 360) that all major new forms of life 'appear in the rocks suddenly and are not led up to by known, gradual, continuous sequences', as we should expect if evolution were true. These absences of linking fossils 'are systematic'.

That means it is a pattern throughout life on earth, right from the beginning. This pattern fits the creation pattern of the Bible and not an evolutionary one. The same can be said of the human fossils. Dr Fleming of Oxford laments that just where we should expect ape-men fossils to link apes with true men, they are missing. He thinks this very frustrating because he takes evolution for granted whether it can be proved or not.

This is why many scientists are thinking up other theories. The old Darwinism in the meantime has gone by the board.

So don't forget. There are no 'gaps' in the fossil record. Records are complete enough to show that no evolutionary types exist; only the types already existing. New forms of life all appear suddenly and complete as if created. This is becoming more and more the pattern as fresh fossils are being found. They support creation and not evolution.

Of course the greatest act of creation is that God can re-create you. He can make you a new creation. The Bible says that, and millions have experienced it. So why not you? Then you'll know there is a Creator!

Leaps or Links?

Fred Hoyle, the famous Cambridge scientist, came clean about it. He wrote in his books, 'Why, even neo-Darwinism does not work', and he says, 'Contrary to Darwin's theory . . . evolution on earth was a series of leaps'. (*Evolution from Space*, Dent, 1981.) So he has come round to state exactly what the Bible says! But, because some refuse to believe it, they have brought out a succession of five new theories.

The first was by De Vries called 'Saltation'. This merely claims that evolution was a series of sudden jumps and not a gradual advance. Obviously then, that is not evolution.

The second was by Schindewolf. Without any evidence for it, he believed that a reptile could lay an egg which, by accident, would hatch out a fully fledged bird! I would rather believe Genesis 1:20, 'God said, "Let birds fly above the earth across the sky." '

The third one is nicknamed the 'hopeful monster theory'. A sheep could be born with two legs, but some ask how it could produce similar offspring if it did not meet a two-legged ram!

The fourth theory was neo-Darwinism. This builds its hopes on mutations. But mutations are faults, not improvements. In experiments they have never produced a different species, only a variant and, more often, a retarded version.

The fifth and last one, by Niles Eldridge, has the fancy name of 'Punctuated equilibria'. This suggests that an isolated population evolved independently, but its fossils have not been found.

Q Is there no *variation at all between the species?*

Oh yes! There are small variations within the type of animal to adjust to the changing environment, but it still remains the same species. Look at the dog for instance. It is still the dog in spite of man's interference by breeding. It is still the dog from the large Afghan hound down to the little yapping toy dog. It is the same with those industrial moths, or the fruit flies. It is often argued that because there are more dark-coloured moths surviving in dirty, smoke-laden industrial areas that this demonstrates an evolution into a new species; also because fruit flies can be damaged in a laboratory by X-rays that this shows evolution can happen by mutations. But this is not so because they are still moths and still fruit flies. So, all creatures from the largest dog to the tiniest fly are all creatures God has made.

No Links for Hominids

Some time ago, I was listening to a doctor of physics. Sadly, he had no training in anthropology. Consequently, he got Neanderthal man all mixed up with Adam. He was in a mix-up with the fossils too!

This kind of approach does not help those studying for their exams. I get many letters from such people who are thankful to have heard my radio broadcasts. Here is one such letter from Bavaria:

> I am 17 years old. Your broadcasts fascinate me. I've learned things about science from you which never would have been mentioned in my class-room . . . I know what our preacher would say but he's not a scientist and I can't disregard the fossils and skeletons that have been found . . . In order to witness to others, I need your help. One friend said she would gladly become a Christian if she could 'get around' the problem of evolution. I won't get the required knowledge in the schools to answer this.

The more knowledge we get from actual discoveries, the more we find that it corrects plausible theories. What is more, they come more into line with the Bible.

AN ASSESSMENT OF ANTHROPOLOGICAL FINDS

Meet Lucy

A great amount of attention has been drawn to finds of early man in Africa, so as an anthropologist you will expect me to give you an assessment of them.

You may be interested to know that while I was at Oxford I was asked if I would join the Leakey family. They have become famous through their finds in the Olduvai Gorge, an area of NE Africa. It is between Ethiopia and the southern Red Sea, a flat waste land of bare rocks called Hadar. It was here that 'Lucy' was discovered – or rather her skeletal remains.

This young lady was only three and a half feet tall, but walked upright like all other humans. Only bits of her skull were recovered, and the front part was missing. So the size of her brain was not men-tioned. Her wisdom teeth were fully erupted, and her wide pelvis showed she was a female. She was discovered in 1981, just when the anthropologists had their transistor radio blaring out the Beatles song 'Lucy in the Sky with Diamonds', so that was how she got her name (otherwise you might have wondered how they knew her name, because she was given the age of three and a half million years old – and no birthday card to celebrate!). She was described as 'The begin-ning of humankind'.

A full description and photo is given by Johanson and Edey. The discovery is in their book entitled *Lucy* (Simon & Schuster, 1981). The outlook of the authors is overtly given by an aggressive attack on the Church of England and an unqualified statement that the fossil record is true, and that we were descended from apes and not divinely created in 4004 BC as the Church insisted. The prologue records the blasphemous utterances of colleagues misusing the name of Jesus Christ.

How do they support their statement that their fossil interpretation is true? Not very well. Like Dr Martin Pickford quoted elsewhere, they admit that no fossils between the ape and humans have been found: 'We have no fossils yet that tell us what went on during the in-between time'. So they fall back very confidently on imagination as follows: 'We can *picture* evolution as starting with a primitive ape-like type that generally, over a long period of time, began to be less and less ape-like and more manlike. There was no abrupt crossover,' the writer continues confidently, 'from ape to human, but *probably* a rather fuzzy time of in-between types. We have no fossils yet that tell us what went on during that in-between time.'

Richard Leakey, the son of L. S. B. Leakey, goes further in his widely read book (*Origins Reconsidered*, Little, Brown & Co, 1992). He not only pictures the progress of the in-between time, he actually draws pictures of a line of ape-men gradually walking more and more upright. Let me state clearly that *no such* skeletons have been found.

Back to Lucy. Johanson and Edey then give a list of humans which followed her. We anthropologists know them well. They are Homo Habilis, Homo Erectus and Homo Neanderthal.

There Johanson and Edey stop, but they remark 'Neanderthal fossils were collected in Europe before anybody knew how to evaluate sites properly or get good dates. Consequently we do not have exact dates for most of the Neanderthal fossils in collection.'

Now I find this surprising. Why? Because we have full succession of types in clear cave layers in various sites in Europe and the Near East.

Can it be that they are trying to forget that the caves for example in Mount Carmel show that man had a sudden start?

How Old Was Lucy?

You are very unpopular if you ask a lady's age, but I must ask how old Lucy really was. Notice what the discoverers say.

'Fossils are almost all exposed on the surface of the ground.'

Now this makes dating very suspect because it makes it difficult to be sure of the fossil's provenance as it is called. This goes for many other fossils also, so whenever Lucy's birthday was, I cannot award her diamonds, either on the ground or in the sky!

When Dr Brain of Pretoria Museum in South Africa showed me his cave specimens, I was struck by the lack of stratification. In Europe we have clear layers, but the South African specimens seemed all jumbled up in a mixed breccia. The skulls were very battered and damaged.

One group of anthropologists at the Cambridge Conference backed Asia as the birthplace of mankind, another group backed Europe, and yet another backed the Middle East.

As the Cambridge Conference committee said, the anthropologists need to get their act together.

No Stooping Ape-men

What picture does the discovery of more fossils give in regard to so-called ape-men? The trend in man-like skeletons is to show that there were no ape-men links between true man and the ape. This may surprise you because of all the propaganda which you get. For example, in Amsterdam I saw posters showing ape-men gradually walking more and more upright (Fig 6.2). In actual fact, no such skeletons have been found.

Fig. 6.2. Row of stooping 'apes'
Showing the false speculation by Richard Leakey in a series of stooping hominids which never existed but which are often depicted in school text books.

I have in my possession an article written in the *New Scientist* which actually laments this fact. It is written by Dr M. Pickford of Oxford. He takes evolution for granted. It never occurs to him to question it. He only laments that, as regards man, there is no evidence to support it. He says: 'The fossil void is particularly frustrating because it was during this time that the earliest human ancestor embarked on a vital stage of its journey towards humanity.' The fossil void he speaks of is the absence of ape-men. But that is what begs the whole question.

Anthropologists now have a great number of human-like fossils and a whole range of ape fossils, but between them there are no ape-men fossils. One would have expected at least a few if man evolved from the ape. So this gives a non-evolutionary picture of man's origins. It is typical of the fossils of other animals before him. There are no evolutionary links there either. The more fossils we find, the more it testifies to separate creation acts. The clear picture is that there are no evolutionary links between the main types.

Powerful Fossil Evidence Against Evolution

Some have asserted that the succession of fossils in the rocks has been falsely concocted on an evolutionary assumption. This is not correct. The fossil record was discovered by geologists a long time before Darwin launched his theory.

Indeed, the fossil record was evidence against evolution. Even Darwin acknowledged this. For Christians, untrained in geology, to attack the fossil record is like shooting themselves in the foot and making themselves ineffective for battle.

Geology Founded Before Darwin

Another misleading assertion is that nowhere is the geological succession complete. This is untrue. William Smith founded geology 200 years ago in 1799, long before Darwin, and so he had no axe to grind. He discovered the succession of sedimentary layers of rock as he journeyed across Britain from south-east England to north-west Wales (Cambria). He found that the rock layers got older and older as he went north-west, generally speaking. His job, a digger of canals, took him throughout Britain.

In some places there were no more than ten successive layers, but where these stopped, they matched similar layers elsewhere with a continuation of layers or strata, e.g. in one place layers **ABCDEFGH** would be followed further north-west by **FGHIJKLM**. Also, the older rocks were much harder, as they had been under greater pressure of rock and soil laid down above them. Many were pressured into microclines – small waves of strata. The great pressure of later soils washed down above them had flattened out the mica grains into horizontal plates. That is how slates were formed. The original geologists did not base their identification of successive strata by the fossils in them, even though some now find it convenient to do so.

The sedimentary layers or varves laid down annually in ancient lakes could also be counted. Even in these old layers, there would be found evidence of earlier rocks now in the form of conglomerate pebbles. That means the pebbles contained material from even an older layer which had become part of the rock of a newer old layer.

Then, of course, there is the evidence of successive earth movements and then, on top of that, layers of rock at a different angle as the result of other earth movements.

My description is very simplistic for you as you may not have had geological training. It is not sufficient to do physical geography while sitting at home. Field geology is necessary.

Witness With the Fossils

The point is this, why 'shoot yourself in the foot' when the rock and fossil successions witness to the order of creation in Genesis? Before Darwin came on the scene, Christian geologists demonstrated this as evidence of creation. Dr Alan Haywood writes (*Evolution and Creation*, Triangle, p 72):

> All the early geologists not only reached their conclusions many years before Darwin launched his theory of evolution, but many of them were Bible-believing Christians and creationists. Among them were William Buckland and Adam Sedgwick. Buckland held the chair of geology at Oxford in the early nineteenth century, while Sedgwick was his counterpart at Cambridge. Both preached the plenary inspiration of scripture and argued in favour of special creation..

Each class of fossil appeared in the rocks without any links which Darwin later suggested should be there, otherwise his theory was false. One and a half centuries have passed and those links have not been found – except frauds or misplacements – so scientists are trying new theories to account for it without God.

Overlaps that Reverse the Fossil Order

Some people not trained in field geology have tried to invalidate the evidence of creation from the order of fossils. They have asserted that a small series of fossils appear in reverse order. The answer is that this appears in geological overlaps. An overlap is like a huge tongue of rock bent back on itself. Originally the fossils were laid down in the usual succession, but a later earth movement has reversed the strata in which they appeared.

On one of my field geology excursions, I was driving a van full of geologists around Anglesey. This island, off north-west Wales, has a huge overlap of about 20 miles. The Armorican earth movement coming up from Wales had pushed the tongue of strata by terrific force over later rocks which were then left below it. The crush marks of debris could still be seen under the overlap. This is a feature well known by those trained in field geology.

How are we to know that this explanation is correct? It is by looking at an exposed rock face where you can see the tongue of the overlap actually turning over. The effect of the overlap is shown in Figures 6.3 and 6.4.

There is a similar overlap in the Alps. In such an overlap, of course, the fossils in that section became reversed in the order as shown in my sketch 'reversed strata'. How then are we to know if a reversed fossil

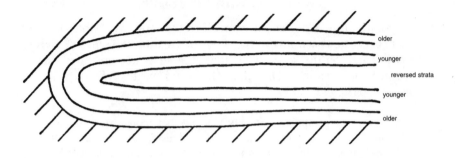

Figure 6.3. The overlap effect, showing reversed vertical order of sediments

order is due to an overlap? It is detectable in the actual bend, as in Mont Blanc.

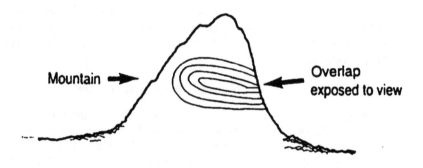

Figure 6.4. Reversed fossil order in Mont Blanc

Conclusion

In this chapter, we have seen how Darwin himself readily admitted that the survival of his theory depended on the finding of missing links. We have furthermore seen that these links are not forthcoming, to the point that now many scientists hold the theory of evolution in disrepute.

Contrary to what most of the media proclaims through nature pro-grammes and to what most of the educational establishment still teach-es, it is the **evolutionists who are unscientific** in their approach, while the anti-evolutionists are very much more true to the observable facts. As Sir Edmund Leach, of Cambridge Anthropological Department, has so aptly put it:

Missing links and the sequence of fossil evidence were a worry to Darwin.
He felt sure they would eventually turn up, but they are still missing and

seem likely to remain so. What we are to make of that fact is still open to debate, but today it is the conventional neo-Darwinists who appear as the 'conservative bigots'.

SUMMARY

MISSING MISSING LINKS

Science supports Genesis' order of life's appearance:

1. But each order appears suddenly.
Are there any links? Darwin admitted that unless links were found, the fossils supported a series of special creations.
Those links have not been found. Fossil scientists, Coffin and Anderson, say, '. . . even more like creative acts than in Darwin's day. Not gaps in fossils found, only an absence of link fossils.

2. Six new theories have been presented by scientists:
explosive evolution; saltation leaps; reptile lays bird's egg; hopeful monster theory; neo-Darwinism by mutations; punctuated equilibria.

3. Mendel's genetics also brought in a new problem for Darwinism.
Darwin thought traits attained in life could be passed to offspring. But genetics showed that only characteristics in the genes were inherited.

4. No stooping ape-men.
Fictional drawings abound. All are quadrapedals or upright-walking.
Meet Lucy 'Beginning of humankind'.
Fossil void between ape and man lamented by Johanson and Edey who found 'Lucy', and Dr M. Pickford.

5. Don't shoot your own foot.
Make fossils your friend. Some Christians dump good evidence. Geological succession discovered 50 years before Darwin. Overlaps in rock strata reverse some fossils.

7 THE GREAT TV COVER-UP

MEDIA PROMOTION OF EVOLUTIONIST FRAUDS

How often do you eagerly switch on your TV set to watch a quality nature programme, only to hear those all too familiar words '. . . and then this gradually evolved into . . .'?

When will the producers of such programmes and the TV companies bring themselves up to date and accept the ever-increasing weight of scientific evidence against evolution and in favour of special creation?

Of course, most of these programmes are fascinating – brilliant photography, beautiful scenery, captivating wildlife, and so on. But you need always to watch them with an analytical eye. Why? Because they almost invariably assume so much of what they say. You can spot big holes in their arguments. They assume there is no God, no Creator, to begin with.

Barren Rocks Before Creation of Life

Recently, I watched a nature programme on invertebrates. The speaker was trying to explain away the appearance of life in the waters. It seemed to happen so suddenly. At the first appearance of life, about 12 different phyla appear together. The rocks were full of them. He then showed how all the rock layers older than them, and therefore lower down, did not have a single fossil. Those rocks were completely barren.

Q How did he explain this mystery?

He said that they represented billions of years of rock layers with no fossils. It made it look as if all the sea creatures in the fossils above had been suddenly created. Every kind of invertebrate was suddenly there in the waters. This is what Genesis 1:20 says, 'And God said, let the waters bring forth swarms of moving creatures that have life'. This would mean that all those non-backboned creatures would appear together and leave their fossils in the rocks. This would explain the barrenness of the rocks laid down before them.

But this TV speaker could not believe in a Creator! There must be earlier creatures, he said, which evolved up to that sudden record of fossils. If so, then why don't we have fossils of those creatures as well? He suggested the usual answer, 'There must only have been soft bodied creatures earlier, whose bodies decayed away without being fossilised.' But soft-bodied creatures **do** get fossilised! Also, why did shell creatures and segmented creatures appear suddenly and not have ancestors leading up to them?

The Bible answer is obviously nearer the facts. God created them when he said, 'Let the waters bring forth swarms of moving creatures with life'. The TV speaker then suggested that a creature very much like a caterpillar was an ancestor. Its name was peripatus, but he did not tell you that peripatus did not appear in the rocks until long after those first sea creatures. He was suggesting this because the rock strata revealed no ancestors before the outburst of life – in effect saying that a fossil found later in the series **must** have appeared before that sudden outburst.

Q But isn't that begging the whole question?

It is. Many museums are deceiving the public by taking a convenient later fossil and replacing it between two forms of life to make it look like an evolutionary link. I could name many cases. Sometimes even a modern animal is taken. It is then given as a suggestion of what the evolutionary link should have looked like if only they had found it.

Ancient Sea Creatures and Old-fashioned Theories

Other nature programmes present further obvious difficulties for evolutionists. On one occasion, the TV speaker showed classes of sea creatures which looked as if they were related but with very real differences.

You may have seen a shellfish with a shell that curls round and round. It is called the nautilus. It uses the empty chambers in those coils to empty or fill in order to rise or lower itself in the sea, just like a submarine – very clever! Now the speaker admitted that the nautilus has never changed during earth's history. There has been no evolution, and yet the TV speaker said that the octopus evolved from it by a series of big changes. He discussed how, step by step, those big changes might have taken place.

If they did take place, then why have we no fossils to record each stage, and why do we still have nautilus unchanged today?

Then he spoke similarly of another family of sea creatures. They were the sea lilies looking like plants: the starfish with five feet to walk on, and the round shelled sea urchin with spikes sticking out all around him. He suggested how they might have evolved one from the other. But, if that were so, why are there no fossil records for each stage of this change? Also, why are these separate creatures still with us in their unchanged form?

They themselves have shown no evolution after 500 million years, the speaker admitted, so why should they have changed one into another early on? Also, they each have very clever separate devices. The starfish's five points are tube feet. Those feet are hollow and are linked to a water cistern in the centre. The cistern floods each foot in succession so that the starfish moves his legs hydraulically!

Isn't it time these agnostic TV programmes were brought up to date? They are still pumping out that old-fashioned, antiquated Darwinism which most scientists have abandoned. 'Darwinism is dead!' Dr Francis Crick said.

Design in Creation

A certain person has been appearing on TV trying to explain how there could be design in nature without a Designer. As many such programmes appear, it is good for a Christian to practise analysing these talks, in order to see the fallacies in such claims. Well, one of the designs this man tried to explain was the design of wings for flight. He claimed that gradually a creature could develop wings and fly.

Now biologists say that such an engineering feat as flying is statistically unlikely to be repeated in nature, yet we find this remarkable accomplishment has been repeated four times in different animal kingdoms. As Anderson said, 'Flight appeared independently four times in geological history'. Very different types of wings are possessed by very different categories of animals and insects. And entirely different phyla, as they are called, have wings. This shows they could not have evolved from each other. The four very different kingdoms of animals in which this happened are:

- The invertebrates, such as insects.
- The vertebrates, such as reptiles.
- The birds.
- The mammals, like the bats.

These are all entirely different families or phyla and are unrelated. Their mode of flight is different; the material of which their wings are made is different; the methods of aeronautics are different. Insect wings are made of very fine material but mammals, like bats, have wings made of skin. Reptiles have wings also made of skin, but birds have wings made of feathers and of an entirely different structure from the reptile wings.

Now to suggest that such remarkable mechanisms evolved without a Designer, several independent times, is even contrary to Darwinism.

Why? Because the selection by environment of thousands of coincidences is unlikely even for one class of animals, let alone four unrelated phyla.

Insects and Symbiosis

Look at the insects, for instance. Their wings vibrate thousands of times a minute. Think of the mechanics behind that, the motor nerve reflex at alternating blade angles! This is how a contributor to the *Creation Journal* described insect wings:

> Nothing can beat an insect for aerial acrobatics. A fly, for example, can loop the loop, hover, reverse direction and land upside down, all in a fraction of a second. It owes that agility to ribbed wings that are subtly engineered, flexible aerofoils. Insect wings have few, if any, technological parallels yet . . . subtle details of engineering and design, which no man-made aerofoil can match, reveal how insect wings are remarkably adapted to the aerobatics of flight.

But there is another difficulty to explain without a Designer. It is called symbiosis. In the fossil record, the insects appear suddenly at the same time as the flowers which needed the insects to pollinate them. Such flowers could not propagate even for one season if the insects were not there.

Moreover, there is no record in the fossils of any evolution leading up to insect wings. No millions of years in which a bit of a useless wing develops to be selected for flight. Evolution says it is only useful things which would be selected. For a wing to function, all the mechanics would be necessary right from the start, and all the genetics would be necessary for it to be reproduced.

Genesis 1:21 gives the solution. It reads, 'God created . . . every winged creature according to its kind'. 'According to their kinds', therefore explains how so many entirely different kingdoms of animal included flying creatures. (Perhaps your translation says that it was the 'birds' which God created. If so, I need to point out that the word in Hebrew does not say 'birds'. It only says 'flying creatures', so it introduces all categories. The insects were the first flying creatures.)

But for anyone who wants to believe that you can have a design without a designer, there is another problem. How would an insect which achieved flight (clever thing!) pass on the information to its offspring? Darwin thought it would be by 'use inheritance'. He knew nothing about genetics, and 'use inheritance' was shown by Mendel to be impossible. Only what was already in the genetic instructions could be passed on.

All the instructions for the elaborate angle elevation of the fins, the motor nerve mechanism for alternating blades at 100 times per second, the power supply to the motor muscles, must all be in the insect's genes already! I think the Bible statement is more logical. We read 'God said'. This must mean the genes and chromosomes are God's speech (Chapter 5). The Designer's instructions were all there!

The Butterfly

Q How could the butterfly evolve from a caterpillar?

Dr F. A. Filby in his book *Creation Revealed* (Pickering & Inglis, 1963, p 103) asks: 'Are we to believe that, for thousands and thousands of years, caterpillars did faster and faster runs up a stalk followed by flying leaps until they became butterflies?'

May we not rather recognise that the Creator designed a marvellous built-in mechanism, which enables them to turn into butterflies in one complete metamorphosis? In the cocoon, the caterpillar turns into quite a different creature, even the cells of his body reorganise. He becomes a butterfly and emerges from the cocoon the opposite way round from the caterpillar. One kind of caterpillar fastens his cocoon to the stalk with a strong silken thread in anticipation – anticipation that he will emerge from the top of the cocoon safely strapped by the silken thread to the stalk!

Dr Filby joked, asked whether a caterpillar practised trial runs – runs before take off for thousands of years! This was because a biologist, writing in the *Encyclopaedia Britannica,* suggested that reptiles took to flying this way. He pictured early reptiles practising swift runs, with long leaps into the air, until they found by accident, after thousands of years, that they had wings to fly with. Dr Filby writes:

> The idea of countless generations of these creatures practising long jumps for some millions of years before becoming birds with feathers is too utterly absurd for words. Besides, there is no fossil record of such things.

Peacock's Feathers

Have you ever admired the beautiful display that a peacock gives in fanning out its tail feathers? Julian Huxley tried to account for the beautiful design of the peacock's feathers by suggesting that the birds with the most striking design must attract the strongest females for the survival of the fittest.

But this ignores a remarkable fact. In that fan-like display of those coloured circles which look like eyes, they all make up a pattern. But did you know that each feather has only one eye? Did you realise that the whole pattern is made up only if the position of the eye on each feather is correct? The eye on one feather must be a certain distance up the feather. On the next feather it must be higher up. Only when the feathers grow to their right lengths and positions do the eyes make the complete pattern. So the gene's instructions for each feather must be different but correct for that feather, so that the complete pattern is the same in each peacock.

Who designed the beautiful pattern for all peacocks and then fixed it so that each feather came in the right place for that wonderful geometrical design? For me the scientific problem is settled by Job 39:13, in the King James version of the Bible. Job has been getting contentious so God asks him, 'Did you give the goodly wings to the peacocks?' The answer is obviously No. Man could not make the peacock's beautiful pattern, and certainly not nature by itself.

Migration of Birds

This thirty-ninth chapter of the book of Job is part of God's answer to Job's personal problems. It starts in chapter 38, showing that it is God answering Job personally, with the words: 'Then the Lord answered Job and said, "Who is this that darkens counsel without 'knowledge."' Chapter 38 continues outlining God's work in his physical creation, all of which shows remarkable scientific knowledge of the universe.

Then chapter 39 moves to the biological creation of animals, that God said he made; he asks Job (who has got too big for his boots) in verse 26, 'Does the hawk fly by your wisdom and stretch her wings toward the south?'

That is an interesting question and brings in the whole mystery of the migration of birds – birds which fly thousands of miles to a destination which their generation have never seen or visited before, yet they seem to obey a built-in programme placed there by God. Certainly it was not implanted by Job's wisdom or man's wisdom or even by the bird's wisdom.

The Lord then said to Job, 'Shall a fault-finder contend with the Almighty? He who argues with God, let him answer it.' Job replies, 'I know that you can do all things. I have uttered what I did not understand; things too wonderful for me that I did not know.' For the same reason, I accept God's implication that **he** gave the beautiful pattern to the feathers of the peacock and birds their migration instincts.

Evolutionist Frauds

A seemingly plausible suggestion was made on a TV programme, that bird's feathers evolved from reptile scales. Sometimes, to support this, the fossil called archaeopteryx is given as a transitional form between reptiles and birds. The suggestion was puzzling to many zoologists because the flying reptile was distinctly reptile but the feathers were modern birds' feathers.

It was that leading Cambridge scientist, Fred Hoyle, who solved the problem. He discovered that the fossil was a fraud. He examined the fossil under a microscope and saw that the birds' feathers had been stuck on with glue! So archaeopteryx joined a long list of evolutionist frauds.

The suggestion that feathers developed from reptile scales has never been tested, neither is there any fossil record of scales forming into feathers. Feathers can be accounted for only by a most wonderful Designer. So you see, **the theory of evolution is a flight of fancy, whereas creationists face up to the facts.**

Engineering Trusses

The bones of a bird are made specially light and strong by being hollow but strengthened by crossed trusses like an engineering truss.

Dr R. E. D. Clark, the scientist, writes (*The Universe – Plan or Accident?* Paternoster, 1961), 'In the bones of a bird, we find that maximum strength is obtained by the use of a hollow stem which enables the bone to withstand lateral pressure.' He draws a diagram to show the general appearance of a section through the metacarpel bone from a vulture's wing. 'The resemblance to an engineering truss is obvious,' he writes, 'but the wing is better designed than the truss, since the struts are not confined to one plane.'

A different blood system also is necessary to energise the very rapid wing movements. The red corpuscles are oval-shaped to provide a quicker supply of energy to the wing movements. Even more significant is that, whereas reptiles have a cold blood system, wings with feathers need a warm-blooded circulation and an endocrine system for moulting of feathers.

Then look at the different styles of flight among birds. Some are made for gliding, with long wing surfaces. Others have triangular wings for quick flights. Similar patterns have been copied by man for the different types of flight required for his plane designs.

Dr Clark described the flight bones of a hawk and shows that they must have been designed by God. That is just what God tells Job in 39:26. I quote, 'Does the hawk fly by your wisdom, Job, or mine, and stretch her wings towards the south?'

Pterodactyls

The TV speaker also said that the bone skeletons of flying reptiles did not show they were designed. Why? Because for every bone there was a similar one in other animals. This is called homology. But this calls even more for a Designer. Why? Because this common design of bones has been adapted for each special requirement by being differently shaped and for flying creatures, differently constructed.

Take the dinosaurs, for example. Their bones are designed to be heavy and thick to take the weight of a huge heavy creature. But the pterodactyl, with its seven-foot span of wings, has light hollow bones.

There is a complete absence of fossils showing any evolution of the wings of flying reptiles. 'When the flying reptiles appear in the Jurassic period, they are fully capable of flight and there is absolutely no sign of intermediate stages.' This is a confession of an evolutionist, E. C. Olson.

But how did the likenesses in bone structure come about? Remember that all the instructions to produce them are in the genetic code. This, I believe, was the record of what God said, the record retained in all genetic codes. The book of physical life. That is why Genesis 1 says that the various creatures were the results of God's speech. The genetic code records what he said.

God Recodes the Instructions

Now when a book is revised, the outline remains, but chapters can be readjusted. This seems to be what God did each time he spoke again. In my book *Who was Adam?* I wrote, 'This is exactly what we find in the Genesis account. The expression 'God said' or its equivalent occurs six times in reference to the progression of living orders of creatures. This would refer to acts of recording.'

Between these acts, the genetic code has a degree of flexibility, for a creature to adjust to its environment. But with all the experiments made on fruit flies and moths, no one has made them into a new species, only variants of their own species. This is what is expressed in the words, 'The waters brought forth abundantly after their kind' (Genesis 1:21) and 'Let the earth bring forth the living creature after his kind' (Genesis 1:24).

When a specialist has delivered a treatise or an author has written a book, it is easier to build up a larger book or revise a book than it is to rewrite it completely. Similarly, the physiological book of life, housed in the cell, has preserved the bones and structure of earlier books. Practically all the bones of the human skeleton are a repetition of those in animals and birds, except that they have been revised or recoded for different uses. It would be natural to retain the complex technical framework of a book of one million pages, such as that written in the living cell. So then, the basic sentences and paragraphs in the physical book of life with their very technical details have been retained for many of the species but have been re-assembled into a different number of chapters for variety among the species.

Fig. 7.1 The bat: a flying mammal   *Courtesy: Creation Science Movement*

Flying Mammals

Have you heard that fable about the origin of the bat? There was a war between the birds and the mice. The battle was raging ding dong. Sometimes the birds were winning and sometimes the mice. There was one mouse which kept changing sides according to who was winning. Eventually (the fable goes), a truce was agreed, but both sides condemned the turncoat to be a bat, half bird and half mouse.

In actuality, the bat is very different from both, except that it is a mammal, the only mammal which flies, though there are over 300 kinds of bats. This again is an argument for a Designer because here flight has been designed for yet a fourth different kingdom of animals – the mammals. The evolutionist story of how it came about is little better than the fable, for several reasons.

First, bat's wings are covered by skin for flying, as are those of the flying reptile, but because it belongs to a different kingdom of animals – the mammals – even evolutionists don't claim that bats are evolved from flying reptiles. Why? Because the flying reptiles would have to evolve into mammals first before becoming bats. Also, because the flying reptiles died out long before them, after the Jurassic age, but the bat did not appear until the Eocene epoch, much later. Also, the bone framework to hold out the wing is different. In the flying reptile, the skin is stretched out over one extended finger, but in the bat, the skin wing is supported by four lengthened fingers.

Also, there are no fossils of mice changing into bats and there are no fossils even of wings gradually evolving. Olson admits that 'The earliest fossil evidence of flying bats is in fully-developed bats of the Eocene epoch.' Again, this is a powerful argument for special creation.

An article in *Creation Update* says, 'It is difficult to imagine any transitional forms. For example, how could a creature with partly-developed wings forage for food or escape predators, being unable to walk or fly properly? Half-developed wings would surely result in extinction in the survival of the fittest!'

So the fact that there is no evolutionary connection between the flying reptile and the bat (yet in both cases the wings are made of skin stretched over a different design of framework) argues for the same Designer making different models.

Talking about models, it also argues for a Designer with much more skill than man, because man has been trying to make things that fly for centuries. Yet he has only succeeded relatively recently and that was by copying the aeronautics of God's flying machines. Three and a half thousand years ago God asked Job, 'Does the hawk fly through your wisdom, or mine?'

Sonic Sight

Those on TV who have tried to explain away the need of a Designer in nature have overlooked the strange phenomenon of sonic sight. The bat has no visual sight but has a sonar system of locating everything by an echo from its high-pitched squeaks.

Have you seen the various demonstrations of bats flying around and avoiding even thin wires whilst catching flies. It would appear that their sonar echo location is almost as detailed as eyesight.

Q But why this strange difference with no evolutionary connection with other animals?

Let me give you a clue. When do they fly? Mostly in the dark, at night. They are nocturnal. Where do they live? Mostly in dark caves.

Doesn't it look to you as if the Creator adapted those ears to be far more sensitive to the high-pitched signal sent out by the mouth? Submarines use a similar sonar system. Would you think it sensible if I suggested that it evolved in the submarine and was not designed and manufactured by human designers?

A recent article in *Creation Update* says:

If the sonar system in the bat of echo-location evolved, then this remarkable system would have had to evolve at the same time as the wing membrane, for without its sonar, no bat could survive. Bats fly in the dark and their sonar helps them to see. They send out high-pitched squeaks of between 50,000 and 200,000 vibrations per second. Bats are provided with special equipment both to send out and receive these signals.

The Human Flying Machine

Human-designed aircraft are equipped with a similar radar system and originally that was so that they too could fly in the dark.

I said that the bat was the only flying mammal. In a sense there is now another flying mammal and that is mankind. But they have designed their flying machines. Would that, too, argue for a divine Designer for flying animals?

You could also make out a case for evolution for the human flying machines. Think of the progress in the design experiments of aircraft. First the flimsy, open bi-planes which went at 60 m.p.h., then the monoplanes, then the larger passenger enclosed planes and now jumbo jets of 700 m.p.h. Does that 'evolution of design' argue for no designer or for a maker of those planes?

Now, the rib skeleton of those planes was altered to suit the new improved designs. In the same way, God uses the bones and framework in all vertebrates and readjusts the DNA instructions so that some bones grow longer or shorter as required for the new model. That is why for every bone in your body there is a similar bone in a horse, but shaped differently for the different model.

God makes this point in Job 39:19. 'Did you give the horse his might? Do you make him leap like a locust?' He who argues with God, let him answer.

Eyes as Eagles

One who had been worried by a TV programme told me, 'He said that there was no need for a designer of the eye. He said it could evolve bit by bit through the sun shining on sensitive skin.'

Q How would you reply to this question?

First of all, the fossil record does not support him. At the first appearance of all forms of life in the Cambrian, every kind of animal has eyes whether it is a worm, a bivalve or a trilobite, they all have eyes.

In fact, the trilobite has a very complex eye for seeing in deep ocean water. Because it appears fully equipped, Levi-Setti says it must have come from outer space (Fig 7.2). Every fish in the fossil record also has perfect eyes. Some fish have bi-focal eyes, without wearing additional glasses! That is because they swim half out of water. Their bi-focal eyes enable them to see above the water at the same time as the lower part can see under the water.

Octopuses, which have no connection with human beings, have eyes just like humans, and in some ways better, because each eye is monitored by a separate brain. They can see each eye's picture separately. There is no squid or octopus to be found with a bit of sensitive skin developing into an eye like this.

Devolution

I mentioned the trilobite's eye and how perfect its fossils are from the very earliest. Actually, its fossil record is the opposite to evolution. It is a devolution. One of the last of the trilobites has lost its sight. It is blind. Very appropriately its name is agnostos, from agnostic.

Then, the insects all have eyes right from their first appearance. They needed them to see the flowers to pollinate them. What is more, they can see colour. They needed to see the colour of the flowers.

Animals and birds have been given eyes according to their requirements. The eagle has telescopic eyes to see right down into the valley from the height of the mountains. It has a telescopic section in the eye. Predator birds are necessary to clear the ground from rotting bodies. They are nature's cleansing department.

All eyes are far more complicated then the electronic camera. For eyes to function, they need a very complicated section of the brain and millions of connecting nerves to it so that the picture can be read and interpreted.

So who made the eagle's eye? God tells Job that he did. He tells him in words which show that he knew all about the eagle's zoom lens – a discovery ornithologists have only recently discovered. God said in Job 39:28, 29, 'The eagle dwells and abides on the rock upon the high crag of the mountain and strong place. From thence the eagle seeks the prey her eyes behold afar off.'

The Miracle Human Eye

Did your camera fall from heaven, already complete with batteries and film? Did your TV set come together accidentally through a storm sweeping into your house or was it a hurricane which blew all the components together with the screws in place?

A man on a TV programme said that this was possible concerning the eye, the human eye. It could all have come together. How? By a series of a million accidents selected by environment.

Actually, your camera and TV set are very simple compared with the complexity of the human eye. The automatic focusing of the

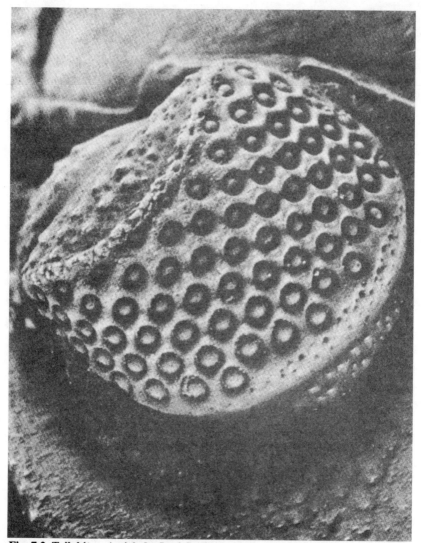

Fig. 7.2. Trilobites: Article by Levi-Setti.   *University of Chicago Press*
From a photographic atlas by Riccardo Levi-Setti
Recently published is a pictorial record of some of the most remarkable animals ever
to inhabit our planet – the trilobites. These woodlouse-like arthropods first appeared
in the early Cambrian seas, about 600 million years ago. How these segmented creatures evolved has long puzzled palaeontologists for it seems they just suddenly arrived
here and spread themselves wide. Did they evolve from the lowly segmented worms
in some enclosed area only to become dispersed when the walls of the confine were
shattered by some cataclysmic happening? For sure they were equipped to travel. Not
only did they have walking legs but also special oar-like swimming legs. I'm surprised
that more attention hasn't been paid to the possibility that they arrived on earth from
elsewhere in the universe! Wouldn't their hard outer skeleton have protected them in
space flight?

camera is simple compared with the very much finer focusing of your iris and lens. The little colour spots on your TV screen only number a few thousand. Compare that with the retina at the back of your eye. Your eye has 20 million nerve endings taking the message of sight to your brain. Yes, 20 million. Your TV set can only read the signals from the studio by a rapid off and on system to stimulate a succession of still shots. Your brain has a similar mechanism to read the moving picture.

Did God intend man to use the telescope and microscope to explore his universe? I believe he did, because the human eye has a very sensitive area in the centre of the back of the eye. It is called the fovea and in the middle of that is an even more sensitive area called the macula. It is so fine and full of communication nerves that it can read the smallest image. Without these, we would know little about the universe or the genes of inheritance in the DNA code. Even more marvellous is the creation of all this each time a child is conceived, because the instructions for it are contained in the cell's genetic code.

Jesus Creates Eyes

I think that this is why Jesus used saliva to heal several blind men. He mixed his own saliva with clay and anointed their eyes. Why saliva? We use saliva in our microscopes to examine the genetic code. The genetic code consists of words your Creator gave to create a baby.

Now the Lord Jesus is the Word. John 1 says he was the Word who created you. So, as I see it, when he made clay with his saliva, that saliva contained his original instructions on how to make an eye for those blind men. Those instructions would use the minerals in the clay to form the eye, even as originally God made man of the dust or clay. Only by the original Designer could such a complicated mechanism of the eye be made. Jesus was the original Designer at the beginning of the universe.

Let's read the account in John 9. 'Jesus said, I am the light of the world.' As he said this, he spat on the ground and made clay of his saliva and anointed the blind man's eyes with the clay, saying to him, 'Go and wash in the Pool of Siloam'. So he went and washed and came back seeing. Spiritually, you receive sight, too. Jesus can wash away your unbelief so that you can see 'The Light of the World'.

Q Did Jesus create eyes and bodies?

When I was at Oxford, I was one of the first to suggest, as in my book *Who Was Adam?* (Paternoster, 1970) that God could use a body cell to create any part of another's body or even a whole human being. That is why God took a body cell from Adam's side to use the DNA code to create a woman.

A number of professors wrote to me and said it was impossible. Why? Because they said that, once a cell had become specialised to reproduce a specific part of a human body, that cell could not be reused to make another. In other words, they were saying a cell from Adam's rib could produce only another rib and blood cell. Years later they wrote to apologise to me. Progress in genetic engineering had shown that even if a cell had become specialised to produce, say, liver or muscle, its genetic code, its DNA, could still be used to produce a complete clone of a human being. Cloning of complete animals are now accepted as fact – see Chapter 5.

But genetic engineers also use only parts of the code to produce only a very small part of a body. Furthermore, they think they will be able to use a gene to correct a disease like cystic fibrosis. Perhaps some day they will even produce an eye for the blind. I think that this is what Jesus did for several blind men. He is the creative Word: the one who created the genetic code in the beginning. That is the implication at the beginning of John's gospel. John states Jesus is the Word:

> In the beginning was the Word and the Word was with God and the Word was God . . . All things were made by him and without him was not anything made that was made . . . and the Word was made flesh and dwelt among us.

Evidence Captured in Amber

Have you ever touched that sticky resin which oozes out of pine trees? There is an interesting history of evidence from it. It shows that evolution did not happen. Do you know why?

That resin is the way that pine trees and all conifers heal their wounds. These conifers are among the oldest types of tree in creation. You can see evidence of them in coal seams. So how does that resin prove that evolution never happened?

Did you know that resin becomes fossilised and turns into amber? Amber jewellery is greatly prized, isn't it? But sometimes you can get a surprise. In that solid, gold-coloured amber, formed a long time ago, you can occasionally get an insect or dragonfly fossilised inside! Through the transparent colour you can see all the wings and legs and body intact. Do you know how it got there?

Well, when that resin oozed out of the pine tree, that insect got captured in the sticky substance and was preserved as evidence – against evolution. Why? For several reasons. That fossil dragonfly, 400 million years old (that's if you accept current time estimates!) was just the same then as it is today. David Attenborough stated on a TV programme that those insects preserved in amber from the coal seam age were just the same as today's. Yes, that is what he said, and many scientists know that is true! There is a whole range of flying insects fossilised in resin, from dragonflies to horseflies. They were perfect for flight right from the start. They had to be, otherwise they would not fly. If they had any ancestors which had useless appendages, and if evolution were true, the survival of the fittest theory would have eliminated them as useless. They would have been selected out before they had been able to fly. This engineering flying masterpiece appeared suddenly. It had no evolutionary links before it and it has no evolutionary links after it.

Mutant Mistakes

Realising the deep flaws to be found in evolution, many scientists continue, almost desperately, to try to find modified explanations that will avoid the implications of a Creator. This approach is often adopted in nature programmes. One such explanation is to claim that the advanced species has resulted from a series of mutations in the lower order of life over millions of years.

I expect you have heard of mutant turtles through children! The public now hears a lot about mutants and mutations. But in actual experiments, mutations are faults. They have never produced anything, only faulty fruit flies with faulty wings and other faults. Sickle cell blood is another mutation fault which causes anaemia, and Down's Syndrome is the result of a genetic fault. All mutations are faulty copying of God's original instructions in the hereditary code. Mutations are not capable of making a more advanced creature. So take your space fiction mutant heroes with a pinch of salt. Yes, the salt of God's truth. You are the salt of the earth if you spread the truth.

What about other explanations scientists are seeking to provide?

Variations Within Species

Have you heard of the biggest dragonflies in history? Quite soon after God created earth's flying creatures, we find one in the rock shales with a nine-foot wing span! Yes, a nine-foot-wing dragonfly! A fossil of it was found in a coal seam and another, even larger than that, has been found.

Q I thought the scientists said that insects were still the same today and therefore you said there was no evolution. What about the evolution of size?

Size in all creatures is variable in the genetic code, according to circumstances. God has given those possibilities, but a species always remains a species. The dragonfly is still the dragonfly today, and the first dragonfly in the fossil record is just as complete as the one today.

According to the Hardy-Weinburgh law, there are 16 possible variants of genetic characteristics, including size, at each fertilisation. That is because the inheritance instructions are carried on two ribbons in each sex, so that makes four for the two sexes. Then for each gene, there are two dominant characteristics, two weak characteristics, and one strong and weak characteristic.

Without going into more detail, this allows for 16 variations, but they all remain one and the same species. Remember that only when both male and female provide all weak (recessive) characteristics can a 'weak' variant come out in the offspring. That is why a characteristic can remain hidden for several generations before it appears again. There are other factors, too. This explains the variations in the human race. I often get asked about this. All scientists are agreed that skin colour and racial shapes are only minor variations. The gene system of all species allows this variation within the same species.

You know by now, of course, that science agrees with the Bible statement of origin. The science of genetics has found proof that we are all descended from a single ancestor.

Can a Crocodile Lay a Bird's Egg?

Because so many scientists have acknowledged that evolution doesn't work, sceptics have come up with new theories to account for the sudden appearance of an entirely new species. One of these theories we have mentioned is called 'saltation'.

Swindewolf proposed that a reptile laid an egg which hatched out a fully-fledged bird. Think of it. Could a reptile like a crocodile lay an egg and find that a feathered bird had broken out? That would neither be evolution nor is there a shred of evidence for it.

Then Dr Niles Eldredge came up with another theory. He called it the fancy name of 'punctuated equilibria'. He says that he came up with the idea because the fossil record just did not fit 'slow evolution'.

Would you be taken seriously if you suggested that a Boeing 747 Jumbo Jet was the result of a tornado sweeping through a junk yard, shooting the rubbish into the air and fitting it all together by chance, to be transformed into an airliner in one night?

Yet this is what one evolutionist seems to be saying about the insects. I repeat his words: 'Some dragonflies developed wings repeating millions of years of evolution in just one night.'

In just one night! – that sounds like belief in magic to me and can be likened to the most sophisticated flying machine suddenly becoming operable in one night.

Yes, you say, but wasn't that after millions of years when faults in the genes were selected by environment and all those faults were put together and made a faultless flying machine?

But environment selects only what is useful, so until that sudden miracle in one night, all the supposed faults were useless, and would therefore be eliminated. The insect could fly only when the complicated machinery was complete for flying.

Has this evolutionist forgotten that the dragonfly started as a grub with no wings, which made a cocoon, went through a miraculous period of change called metamorphosis, then crawled out complete with wings and knew how to use them with a mechanical skill which puts even a helicopter to shame?

I prefer the Bible statement that 'God created the flying creatures of every kind, that they may fly above the earth'.

Those Black Holes

You may have seen TV programmes of Stephen Hawking, the Cambridge Professor who suffers from motor-neurone disease. He promotes deep theories about Black Holes and Big Bangs. One theory was that a time comes when all history runs backwards like a film reversed or a video run backwards. The shattered cup pieces fly together again.

The scientific world finds him very entertaining if only because he constantly changes or modifies his theories. They are theories about time and space and relativity and quantum mechanics. To his credit, he has acknowledged some mistakes.

What effect does it have on you – I mean all this constant revision and change of scientific theories and speculation about God? For myself, it makes me glad that God himself has revealed the truth. He has not left us to flounder and wallow in the world's wisdom. He has spoken, he says, through the Bible and through the Lord Jesus Christ.

You can be all confused by these changing theories if you don't know God has spoken. Hebrews 1 says: 'God at various times and by many methods spoke in old times by the prophets, and has finally spoken to us by his Son.'

Jesus himself said: 'I am he who came down from heaven . . . The words that I speak to you I speak from God the Father.'

Stephen Hawking hoped that he had come up with a complete theory to answer the question, 'Why is it that we and the universe exist?' He thinks that, 'If we find the answer to that, it would be the ultimate triumph of human reason, for,' he says, 'we would know the mind of God.' He calls it his 'Theory of Everything'! Well, how is this for a reply? 'Who has known the mind of the Lord? We do. We have the mind of Christ.' And 'in the wisdom of God, the world by its own wisdom knew not God . . . because the foolishness of God is wiser than the wisdom of men' (1 Corinthians 2:14–16).

Scientist Believers

One of the impressions these nature programmes give is that there is a consensus among scientists – that all support what is being said on the programmes! Do you get the impression that most scientists do not believe the Bible? Actually, this is far from being a true picture. Dr Malcolm Dixon of Cambridge worked out statistics and found that there were as many believers among scientists as there were among non-scientists.

Q So how is it then that the public get the wrong idea?

One reason Dr Dixon gives is that the news value of one heretic bishop outweighs the views of 50 bishops who believe the truth. Another reason he suggests is the success of the propaganda by atheistic communism. It was sponsored into all countries. Unfortunately, it is not widely known that atheistic communism poured money into the cheap publication of science books for universities and colleges.

Is there any other reason why the public get the wrong idea? Yes, I think, too, that there is another reason. It is people's eagerness to accept any theory which will give them an escape from or an excuse not to believe in God. As St Peter wrote, 'They greedily run into error'. Dr Malcolm Dixon went on to show that, contrary to general opinion, a major proportion of the scientific progress of the last two centuries was made by scientists who were Christians. Also that their Christian faith actually helped them to make the right discoveries. (*Enzymes*, by Dr M. Dixon, head of Enzyme Biology Dept., Cambridge, 1958.)

I could give you a lengthy list of very famous scientists who were Christians: Newton, Faraday, Boyle, Mendel and many many others. Even Einstein admitted that he believed in God!

Well, I belong to a UK scientists' Christian fellowship called Christians in Science which has over 300 members. A large proportion of them hold important positions in our universities. Also, I belong to another affiliation which opposes evolution on scientific grounds. So you see, the idea that Christians lose their faith when they become scientists is quite wrong. On the contrary, many unbelievers are seeing that evidence of truth points to God and are then becoming believers!

Truth at the British Museum

In 1981 – to mark its centenary – the British Museum opened an exhibition on Darwinism. Visitors were taken aback to see two notices at the entrance to the exhibition. Both asked about the origins of the living creatures, but gave two opposite explanations.

The first notice stated: 'One idea is that all living things have evolved from a distant ancestor by a process of gradual change – an explanation first thought of by Charles Darwin.' The second notice stated: 'Another view is that God created all living things perfect and unchanging.'

This produced an outcry in the press, but 22 of the Museum's biologists quickly replied, 'Are we to take it that evolution is a fact, proven to the limits of scientific rigour? If that is the inference, then we must disagree most strongly.'

So I feel it is safe to predict that it will not be long before the die-hard Darwinian TV producers will have to give way to the facts, and we may begin to see a more balanced approach to nature programmes. Certainly we should pray that God will soon grant this.

We are seeing that it was because of ignorance that many scientists have been schooled in anti-creation ideas. As scientific understanding increases, we have found that it always comes round to proving the Bible correct. That is because the Creator knew what he was talking about, and that is why **more and more scientists are admitting the existence of a Creator.**

Fraudulent Museum Displays

Many museums do not tell the public that they have assumed an evolutionary process and inserted a fossil to look like a link 'in the interests of completeness', but which has been taken from another place in the fossil record. There are many instances of this for example, the graptilites are often rearranged into an evolutionary-like succession, but actually the most complicated varieties come first. The same applies to trilobites, and Morley Davis says so in his *Introduction to Palaeontology* (1920), but when his book was revised in 1961 by C. J. Stubblefield (Allen & Unwin) the remark was omitted!

The archeoptrix fossil was supposed to have feathers, but Professor Fred Hoyle found they had been stuck on with glue. In reply it was said there are nine other similar fossils but a recent examination reveals that none had feathers.

Under the heading 'Embryonic Fraud Lives On', the *New Scientist* of 6 September, 1997 reports that Heakel's fraudulent drawings of alleged embryonic evolutionary parallels are still displayed in museums today. He was convicted of fraud by Jena University over 120 years ago!

SUMMARY

THE GREAT TV COVER-UP

TV propaganda for evolution hides present scientists' doubts.

Barren rocks before sudden creation of 12 phyla of marine life.
As Genesis 1:20 says, 'God said, let waters swarm with moving creatures'. The Cambrian strata has swarms of fossils – suddenly. David Attenborough on TV said there must have been soft-bodied creatures earlier which left no fossils. But soft bodies do leave fossils. Furthermore, sea urchins of the Cambrian period are still similar today.

Flying aeronautical marvels of four different kingdoms of animal.
All contrary to 'survival of fittest' theory:
• Insects (preceded by metamorphosis in cocoon) (amber evidence).
• Reptiles 'practised swift runs and leaps for thousands of years until they could fly' (*Encyclopaedia Britannica*).
• Birds: mechanism of interlocking feathers quite different from scales.
• Mammals like bats – no fossils of mice changing into bats.

No evolutionary record of any of these. Professor Hoyle found Archaeopteryx to be a fraud.

Gen. 1:21 God created every winged creature.
Job 39:13 God created the peacock's wings.
Job 38:26 Migration of birds by God's wisdom.

Sight: from first fossils, all have eyes, even worms.
• Sonic sight for bats (dark caves).
• Telescopic sight for eagles.
• Trilobites had complex eye for opaque deep water.
• Octopus eyes like human's (yet entirely different kingdom).
• Human eye: 20 million nerves from retina to brain. Automatic focusing and light meter of iris and lens.

22 British Museum biologists said in 1981 'Evolution is not a fact'.

8 THE CONVERSION OF CHARLES DARWIN
THE EVIDENCE SOME SEEK TO HIDE

Charles Darwin (1809–1882) was born into a generally agnostic family. His mother died when he was only eight years of age and this childhood tragedy appears to have significantly influenced his later outlook on life. His father was a respected physician and would have liked Charles to continue in his footsteps, an ambition which was never realised owing to the young man's sensitive nature and his intense dread of blood and human suffering.

After his father reluctantly realised that Charles was unsuited for the medical career, for which he had been preparing at Edinburgh, he determined to send him to Cambridge to be trained for the Anglican ministry – a surprising decision by someone who was a self-declared atheist – but he was never subsequently ordained.

It is a favourite theme drummed out by the media that Darwin was a believer at first and that science changed his views, but apparently, according to Desmond and Moore in their new book on Darwin, he had no real faith as a young man. He did not believe in miracles and his grandfather described his beliefs as half-Christian – 'a feather bed to catch a falling Christian'. The authors wrote that, while at Cambridge, Darwin seems to have made no contact with the famous Charles Simeon who was the stalwart for biblical faith.

Darwin's conversion at the end of his life, largely ignored by the media, must have been a first-time conversion, not just a restoration from backsliding.

Some time after returning from his voyage on *HMS Beagle* (1831–1836) Darwin had, publicly at least, rejected any faith he may have had. He was still a young man when he began to formulate the hypothesis which would later be known as his Theory of Evolution by Natural Selection.

At that time he did not think that the theory of evolution ruled out a Creator, as he made clear in his *Origin of Species*. Towards the end of his life, however, **Charles Darwin admitted his misgivings about evolution**. 'I was a young man with unformed ideas. I threw out queries, suggestions, wondering all the time over everything and to my astonishment the ideas took like wildfire.

Little has been said by his supporters about the questioning that went on in his own mind regarding his new theory. Fewer still of his followers are willing to admit that he maintained, throughout his life, a considerable inner turmoil (which seems to have been the major cause of the chronic illness from which he suffered).

Darwinians reject violently the mere suggestion that he came to faith in Jesus Christ in his old age. One of Darwin's biographers is Ronald Clark. He published his book in 1984 entitled *The Survival of Charles Darwin*. In it, he denies that Darwin was converted. This is what he said: 'A deathbed conversion was obviously called for, and if one did not exist, it had to be manufactured.' Thus he implies that the conversion was a fraud.

Testimonies to Darwin's Conversion

Despite all this, there is substantial evidence to support the claim that Darwin was converted to Christ a few months before his death. His conversion was reported by Lady Hope who claimed to have visited him and read the New Testament to him. Some Darwinians have tried to make out that this report 'was an absurd fabrication'. Others have said, 'There is not an iota of truth in the charge' and 'That's the kind of story the evangelicals would manufacture'.

However, Dr Croft of Salford University has published a book in which he brings loads of evidence that Charles Darwin was indeed converted about six months before he died. In fact, there was quite a revival going on at the bottom of his garden, in the village of Downe in Kent, where many of his servants were converted as well. I will give you the evidences one by one, as Dr Croft does in his book *The Life and Death of Charles Darwin* (Elmwood, 1989). It turns out that Lady Hope was not the only one to testify to Darwin's conversion.

In what way do the agnostics say that Lady Hope's report was a fraud? The first accusation was that there was no such person as Lady Hope. In reply, Dr Croft looks up the reference books to find she was quite a famous person. She was the daughter of General Sir Arthur Cotton. If that was not fame enough, she was married to the First Admiral of the Fleet, Sir James Hope.

The catalogue of the British Library tells you also that she was a well-known author of 37 books and pamphlets. These were mainly evangelical tracts and temperance pamphlets. It is quite understandable that she should go to talk to Darwin about faith, also about temperance, for Darwin was a stout supporter of temperance, as he had a horror of drunkenness.

Yet some have said Darwin could not have been converted because there was no such person as Lady Hope! Lady Hope said she was invited to talk to him. She found him reading his Bible. He told her that the letter to the Hebrews was his favourite book, 'The Royal Book' he called it. 'Isn't it grand?' Yes, it is that book which speaks about the all-powerful cleansing blood of Jesus Christ, who can wash away every sin and save a person to the uttermost.

Are there others who knew Lady Hope? Dr Croft looked up the records and found that there were. The famous Lord Shaftesbury knew her well. So too did Booth Tucker of the Salvation Army and others like James Fegan – an evangelist – and the the Revd Ishmael Jones.

Now it was in 1881 that Lady Hope said that Charles Darwin was converted and it was that same year, on 21 December 1881, that the Revd Ishmael Jones wrote an article in the *Christian Herald*. Here is his article as published in Dr Croft's book:

I once attended a meeting at Dorking (in Kent) which was addressed by Miss Cotton (now Lady Hope) who did such a good work for the Gospel, and for Temperance. She said that when first she saw the necessity of adding temperance to spiritual work, she was anxious to obtain a pledge-book. She was told that the last man who signed it was an old drunken shoemaker and that he had signed it twenty times and broken it on each occasion. Miss Cotton asked the address of this man and resolved that she would commence her temperance work with him. She went to his shop and asked him if he would make one more effort for freedom. He replied that it was no use as he had tried many times before. She knelt down by his side and prayed while he went on hammering away at the shoe he was mending. Still she kept praying until at last she found that his work ceased and he said to her, 'Miss, I believe there is hope for me.' Lady Hope visited him day after day to encourage him and he gained victory, and for years he has been a steadfast Christian in the town of Dorking.

A Horror of Alcoholism

Now you will notice a lot has been said about temperance. Lady Hope was the leader of the Temperance Movement and Darwin was an ardent supporter of that movement. What was his concern? It was because both his grandmother and his great-grandmother had died of drink. Charles Darwin's son, Francis, wrote therefore, 'He had a horror of drinking and constantly warned his boys that anyone might be led into drinking too much.'

Is it any wonder, then, that Darwin would invite Lady Hope to visit him? After all, she was the leading figure in the national Temperance Movement!

Pat Sloan wrote in the agnostic magazine *The Humanist*. She referred to Lady Hope as 'that elusive Lady Hope'. But how can Lady

Hope be elusive when she is known to be the daughter of General Sir Arthur Cotton and the wife of the First Admiral of the Fleet, Sir James Hope, and when the British Library says she is a well-known author of 37 works?

Lord Shaftesbury, indeed, wrote a foreword to one of Lady Hope's books in 1878, describing her as 'a pious, amiable and accomplished young lady', whose exertions were 'founded on an intense love of the gospel'. That sounds to me just the right person to visit and report Darwin's conversion!

I have mentioned the report in the *Christian Herald* in 1881. Some years later another report in that same paper appeared. It was an interview by Booth Tucker who was a Commissioner in the Salvation Army. He questioned her at length about the conversion of Charles Darwin. She confirmed all that she had said. Here are her words as they were reported in the *English Churchman*.

Lady Hope's Report

It was one of those glorious autumn afternoons that we sometimes enjoy in England, that I was asked to go in and sit with the well-known scientific author, Charles Darwin. He was almost bedridden for some months before he died. I used to feel, when I saw him, that his fine presence would make a grand picture for our Royal Academy; but never did I think so more strongly than on this particular occasion.

He was sitting up in bed, wearing a soft embroidered dressing gown, of rather a rich purple shade. Propped up by pillows, he was gazing out on a far-stretching scene of woods and cornfields, which glowed in the light of one of those marvellous sunsets which are the beauty of Kent and Surrey. His noble forehead and fine features seemed to be lit up with pleasure as I entered the room. He waved his hand towards the window as he pointed out the scene beyond, while in the other hand he held an open Bible which he was always studying.

'What are you reading now?' I asked as I seated myself at his bedside. 'Hebrews!' he answered, 'still Hebrews, the Royal Book, I call it. Isn't it grand?' Then placing his finger on certain passages he commented on them. I made some allusion to the strong opinions expressed by many persons on the history of the Creation, its grandeur and then their treatment of the early chapters of the Book of Genesis. He seemed greatly distressed, his fingers twitched nervously, and a look of agony came over his face as he said, 'I was a young man with unformed ideas. I threw out queries, suggestions, wondering all the time over everything; and to my astonishment the ideas took like wildfire. People made a religion of them.'

Then he paused and after a few more sentences on the holiness of God and 'the grandeur of the Book', looking at the Bible which he was holding tenderly all the time, he suddenly said: 'I have a summer-house in the garden, which holds about thirty people. It is over there,' pointing through the open window. 'I want you very much to speak there. I know you read the Bible in the villages. Tomorrow afternoon I should like the servants on the place, some tenants and a few of the neighbours to gather there. Will you speak to them?'

'What shall I speak about?' I asked. 'Christ Jesus' he replied in a clear emphatic voice, adding in a lower tone, 'and his salvation. Is not that the best theme? And then I want you to sing some hymns with them. You lead on your small instrument, do you not?'

The wonderful look of brightness and admiration on his face as he said this I shall never forget, for he added: 'If you take the meeting at three o'clock this window will be open and you will know that I am joining in with the singing.' How I wished that I could have made a picture of the find old man and his beautiful surroundings on that memorable day!

Details Confirmed

Dr Croft has found plenty of evidence that Charles Darwin was indeed converted to Christ before he died, thus fully substantiating Lady Hope's visit and report.

Darwin referred to the special musical instrument which Lady Hope used at her meetings. Darwin said, 'You lead on your small instrument, do you not?' Apparently, it was Lady Hope's practice to use a small harmonium in her meetings. She refers to it in one of her books as follows:

> . . . a small instrument for hand-playing only, size about two and a half feet by one and a half, five inches deep and placed on the knee, played with one hand and is called a Book Harmonium. This instrument is most suitable for leading the singing in hospitals, cottage meetings, etc. 'It is a treat' the poor sick ones say, 'when we have sung some hymns together in the largest ward of our little hospital.

Charles Darwin knew all about her little harmonium so that detail is confirmed.

Another detail which some denied was that there was a summer-house in Darwin's garden. Darwin had asked Lady Hope to hold an evangelistic meeting there, but Henrietta Lichfield, writing over 70 years later in *The Scotsman* said there was no such thing as a summer-house in Darwin's garden. But Sir Hedley Atkins said there was a summer-house and he should know because he was curator of the Down House Museum, and Darwin had lived at Down House. (Fig 8.1).

Sir Hedley Atkins was also past President of the Royal College of Surgeons and he wrote, 'There was a summer-house at the end of the sandwalk on Darwin's estate.' Therefore Henrietta Lichfield was wrong in her published statement. Sir Hedley Atkins adds that 'perhaps Henrietta was carried away by her indignation'.

Why is it that some seem so keen to deny that Darwin was converted?

Figure 8.1. Down House in the Kent village of Downe in 1872, after Darwin's many additions   *Courtesy: The Mansell Collection*

They seem to be afraid of admitting that he turned to Christ in the last years of his life. The same Henrietta Lichfield claims two more things: that he never recanted any of his scientific views and that neither servants nor villagers sang hymns to him on his lawn.

So there was a summer-house! Now let's look at the information Dr Croft brings about meetings on Darwin's lawn. It seemed there was quite a revival going on.

Darwin's Revival Meetings

Dr Croft quotes ten separate sources about these evangelistic meetings on Darwin's lawn and he even quotes from a letter written by Darwin to an evangelist. The evangelist was James Fegan, who was well-known in the last century. Moreover, he was a friend of Lady Hope and the organiser of those meetings.

Fegan's report of these revival meetings is given by Darwin's own wife, Emma, in the book *A Century of Family Letters,* vol. 2, p 244. In it, James Fegan said:

> The services I held were attended sometimes by members of the Darwin family and regularly by members of their household. Indeed, when I had a Mission in Downe, the Darwin family were considerate enough to alter their dinner hour so that their household might attend – but this was char-

acteristic of all who served them. At the services, Parslow, the old family butler was converted to God and brought into Church membership, also Mrs Sales, the housekeeper, was brought into the light, and others.

We definitely know that services were held during the February (probably 14th–16th) of 1881, for Emma wrote the following letter to her daughter: 'Hurrah for Mr Fegan! Mrs Evans (the cook) attended a prayer meeting in which old M made as nice a prayer as ever you heard in your life . . .' (Old M is described in a footnote as 'a notable old drunkard of the village'.)

Fegan's Orphan Boys

We now have a great deal of information about James Fegan. As well as being an evangelist, he was a great humanitarian who had built a home for orphan boys at Stony Stratford. During August 1880, Fegan brought 67 of these orphan boys to Downe where Darwin's home was, for a camping holiday. They also sang hymns on Darwin's lawn. Darwin was a great admirer of Fegan and gave each of the lads a six-penny piece, which was worth a lot then. Dr Croft tells us that it was the following year that Fegan held revival meetings in Darwin's village. Now the weather turned very cold, so Darwin invited Fegan to hold his meetings in his school room and that is where so many of his household were converted.

So if somebody says to you, 'Evolution explains everything without God!' you could say to them, 'Darwin says there is a better theme; it is Jesus Christ and his salvation'.

Darwin's Second Thoughts

The other objection we must deal with is that Darwin 'never recanted any of his scientific views'. However, the following report was published in the *Bromley and Kentish Times* with the recollections of a Mr A. H. Nicholls who was closely acquainted with the servants of Darwin's household who had nursed him through his final illness:

> This lady who had been in attendance on Darwin prior to his death had informed him that he requested her to read the New Testament to him and asked her to arrange for the Sunday School children to sing, 'There is a green hill far away'. This was done and Darwin, who was greatly moved, said, 'How I wish I had not expressed my theory of evolution as I have done.'

It is probable that the 'lady who nursed Darwin' was Mrs Evans. She had been with the Darwin household as a nurse for many years and ,as she was a member of the Gospel Hall congregation, she could have

Figure 8.2. Cartoon of Charles Darwin showing prevailing humour in the mid-nineteenth century
Courtesy: Punch magazine

easily arranged for the Sunday School to sing an Easter hymn for Darwin.

Thus we now have two independent accounts that support the fact of Darwin's conversion. If one accepts Lady Hope's account, one must also presumably accept the accompanying claim that Darwin regretted his evolution theory and stated that, 'People made much more of it', 'The ideas took like wildfire' and 'People made a religion of them'.

There is no doubt that towards the end of his life, Darwin had realised that individuals were using his theory for all sorts of repugnant ideologies. It is known that he was extremely unhappy about this, for in a letter to Dr Scherzer, written in 1879, he wrote, 'What a foolish idea seems to prevail in Germany on the connection between Socialism and Evolution through Natural Selection'.

The thought that Haeckel was urging the German peoples to accept their racial superiority and to adopt a policy of racial 'weeding', with the argument that the extermination of 'lower' races was all good – in the name of Darwin's natural selection – must have made him feel wretched. Hitler later developed his theme. It was Haeckel who made fraudulent sketches of the supposed evolution of the baby in the womb which he called, 'recapitulation'. This theory has been pronounced by science as incorrect. Haeckel himself confessed later that his drawings 'were frauds'.

Furthermore, Darwin was also sensitive of how Karl Marx was applying Darwinism to justify revolutionary charge. This also must have proved distressing for him, so much so, that he refused Marx permission to dedicate the English edition of *Das Kapital* to himself.

Thus there is substantial evidence to support the belief that Darwin did express regret, regarding the consequences of his theory, in his conversation to Lady Hope. Furthermore, we have seen all the evidence from many people from many quarters that Charles Darwin was converted to Jesus Christ in the last year of his life. All the objections to Darwin's conversion have been fully answered.

Darwin and the Occult

To what extent can we attribute Darwinism to the occult? Perhaps more than you think. It is not generally known that in 1857 Darwin consulted a clairvoyant and in the years that followed, according to Dr Croft, he attended seances and met mediums.

When I was at Oxford, I attended a lecture by Sir Alistair Hardy. He told us what it was that changed him from being an atheist into believing in the supernatural. It was that a medium told him about some personal things which he was sure that nobody else could possibly know about. What is your reaction to that? Perhaps you say, 'Well good came out of that'.

But I know of others with whom it started innocently, but eventually it became evident that they were in touch with evil spirits and they had to be delivered from their power. 1 Timothy 4:1 warns you that in 'the latter days, many will depart from the faith and give heed to deceiving spirits and doctrines of devils'. Certain court cases are evidence of this today, where gunmen have been provoked by evil spirits to fire at random into crowds.

Notice that phrase 'doctrines of devils'. Doctrines or teaching include deceiving theories. St Peter wrote about one to come in the latter days, of a theory which would deny that God created things by his word. Peter says this would lead to lust and lawlessness; there is plenty of that around today. Also, St Paul warns you against what he calls 'the great lie'. 'In the latter days,' he says, 'all will believe the lie who don't want to be saved.' So a person who does not want to be saved leaves himself open to deception.

The Bible clearly forbids the occult and spiritism, because Satan is

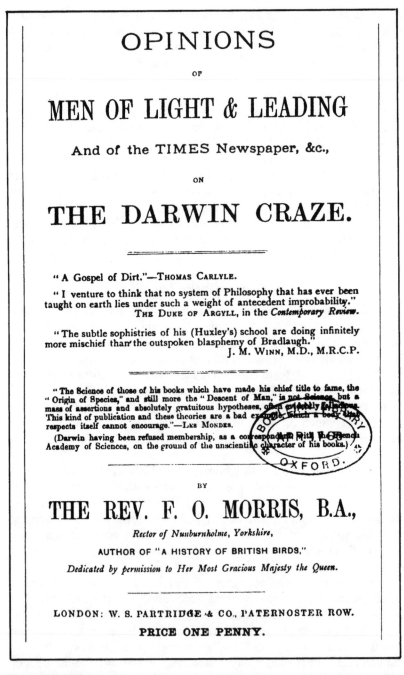

Figure 8.3. Collection of adverse opinions of Darwin's theory (published in 1885)
Note comment by Les Mondes: '. . . a mass of assertions and absolutely gratuitous
hypotheses, often evidently fallacious.'   *Courtesy: Bodleian Library, Oxford*

a great deceiver. 'He deceives the whole world,' Revelation says. That is why I'm not surprised when I see TV programmes which deceive the public!

When Darwin visited his first clairvoyant, she shrank back in terror and exclaimed she could see within him 'a most appalling picture of horrors'. Was not Nazi-ism based upon Haeckel's propaganda of Darwinism? Haeckel convinced the Nazis that to eliminate and massacre inferior races was part of the philosophy of the survival of the fittest. Karl Marx also based his philosophy upon the same principles. The world is now seeing that systems based upon the survival of the fittest are failing and falling apart.

Revelation 12 describes the devil as Satan who is the deceiver of the whole world and Jesus said that the devil was a liar and murderer from the beginning and the father of all lies. He has thousands of years experience at making lies look like the truth.

The Wedgwood Potter's Vessel

Darwin was like a shattered potter's vessel which God in his grace restored. It is appropriate that Charles Darwin married the daughter of the famous pottery manufacturer Josiah Wedgwood. Her name was Emma. She was a sincere Christian who read her Bible daily. Eventually, it was to help Darwin come to a true faith.

I used to have a ministry in the Potteries in England. Opposite Stoke station in the Potteries centre stands a statue of Josiah Wedgwood in a knickerbocker suit of Georgian times. In his hand he holds one of his famous Wedgwood vases, ready to dash it to the ground if it was not perfect.

God warned Jeremiah, the Old Testament prophet, he could do this to anyone. In chapter 18 he said:

Go down to the potter's house and there I will give you a message. So I went down to the potter's house and I saw him working at the wheel, but the pot he was shaping from the clay was marred in his hands, so the potter formed it into another pot. Then the word of the Lord came to me . . . 'Like clay in the hand of the potter, so are you in my hand . . . If a nation I warned repents of its evil, then I will not inflict on it the disaster I had planned.'

Charles Darwin's faith and health became marred by false science, but our gracious God did not scrap Darwin. His Creator was able to remake him in the last year of his life.

Many nations were deceived by Darwin's survival of the fittest theory and experienced disaster. Darwin himself was shattered but restored like the potter's vase when he repented and believed. He went down to Potter Wedgwood's house at Maer and married his Christian daughter Emma in 1839 and then, nearly 50 years later, with his new-found faith, we find him enjoying Bible reading with his Christian wife.

Darwin's Support for Christian Missionaries

Charles Darwin became an admirer of Christian missionary work during his voyage on *The Beagle*. In his *Journal* he praises the work of missionaries in Tahiti: 'The missionaries have done much in improving their (the Tahitians') moral character, and still more in teaching them the arts of civilisation.' Later he adds: 'I think it will be acknowledged that every well-wisher of Tahiti owes no common debt of gratitude to the missionaries.'

Again in New Zealand – where he was appalled at the horrors of cannibalism – he acknowledges what the Christian missionaries had done to eliminate this evil:

> I took leave of the missionaries with thankfulness for their kind welcome and with feelings of high respect for their gentleman-like, useful and upright characters. I think it would be difficult to find a body of men better adapted for the high office which they fulfil.

Revealing his relief at finally leaving New Zealand, he adds: 'I look back but to one bright spot and that is Waimate, with its Christian inhabitants.'

But it was the Yaghan Indians of Tierra del Fuego who most attracted Darwin's attention. When first he encountered them, in December 1832, their 'savage and wild' appearance and their barbarous ways made an indelible impression on him. Such was their state that he wondered if in fact they might be one of the 'missing links' he was looking for.

Later, in correspondence with his lifelong friend, Rear Admiral Sir James Sullivan, Darwin reveals his great surprise and incredulity at the changes taking place amongst the Tierra del Fuego Indians as a result of the missionary efforts to evangelise and educate them. His admiration for this work led him to become a supporter of the South American Missionary Society (SAMS) during the last 15 years of his life. His support started in 1867 with a donation of £5 (more than £300 in today's money!).

Rear Admiral Sullivan was a member of the SAMS Committee, who had kept Darwin regularly updated with news of missionary endeavours. On 30th January 1870, Darwin wrote to him: 'The success of the Tierra del Fuego Mission is most wonderful, and charms me, as I had always prophesied failure. It is a grand success. I shall feel proud if your Committee think fit to elect me as an honorary member of your Society.'

Four and a half years later, on 6th June 1874, Darwin again writes to Admiral Sullivan to express his amazement at the changes occurring amongst the Fuegians. Seven years later, on 20th March 1881, Darwin writes: 'The account of the Fuegians interested not only me, but all my family. It is truly wonderful what you have heard from Mr Bridges about their honesty and about their language. I certainly should have predicted that not all the missionaries in the world could have done what has been done.'

Sir James later recalled that not many weeks before Darwin's death, Darwin had sent him the annual subscription to the South American Missionary Society with the comment: 'Judging from the *Missionary Journal* the Mission on Tierra del Fuego seems going on quite wonderfully well.'

Would it be wrong to suggest that the God of all mercy was using the labours of these missionaries not only to bring salvation to the Fuegians, but also to begin a 'knocking at the door' process in the hardened heart of one Charles Darwin, who finally succumbed to the perseverance of the Lord and opened his heart to the Saviour in the last months of his life?

How appropriate the opening phrases of Hebrews were for the founder of the Theory of Evolution. One could surprise a doubter by inviting him to read Darwin's favourite book, which begins by stating that 'God who at various times and in different ways spoke in time past to the fathers by the prophets, has in these last days spoken to us by his Son . . . by whom he created the universe. The Son is the radiance of God's glory and the exact likeness of his being and upholds all things by his powerful word.'

SUMMARY

USEFUL POINTS FROM DARWIN'S LIFE

1. Darwin's conversion reported by Lady Hope. Who was she?
- Daughter of General Sir Arthur Cotton
- Wife of Admiral Sir James Hope
- Author of 37 books (British Library)
- Temperance worker

2. Also reported by:
- James Fegan, evangelist, temperance advocate
- Ishmael Jones in *Christian Herald* periodical
- Booth Tucker of Salvation Army
- A. N. Nichols who also heard Darwin's regrets re evolution

3. Mission conversions on Darwin's lawn reported by:
- Darwin's wife Emma
- Darwin's butler
- The *Bromley and Kentish Times*

4. Accuracy confirmed by:
- Sir Hedley Atkins, President of Royal College of Surgeons
- Darwin's reference to harmonium and summer-house meetings
- Darwin's letter to evangelist J. Fegan
- Dr L. R. Croft of Salford University

5. Darwin:
- Regretted the results of his theory
- Regretted use made by Karl Marx, etc.
- Regretted use made by Haeckel
- Admitted that fossil record looked like special creation
- Made donations to South American Missionary Society

9 THE GARDEN OF EDEN

THE ORIGIN OF FARMING

Treasure Island! What adventures that story conjures up. Do you remember the story of the map? The map showed the Island in the warm Pacific Ocean. It described where the pirates buried the treasure and how to find it through the palm trees waving in the breeze. The adventurers believed the map and set out full of faith to find it.

The finding of the Garden of Eden has also been an adventure. Unfortunately, many seekers who were anthropologists did not believe the geographical area described in the Bible. In fact, they had never taken it seriously. Gordon Childs, a pronounced atheist, thought it must have been in Europe, but found he was wrong.

Of course, they did not call it *Eden*. They called it the place where farming started.

Where Was the Garden of Eden?

Where did farming begin? Archaeology has traced the geographical centre right back to where the Bible says. At first they looked at other places thinking that farming started there – Europe, then Egypt, then Palestine, then the fertile crescent of the Middle East. If they had looked where the Bible said it started, they would have saved a lot of wasted time.

In Genesis 2:10–14, the exact location and topography of the Garden of Eden are described. It was in the headwaters of the four rivers Pison, Gihon, Tigris and Euphrates. These rivers rise on the plateau heights of Eastern Turkey.

The height of this inland plateau varies from 3,000 to 4,000 feet. Around it is a rim of mountains rising to 12,000 feet and then the main peak – Mount Ararat – towers above them all. (See my photograph, Fig 9.1.) The text refers to the sources of the rivers being fed by one main source. Those who have explored this area find that the melt waters from the glaciers at the foot of the mountains flowed as rivers into Lake Van which, at the time of the first farmers, covered a much larger area.

The excavations and pollen core samples prove that the type of farming in this Garden of Eden was just as described in Genesis 2. It was what was called dry farming. In other words, the garden plots did not depend upon rain, just as the Bible says: 'God did not cause it to rain upon the ground'. How then was it watered? Streams of water

Figure 9.1. The Mountain of Ararat
The workings in the foreground are on the 1,000-metre plateau beyond which is the Garden of Eden where the four rivers meet. A derrick can be seen to extract water from below ground. Mount Ararat rises to a height of 5,000 metres above sea level.

coming out of the rocks were kept back in the garden by clay walls banked up around the garden. That is the evidence we found.

How We Know that Farming Started Here

It is proved by three branches of science:

1. Archaeological succession. That is the layers of rubbish, pots, tools and buildings which succeeded each other in order of time, layer upon layer.
2. Biological origins. That is where wheat originally grew and from where farm animals actually originated.
3. By radio-active dating. The radio-active dating came much later and only confirmed what had been discovered by the other two methods.

In answer to some objectors to radio-active dating, the method has been corrected. It only shows a small difference, but the picture looks the same. In any case, it is a biblical picture. Wrong ideas of scientists have been brought more and more into line with the Bible. Many anthropologists are unaware of this.

The Spread of Farming

In my book *Who was Adam?* I give an outline of **how farming spread to the rest of the world from the Garden of Eden.**

Those who migrated into Europe have been traced as the Danubians who pioneered central Europe by river or the sea farmers who came by coastal routes. 'These New Stone Age farmers sailed the length of the Mediterranean bringing with them their cattle, sheep and pigs in their boats. They would tie up their boats and land their domesticated animals as they migrated further and further west along the northern shores of the Mediterranean Sea' (*Who was Adam?* p 59). Eventually, they went through the Gibraltar Straits and landed in the west of England, Wales, east of Ireland and north of Scotland. Some went even further to Scandinavia.

A second migration travelled eastward. How did they eventually reach America? Firstly through India, where migrants divided into three regions dependent on wheat, rice or sorghum. Then they went on to China. We have the evidence – their reaping knives can still be dug up in China along the Yellow River. Pottery of the Third New Stone Age era then reached Japan. The farmers migrated through north-east Asia and then across the Bering Straits to America. In the 1920s, Vavilov thought that the American Indians had invented their farming independently, but this is not so since Graham Clark of Cambridge shows that the bone handles with slots to hold flints for reaping have their origin in Eurasia – that is, Turkey, China and east Siberia. Darlington and others have confirmed this showing how maize and beans replaced wheat .

A third migration went south into Egypt and then to Africa.

Moses Gets it Right

Well, that is interesting for you who live in these countries but even better is to know that it is all correctly recorded in the Bible. The remarkable fact is that **the Bible gets all the cultural succession right as well as the migrations**. What do we mean by that?

It is largely the materials with which man made things that is the culture. If you found a kitchen utensil made of plastic, you would know that this was not made until the middle of the twentieth century because of its material. If you found a digital watch, you would know that it was still later this century when digital watches began to be made. So then, we are able to tell, both by the materials of which tools are made and also by their design, the historical order in which they were made.

Now, the order in which man used materials was stone, copper-stone, bronze and then iron. The amazing thing is that the Bible gets this order right. Why amazing? Because the Bible is speaking of cultural material thousands of years before Moses lived. How did Moses get it right in the first five books of the Bible? It must have been because God told him.

Some of the material in the first book of the Bible looks as if it came down to Moses on tablets. These tablets would be those records handed down from Abraham to Joseph and then to Moses; even so, by their accuracy their genuineness is proved because people living in Moses' time would not get the background culture correct and certainly any living after Moses would not get the culture details right.

Now, Abraham lived 2000 BC. How would he know for instance that Adam lived in the Stone Age? That was some thousands of years before him. Also, how would he know that native copper was not discovered and used in tools until the Copper Stone Age? All that is accurately described in Genesis chapter 4 and scientists know this. Later on, techniques brought in bronze alloys. The Bible gets that right too. Last of all comes the Iron Age.

Now the Iron Age had to wait until the Hittites discovered how to smelt iron-ore. Iron was very tough and difficult to reduce. Only the hottest furnaces could do it. The Hittites kept their secret to themselves for 400 years. Even Pharaoh of Egypt pleaded with the Hittites for their secret. Their iron weapons and iron chariots were their secret weapon. Quite correctly, the Bible talks about the Hittite chariots of iron.

Yet the critics, always eager to find fault with the Bible said, at first, that there were no such people as the Hittites! Then the archaeologists discovered all about them. Yes, the Bible was right again! The Bible was also right when it said that the Israelites were not allowed to have iron weapons until King Saul's time.

This all shows that **the incidental background detail to the Bible stories is correct.** The background about materials which were used to make things would not be known if those early books were written after the time of Moses, as some have tried to pretend.

What would it matter to a later writer whether a tool was made of stone, copper, bronze or iron? Such background details show the accuracy of the Bible accounts. If this accuracy is even in the background details, it shows how you can rely upon the details which matter; especially when it tells you truth which fallen human nature wants to ignore.

An Answer to Doubters of Eden's Location

Some have different ideas about where the Garden of Eden was. Some have said it was in Mesopotamia, or even in the delta of the Persian Gulf at the mouths of the Tigris and Euphrates rivers.

Don't be deceived by 'tourist ideas', or comments by amateurs who have done no empirical research. There is a clear geographical location given in Genesis 2:10–14.

* *First.* Eden was at the source of the rivers (v 10) so it was *not* at the mouths of the rivers or halfway down as some suggested. Rivers start in mountains, not in valleys. The sources of the Euphrates and the Tigris are in Eastern Turkey, high up on the plateau. They are fed from the streams from the surrounding mountains of the Ararat range. Mount Ararat itself is 17,000 feet high, and the surrounding range of Tauros-Zagros mountains is 12,000 feet high. These feed Lake Van, on the high plateau which is an average of 4,000 feet above sea level.
* *Second.* The identities of the rivers Pison and Gihon are clearly given in the London Geographical Institute maps. The present names of these rivers are Halys and Araxes. The Halys rises in Eastern Turkey and flows north to the Black Sea. The River Araxes rises in Eastern Turkey and flows north-east into the Caspian Sea.
* *Third.* The map in Figure 9.2 shows the headwaters of these four rivers.
* *Fourth.* As well as my own research in the area, other anthropologists and archaeologists have given the following reports from the sources of these four rivers:

> The source of water for Eden was Lake Van fed by streams from the surrounding mountains. In Eden itself, the high pressure out-blowing winds must have kept the enclave free from rain. Even today in altered conditions, Lynch speaks of the clear skies. Wreaths of smoke are never seen on the tops of mountains and whatever clouds may have climbed the barrier of the peripheral ranges are suspended high in the heavens, seldom obscuring the sun (Flannery).

World Conference of Prehistoric Archaeologists

In a symposium of world prehistoric archaeologists, Flannery describes the dry farming which was practised in the Near Eastern Eden by the early farmers. He says that about 10,000 years ago, the oak woodland belt expanded over the Uplands of Turkey and Iran, even into the areas of the Zagros mountains which had formerly been treeless steppe. He points out that a small rainfall and high plateau altitude would prevent dense forests growing. This absence of forest

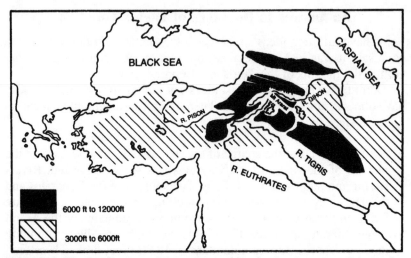

Figure 9.2. The headwaters of four rivers rising in the Ararat and Armenian mountain ranges
This answers the description given in Genesis of the location from which farming began.

would enable certain species like wild cereal grasses to grow as thick as a cultivated field, free from weeds. This, then, was **the reason that farming commenced and thrived in an elevated plateau and not in lowland valley**s. He tells how Harland, another anthropologist, reaped such an area of wild wheat harvest with a flint-bladed sickle. He harvested enough wild wheat in an hour to produce one kilo of clean grain. This wild grain, after chemical analysis, proved to be almost twice as rich in protein as domestic wheat.

A family of experienced plant collectors, in three weeks without even working very hard, could gather more grain than the family could possibly eat in a year. Later he adds: The spread of early dry farming complex across the Near East is striking.

In *Who was Adam?* I suggested that verses 5 and 6 of Genesis chapter 2 describe the desolate condition following the retreat of the ice from the area which was to become the Garden of Eden. The source of these floods, which have left their evidence in the Armenian heights of Asia Minor, must have been from the peri-glacial ice-melt characteristic of conditions existing at the end of the last ice age. This correlates well because the dates of the end of the ice age and of the commencement of farming are the same, namely 10,000 BC. The greenhouse canopy theory could give similar effects.

As a certain theologian questioned the presence of what are called peri-glacial conditions, we will quote the evidence from contributors to the symposium referred to above. Charles Reed says, 'The Taurus-Zagros mountains of the Near East had been heavily glaciated but

12,000 years ago these glaciers were melting back towards their highland sources.' Flannery adds his evidence:

> In the Zagros mountains, the climate was arid and cold during Wurm 11 (a phase in the last ice-age); pollen analysis indicates Artemisia steppe. The transition to post-glacial was marked by increasing humidity of mists and floods. It was in this kind of setting that the first steps toward plant and animal domestication were made.

Charles Burney in *The Peoples of the Hills* also gives a description which gives an insight into the conditions which are described in Genesis 2:5,6 as a prelude to the development of the Garden of Eden:

> From the results of palaeo-climatology, it seems apparent that during the last glaciation, the climate snow line was as much as 2,700 feet lower than that of today. With this went an alpine vegetation (described in Genesis 2:5,6) in the highlands of eastern Anatolia (Eastern Turkey) and in Caucasia, with meadow and scrub and some glaciers. Two radio-carbon dates show that loess ceased to be deposited (by glaciers) by about 9000 BC, suggesting that by then the dry northerly winds [which brought the rainless climate in Adam's time – author], blowing during the glacial periods from the steppes of Eurasia, were no longer prevalent.

ADAM'S DRY FARMING

Flannery also draws attention to dry farming by the early farmers. At Ali Kosh 9,500 years ago, cereals were planted in swamp conditions. The small early dry farming village on the Kozistan steppe of southwest Iran, also produced 10,000 identifiable bones from 35 species of domesticated animal. A typical dry farming garden is shown in Figure 9.3.

It seems strange to some why the first farmers should choose such mountainous districts and arid conditions in which to develop their cereal growing experiments. Here Vavilov's comments help us. He is an archaeologist. He said that the origins of plant domestication were in mountainous zones because the ancestors to cultivated plants would be unable to grow in dense plant communities of perennial trees, shrubs and herbs. The wild wheat and barleys were restricted to disturbed soil along river banks or on gravel screes and places where the poor and intermittent rainfall was insufficient to support other vegetation (weeds) which would overwhelm and choke them. They may well have germinated near great glaciers, scrub-deserts and **dry intermountain basins.**

Q Are there others who also have done fieldwork in this area of Eastern Turkey and Northern Iran?

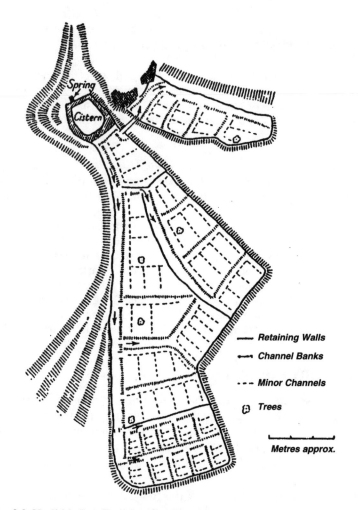

Figure 9.3. Neolithic Dry Farming Garden
Rainless area irrigated by water seeping through rocks (Genesis 2:6) typical of dry farming methods in the Garden of Eden area and still used today in Arizona by the Pueblo Indians.

Courtesy: C. Daryll Ford 'Habitat, Economy and Society' Methuen

I have already identified the sources of the four rivers rising in Eden. Now read the description of the ecology as given in my doctorate thesis, pages 130–132:

One has to cross the central tableland toward the mass 5,000 feet up which contains the headwaters of the Euphrates. Here the rivers flow in deep canyons eroded in the volcanic soil where the grain river, Arpa Chai, flows on to join the Araxes which is Gihon, one of the four rivers of Eden. We press eastwards towards the sources of the other rivers once fed by a vast lake which has since shrunk into Lake Van of pale ice-blue which is dwarfed by the snow-capped Ararat towering up behind it to 17,000 feet. This high altitude is the roof of the world to West Asia.

Lord Kinross describes the common source of Eden's rivers Tigris and Euphrates whose waters mingle in marshland when in flood (*Within the Taurus*, Murray, London, 1970, p 136):

> As we would expect from the description in Genesis, the waters seep through porous rock to be precipitated north, east and south through headwaters of the Halys to the Black Sea, the Araxes to the Caspian and the Euphrates and Tigris by endless stages to the Persian Gulf. According to Genesis 2:10 and following, these waters 'flowed out of Eden to water the garden and there it divided and became four rivers. The name of the first is Pison (the Halys) . . . the name of the second is Gihon (The Araxes) . . . and the name of the third is Tigris, which flows east of Assyria and the fourth river is the Euphrates.

Verse 6 of Genesis chapter 2 tells us water, or floods, rose from the face of the earth. Water seeped through the rock layers and came from miles away. Professor Daryll Ford describes the remarkable sight of similar farming in Arizona, practised by the Pueblo Indians. Amidst the dry and desert, you see Pueblo gardens, lush green, bright with colour and flourishing corn. The water flows through porous rocks and mud walls have been built around the gardens to hold the water so that the crops are irrigated. In the Garden of Eden, this is the kind of fossil palaeo-cultivation which excavation has revealed, not made possible by rain but by flood water from distant mountains seeping through porous rock, making the desert 'blossom as a rose'.

One could see the cirques and cols on the skyline where erosion had eaten back into the mountains, leaving evidence of the piedmont glacial streams which had united to feed from one source (according to Genesis) the four rivers with ice-blue meltwaters. Pliny claims that even as late as his time in the first century, Lake Van was vast enough to connect the River Gihon with the Tigris. Raised beaches indicate that a higher level of water for a long period has eaten away and made a beach platform. At Lake Van, they can be seen today at 1,600 feet and 320 feet above the present level of the lake.

Charlesworth, whose massive work every geologist knows, describes the effects of glaciation throughout Armenia and Persia. He says that pluvial lakes occupied the inland basins and included the salt lakes of Urmar, Tuz, Golu and Van. Burney more recently said, 'Some evidence exists to support the theory that large lakes, since either drastically shrunk or completely vanished, existed in early farming times over much of these areas, with tell-tale deposition of alluvium.'

Eden's Granaries

This Garden of Eden constituted one of the granaries of Armenia long after the opening saga of our present race. Lynch describes how the extraordinary fertility is induced by the intermixture of the lavas with alluvial or lake deposits. The black earth of the plains about Akhalkalaki is famous and the soil in the neighbourhood of Alexandropol derives its richness from a peculiar kind of lava side by side with the sediment of a former lake. The southerly extension of these vanished waters is marked by the belt of high ground extending from Alagos across the plains to the Arpa Chai.

Concerning the actual location of Eden, R. C. Kuttnerin, in *Race and Modern Science*, says that 'the single district of origin of farming was on the northern side of the Near East in Anatolia, Turkey and to have arrived much later on the southern side in [what is now] Palestine.'

The following analysis of the Hebrew text was made by G. T. Manley before the discoveries concerning the Turkish steppe plateau and so its harmony with the above is all the more impressive. He said (*The New Bible Handbook*, IVF, 1947):

> The Eden of Genesis 2 is probably the same word as the Babylonian 'Edinnu', which denotes a plateau or steppe. The land which lies east of the upper reaches of the Tigris was known by the Kassites as Cush (verse 13), which implies that the ancient name of the Gihon was the modern river Araxes and that Eden was the region assigned to it by Sumerian tradition, at the headwaters of the great rivers of Mesopotamia. 'The cool evenings' mentioned in Genesis 3:8 would be typical of the high plateau.

How Did Farming Begin?

Adam, as the first farmer, was a very clever man. We have discovered the actual tools which the first farmers invented. They very cleverly took wild grasses and, by cross fertilisation, developed two rows of seeds into six rows of hexaploid ears of wheat. Anthropologists have been puzzled about what started the first farmers doing all this. (See Figure 9.4.)

The first farmers also skilfully controlled the breeding of sheep and other farm animals. The whole thing was so revolutionary that anthropologists have called it the New Stone Age Revolution. That is a similar term used for the Industrial Revolution in recent history. The Bible solves that problem. The second chapter of Genesis says that it was God who showed Adam how to farm. Verse 8 says that he 'placed the man in the garden to cultivate it and maintain it'.

We have seen also how God brought the animals to Adam. Some of them he must have domesticated. Archaeology also shows that the

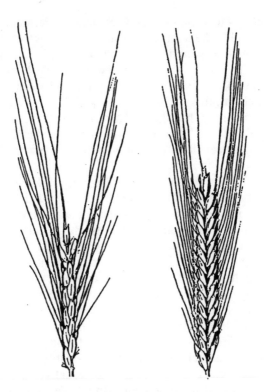

Figure 9.4. Wild grasses of the Middle East developed by man into cultivated wheats and barleys
(*left*) The diploid wheat *Titicum boeoticum*, wild ancestor of Einkorn, the remains of which have been found in the Garden of Eden area; (*right*) *T. Monococcum*, cultivated Einkorn. Approx. nat. size. *After E. Schiemann.*

Courtesy Sonia Cole, The Neolithic Revolution, British Museum, 1959

selection and breeding of farm animals started while the first farmers lived in caves. That is where we have found some of the first evidence. When you go to Palestine, your guide will show you that, even in the time of Jesus Christ, many lived in caves or partly in caves. In fact, the carpenter's shop is represented as partly a cave. Those chalk caves could be made very comfortable.

But, before wheat could be sown and reaped and milled into flour, Adam and his descendants had to invent tools to do all this. Remember that the use of metal was not yet invented. The first farmers had to do it all with stone tools, which took great skill to make. They were made mostly out of flintstone and volcanic glass. We can get an idea of their great skill by comparing it to flint knapping two centuries ago. The flints were chipped to the right size and shape by people called flint knappers. The skill of these flint knappers was simple compared to the complex patterns to which the New Stone Age farmers chipped their tools. They would take a large flint and know exactly where and how to strike it. Then they would take the blade and chip it into a knife. This they would do by a method called pressure flaking. With a bone point, they would press off tiny flakes until they had made very beautiful shapes for their farming tools.

How did they reap the wheat? They used flint sickles. These were flints they had cut small and sharp and then placed and glued in a row in a grooved reindeer rib or curved wooden tree branch. Some typical tools are shown in Figure 9.5.

How did they remove the husks off the grain? The early grains had very tough husks, so first they scorched them in their ovens. Some of the grains left in the ovens were found by archaeologists and that is how we were able to map out the progress that Adam's farmers made. Later, they developed wheat and barley which did not have such tough husks. Husking trays made in clay were then invented. But it was some time before pottery itself was invented. Pottery was made by the women. You can see their fingerprints inside the pots. Probably the invention was accidental. They started as woven wickerwork baskets, which were then lined with clay to make them hold water. When they put them over a fire to boil the water, they found the clay baked into a pot. For a long time afterwards, it was fashionable to make pots basket shaped and to decorate them to look like basketwork.

How did they mill the grains into flour? We have discovered their simple milling stoves. They were trough shaped. The grains were put in this and then a flattish shaped stone was rubbed over them. This pushed out the milled grains as flour into a stone dish.

But before all this, they had to dig up the ground to sow the seed. How did they loosen the soil before sowing? They used what is called a digging stick. This can loosen only light soils. Consequently, the first farmers to migrate from the Garden of Eden could follow only the light soils into Europe.

In order to push the digging stick into the soil, they threaded a stone weight on to the stick, then pushed with the foot on the stone. To do this, they bored a hole in the stone through which the stick was jammed. This was called the digging stick weight. We have found these all over the world brought by those migrating first farmers – the descendants of Adam.

Figure 9.5 shows you a picture of the flint tools which must have been similar to those Adam used. Stone Age farmers were still using similar tools until recently in remote parts of the world. In New Guinea, some were using them as recently as the 1950s. These, too, had migrated all the way from the Garden of Eden.

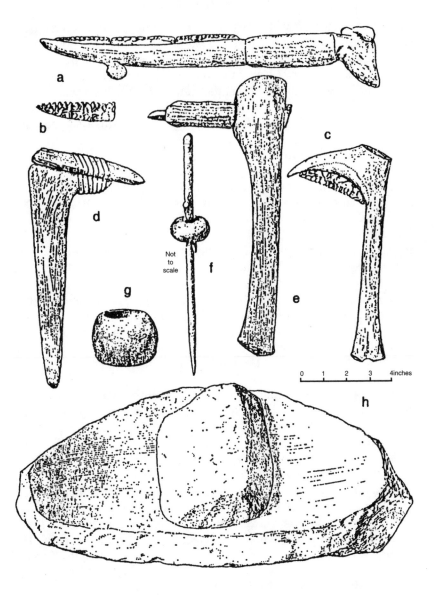

Figure 9.5. The tools Adam used may have been like these (one-fifth size)
(a) Goat-headed antler sickle with flint teeth restored; Natufian. *After Curwen*; (b) Flint saw-blade; (c) Crescentic flint sickle-blade in an antler halt; (d) 'Neolithic' hoe (or adze) with polished stone head; (e) Pick; (f) Digging stick with stone weight; (g) Stone weight enlarged; (h) Quern and rubbing-stone for grinding wheat.

Courtesy: K. P. Oakley, British Museum

Surprise in Denmark

People were amazed when they saw a man chopping down birch trees in Denmark. What was it that was so unusual? He was not using a chain-saw driven by a motor. Surely he could saw through trees in seconds with a chain-saw? It wasn't even a steel axe which he was using as he laid blow upon blow upon the trunk. The axe-head was a peculiar colour. It looked as if it were made with stone and it was ground and polished too. It was toffee coloured. The axe-man stopped and lowered his axe.

'What is the axe made of?'

'Flintstone!'

'What, no chain-saw, not even a steel axe! What's the idea?'

The man raised the axe and looked at it. 'This axe-head is 4,000 years old. It was chipped into shape and then ground into shape. It is like the stone axes which the first Stone Age farmers used as they migrated through Europe. This one had never been used. I'm an anthropologist seeing how many trees I can shop down with it. I've now chopped down 100 trees!'

The anthropologist then started to chop another tree, but the stone axe split into pieces. Yes, he wanted to see how many trees a stone axe would chop down. It felled 100. (See Figure 9.6.) The ground and polished stone axe was another tool which was typical of the first farmers. How did they get to Denmark? The farmers migrated from the Garden of Eden in Turkey.

It must have been after Adam and Eve sinned and were expelled from the Garden of Eden that their descendants moved to thicker wooded areas in Turkey and then through the forests of Europe. Even before they used their digging sticks, they had to clear an area first into which they would sow their crops. It was hard work as Genesis 3:19 says and there were weeds too.

When they reached the British Isles, they established four axe factories, in England, Ireland, Scotland and Wales. We can tell which factory any axe came from because of the type of stone it was made from.

I was speaking to a native Christian of New Guinea recently. His culture was still using the polished stone axe until after the Second World War. His face was aglow with the joy of the Lord since he had received the Lord Jesus Christ as his personal Saviour. He had rediscovered the secret of paradise of Eden. You can discover that secret too!

Man's First Friend

Recently, the media showed the most amazing dog I have ever seen. He was of the collie type of good average size. The owner was a

Figure 9.6. Photographs of tree-felling with Stone Age axe
Tree-felling in Denmark using a Neolithic polished stone axe-head. Three men cleared 600 square yards of birch forest in 4 hours and more than 100 trees were felled with the same axe-head, which had not been sharpened for about 4,000 years. *After Jorgensen.*

C ourtesy: Sonia Cole, The Neolithic Revolution, British Museum, 1959 bricklayer. He was up on scaffolding of iron tubes and planks when to his astonishment, his dog, only a year old, climbed the builder's ladder, walked along the planks and brought the bricklayer his trowel which he had dropped to the ground. The man was astonished because he had never trained the dog to do this! The dog wagged his tail and began to carry a brick to the man. Then, most astonishing of all, the dog balanced himself along the scaffolding tube where there were no planks, better than a cat could and made his way down to the ground. The dog continued to give this help and is now a regular bricklayer's mate!

Did you know that we anthropologists have found that the dog is man's oldest friend and the dog and the cat are man's oldest pets? Did you know that science has found that it all started in the Garden of Eden?

Yes, and this has helped us to pinpoint where the Garden of Eden was. The dog skeletons show they were among the first animals to be domesticated. In fact, when you watch sheepdog trials, remember that the dog probably helped man's first domestication of sheep. Yes, we have found their bones as well, in the Garden of Eden – the first dog skeletons and then the sheep bones.

It must have been when God brought the animals to Adam that started what scientists call 'the domestication of animals'.

Q Has science been used to discover how farming started?

Yes, it has. We have discovered it recorded in the animal bones associated with the first farmers, who, the Bible tells us, were Adam and his descendants.

The bones of dogs and sheep which have been discovered reveal that they were the earliest farm animals. Remember this when you see those fascinating sheepdog trials. It is quite remarkable how the dogs answer the instructions of the shepherd by whistles and codes, to take the sheep around bends, back over hills, separate them into groups and guide them into the folds. The dog is man's oldest friend (Fig 9.7). Evidence from the caves and open sites of the Garden of Eden show us how it all started.

They Came From Eden

But what of the farm animals? Science has found, just as Genesis says, that sheep and goats and cattle all started in the Garden of Eden at that time. But they don't call it the Garden of Eden.

Q Why do you call it the Garden of Eden?

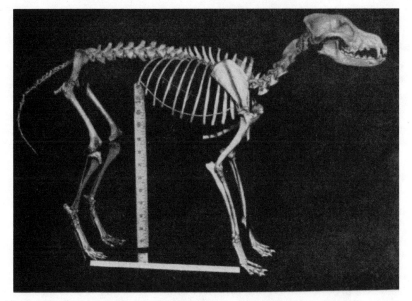

Figure 9.7. Skeleton of Dog – Neolithic Man's oldest domesticated friend.

Courtesy: Sonia Cole, The Neolithic Revolution, British Museum, 1959

Because the area where scientists say that animals were domesticated is the same place where the Bible says animals were domesticated. And the Bible calls it the Garden of Eden.

Professor Flannery reported to a big meeting of anthropologists that as many as 10,000 bones of domesticated animals had been found in that region at Ali-Kosh. Among them, the number of species identified was 35, yes, 35 species!

Dr Helbaek, the archaeologist, says that some hunting still went on. The first chapter of Genesis indicates that as well. He says that they hunted red deer, wild asses, cattle, boars and leopards. The cave drawings also bear this out. But when Adam's descendants bred sheep and cattle for food, they became independent of game hunting. That was now more of a sport. By breeding these animals, their food supply was more constant. This meant they could settle down in houses, villages and even towns. And this is just what the Bible says and what science has found.

If you are a farmer, remember that God has placed the welfare of animals in your hands. He requires you to be kind to all animals. You may not be a farmer but you can still be kind to your pets. Do that and you show God's love. God brought the animals and birds to Adam to see what he would call them.

Q Have we got any evidence of the domestication of animals by Adam?

Yes. When I was qualifying as an anthropologist, I was fortunate enough to attend lectures by the world's leading authority on the origin of pets, Professor Zeuner.

It is ironical that, although he was an atheist, he confirmed the truth of what Genesis says about pets. Equally ironically, in the same university, the theologians were teaching that it was all a myth!

Zeuner tells us that the domestication of both the dog and the cat started in the Near East. Skeletons of dogs have been found in the caves where domestication began – the caves in Eastern Turkey and Iran where the Garden of Eden was situated.

Q Were these the only animals Adam tamed?

Oh no! We know what other animals Adam tamed because we have found their bones in the sites where farming first began and spread to the rest of the world. These were sheep, goats and cattle. These, along with the dog and cat were all domesticated in the Garden of Eden. People are surprised when I tell them that their sheep came from the Garden of Eden. This is what scientists have discovered. If you buy the book on the New Stone Age revolution from the British Natural History Museum, you will see the drawings of sheep and other animals with maps showing the dates of the migrations of farmers. According to anthropology, even the sheep in New Zealand or South Africa or America all came from the Garden of Eden, because originally sheep were native only to Turkey and Northern Iran. We can even trace how the descendants of Adam bred their sheep to produce softer wool and better meat.

Genesis chapter 2:19 reads, 'The Lord God formed every beast of the field and every bird of the air and brought them to the man to see what he would call them and, whatever the man called them, that was their name.'

The Uniqueness of Human Speech

Note here that Adam was able to talk to God. Experiments show that the speech areas of the brain are a built-in package and did not evolve from grunts and growls. Notice, too, that the older a language is, the more structured and complicated are its grammar and parts of speech.

The implication here is that human speech was in existence from the beginning of time and at an advanced level of communication.

Roger Lewin and Sue Savage-Smith experimented to make an ape speak, but they found that the ape does not possess the articulatory organs required to make words. (Reported in *Kanzi – The Ape at the Brink of the Human Mind*, Doubleday, 1994.) They explained that the ape does not possess the human larynx. To make words, an ape needs to be able to voice consonants in order to break up the vowel sounds into words. Lewin and Smith contrast this lack of facility with homo sapiens. It is significant that even the human baby does not have the larynx in position for speech at first. This development comes only when the baby is weaned, the reason being that, when the baby is feeding at the breast, it needs to breath and suck at the same time without choking. When weaned, the larynx descends to the same level as the throat so that the breath can also be used for speech.

The tube for transporting air is the windpipe or trachea and the tube for transporting food and drink is the oesophagus. Most animals are safeguarded from choking because these channels are separate throughout life, so they cannot redirect breath through the larynx for speech. This means that any animal may have more understanding of human words than it is able to articulate itself. Darwin referred to the dog as an example of this, which understands the words and whistle signs as illustrated in sheep-dog trials, but can only bark or whine.

The Ecology of Eden

The description of the ecology of the Garden of Eden in the Near East matches that of primitive dry-farming communities known to anthropologists such as that of the Hopi Indians of Arizona. The Adamic type of horticulture relied on irrigation: 'Streams came up and watered the earth' (NIV, RSV, NEB). The word *ed* (Hebrew) corresponds to the Sumerian *id*, 'river' (or 'flood' as in RSV margin). The statement in 2:5 that 'No *siah*' and 'No *eseb*' of the field were yet in existence was intended to imply that these were part of the garden when it was ready. The word for field '*sadeh*' refers to arable land and indicates that '*siah*' and '*eseb*' were particular types of plant suitable for human use. They may be understood as indicating low bushes bearing berries and the natural grasses from which cereals might be obtained.

EVIDENCE FOR THE DISPERSAL OF FARMING FROM EDEN

C. D. Darlington, writing in *Patterns of Exploitation* says:

> The view that agriculture arose in several places independently must be revised. Prehistorians were misled by Vavilov's theory of crop origins in 1926 set out in his book, *Agricultural Origins and Dispersals,* and followed up by Saur, Coon and Wissman, who expounded them fully. But the study of the last forty years historically and geographically has led us

to believe that Vavilov's centres of diversity were not so much primary as secondary – not so much the sites of origin as places of development.'

More than a hundred scientists of related disciplines came to a conference from all over the world to discuss the subject of farming origins. Their papers considered all angles – botanical, zoological, anthropological and archaeological. The symposium 'The Exploitation of Domestication of Plants and Animals' is a record of their findings. C. D. Darlington, a contributor, writes:

> What we see today is the decisive evidence that agriculture in the Old World arose in a single connected region, a nuclear zone of Anatolia (Turkey), Iran and Syria before 7000 BC or 9,000 years ago, and that it arose here at a time when no other region of the Old World shows evidence of any similar settled life.

Gradually in India, the division into three regions depending on wheat, rice and sorghum had been stabilised. In East Asia, pottery associated with the third Neolithic stage had reached Japan six millennia BC.

In China, reaping knives showed that wheat had preceded rice seven millennia BC according to W. Watson of the symposium. The knives occurred in a full Neolithic context or on sites where grain had been recovered. These knives were distributed mainly along the middle course of the Yellow River, to the north-east as far as Liaotung. Here, then, the wheat of the Near East was the primary crop, but rice took over as a secondary development, being more suitable and acceptable to East Asian economy.

Agriculture reached Japan by the sixth millennia BC. Pottery is associated with it. As pottery was invented in the Near East three stages after the origin of farming, the fact that in Japan the first farming is 'Pottery Neolithic', shows that it is later and fits in with the time lag of diffusion from the Near East.

The long journeys by caravan through the Gobi Desert were an ancient means of rapid transference of culture between Western Asia and East Asia from whence the New World early Mongoloids came.

However, the South East Pacific was still of New Stone Age culture until recently. It reached Melanesia 6000 BC but the Maoris occupied New Zealand only 1,000 years ago.

What About the Americas?

In contrast, the old land bridge at the Bering Straits brought farming early to North America. The earliest maize growing in America is dated by radio-carbon as 3650 BC from Bat Cave, New Mexico, comparatively near the Pueblo maize growers. In South America, dates around 2500 BC have been obtained.

Maize was not the earliest plant to be cultivated in the New World however. Gourds, lima beans and squashes came before it. The symposium of world specialists *The Domestication and Exploitation of Plants and Animals* published proceedings in 1969 which said that the first plants to be cultivated in the New World are dated by radio-carbon at 6500 BC. This was the American bean, *phaseolus*, in Mexico.

The great question is – how did cultivation arise in America? Did it commence as an independent revolution or did it come via Asia from the Middle East? If the latter, then why was not the staple crop originally wheat instead of maize? C. D. Darlington of the Botany School, Oxford and contributor to the above symposium, considers that cultivators moving from old areas to new ones adopted new crops as they went. Wheat was replaced by its own weeds, rye, oats and buckwheat in the northern regions, and in the southern regions by its own millet.

There are some who prefer to think that an independent Neolithic revolution started in the New World. They have failed to revise Vavilov's theory of crop origins made in 1926. Subsequent investigation has supported the evidence that Vavilov's centres of diversity were not so much primary as secondary – not so much the sites of origin as places of development. Indeed, Graham Clark of Cambridge points out that the North American bone handles, slotted to receive flint flakes, have their origin in northern Eurasia.

Perhaps the similarities between the American Pueblo culture and Çatal Hüyük indicate an ancestry in Turkey which reached America via the Bering Straits from East Asia. The American Indians, who were the original inhabitants, have grown maize as their subsistence crop for a very long time.

Leguminous Plants

We must not forget that the early farmers of the Near East not only grew cereals but also cultivated leguminous plants such as beans, peas and lentils. Recently, lima beans, gourds and squashes have been found in a cave near Ocampo, Mexico and tentatively dated at about 6500 BC.

Henry T. Lewis of Albert University draws our attention (*Man*, June 1972, p 206) to legumes being the earliest vegetation cultivated by man before wheat, barley and oats. He quotes Helbaek, the widely-accepted authority on ancient horticulture. 'The large seeded annual legumes – for instance, the horse bean, pea, vetch, vetchling, chickpea and lentil – appear in early horizons in the Near East. They seem at times to have attained an economic value almost as great as that of the cereals.'

Lewis adds, 'They were not simply displaced, however, rather they played an important complement to hunting and gathering until the raising of cereals and the herding of sheep and goats became the primary strategy.' It is this form of hunter horticulture – the earliest stage – which seems characteristic of that which reached America first. This was to be expected as the Bering Straight land bridge would filter out other elements of photo-neolithic farming.

Although the legumes may have been part of the economy of the early farmers in America, the local wild maize would be a further secondary crop. Thus a pattern similar to that in China, of a secondary native plant replacing the primary species by which farming was introduced, would be repeated in America. Its areas of development could have been in a number of centres of the New World long after the art of farming had first reached America. It had probably come with the early Mongoloids, whom we now know as the American Indians.

These early Mongoloids or American Indians migrated into America from Mongolia, Manchuria and Siberia. They are the originals or the aborigines of America because they are the oldest surviving peoples, whose ancestors set out from the Garden of Eden.

GOD'S STORY UNFOLDS

You may sometimes have heard people suggest that the second chapter of Genesis is a separate creation account. Some higher critics sitting in their studies, without archaeological knowledge, try to make Genesis 1 and 2 contradict each other. They say there is a different order of creation in chapter 2; the second chapter says the Lord God created the vegetation and trees first, then man, then the animals.

Apparent textural variations between Genesis 1 and 2 can be accounted for to some extent by the method used for identifying clay tablet records (see Fig 14.1) before scrolls were in general use and by the arbitrary provision of our present-day chapter numbers.

Anthropologists find that there is no contradiction. Professor D. Wiseman, former head of Assyriology, University of London and Dr Millard, formerly of the British Museum Archaeological Department, have shown that Genesis 2:4 is the summary of what has gone before. It was the label, so to speak, which identified the first tablet which gave the creative account:

> This is the summary of the events in the creation of the heavens and earth which the Lord God had made.

Genesis 2:5 could then be the start of the second tablet which contained the next instalment telling of the domestication of animals and of the first farming horticulture.

The domestication of animals and plants was a very important step.

It enabled man to control his food supply and therefore be able to settle down in houses and villages in the way we have described.

SUMMARY

GARDEN OF EDEN

1. Where?
Source of four rivers, therefore highlands of Eastern Turkey, not Mesopotamian valley. 'Eden' means high plateau.
Lake Van: former source of rivers Pison into Black Sea, Gihon into Caspian, Tigris and Euphrates into Persian Gulf.
Evidence: Pollen core samples. Archaeological succession (pottery, etc.) World Conference of Archaeologists.

2. Origin of farming
Where Bible says Adam started. Gen 2:8,15
Dry farming techniques – no rain. Gen 2:6. *'ed'* = water not mist.
cf Pueblo-style dry farming or 'flood water farming'.
Flint tools before metals of Gen 4:22. Adam's tool kit.
First domestication. God brought animals to Adam. 35 species found at Ali-Kosh.
Cereals native to that area. Wheat, barley, legumes.

3. Migration to World (Evidence: stone axes, digging sticks)
Europe: along Danube and Mediterranean shores.
East: India, China Yellow River (reaping knives) to America across the Bering Strait.
South: Sahara 'desert' lush vegetation (before Flood) to Africa.

4. Tablets of Gen 2:4 onwards are *not* a second creation account.
Toledoth tablet method v. 4 sums up before sequel is added (Fig 14.1). Higher critics did not know this and still ignore archaeological evidence.
Two names for God on one tablet source was common usage 2500 BC (Ebla tablets use Lord and God together, i.e. Yah and El).

10 EVIDENCE FOR 'THE FALL'

THE PURPOSE OF ANIMAL SACRIFICE

The biblical 'Fall of Mankind' records how the ancestors of mankind fell from God-fearing innocence into a sinfully biased nature with all its consequences. The Fall is basically man's inclination to disobey God.

To Adam, God said, 'Because you listened to your wife and ate from the tree about which I commanded you, saying you must not eat of it: cursed is the ground because of you; through painful toil you will eat of it all the days of your life' (Genesis 3:17).

An Age of Innocence and Belief in One God

What evidence has science for the Fall? This is a question which was asked recently. Surely we should expect an absence of weapons and scenes of destruction in the age of innocence which must have preceded it! It is possible that there may be a brief age of purity indicated archaeologically although little material evidence should be expected.

There appeared to be no need for weapons of war or fortification in the earliest New Stone Age or in the first wave of farmers migrating from the initial centre. Mellaart remarks about the absence of war in early Çatal Hüyük (more about this New Stone Age city in Chapter 12). This was so with the first Danubians who moved through Central Europe, also with Mediterranean coastland migrants who brought their cattle by boat and with the first pre-pottery Neolithic migrants of the Balkans. These are the three main Western streams of migrating farmers.

Likewise, concerning morals, the commonplace sexy fertility figurines were absent in those three streams. As for Çatal Hüyük, even though the Fall would have already taken place, Mellaart remarks, 'It significantly lacks the element of sexual vulgarity and eroticism that is almost automatically associated with fertility' ('A Neolithic City in Turkey', in *Scientific America*, 1964). He suggests the reason might be that the religion of Çatal Hüyük was created by women!

Socially too, there were no class distinctions among these Western migrants. All were equals. In other words, it was not a stratified society.

The Consequences of the Fall Become Evident

There was a marked difference from the Danubian pioneers when the second Danubian Neolithic peoples traversed Europe over a thousand years later. They built strong stockades around their settlements and provided themselves with effective weapons. Sexy figurines were part of their household goods. The figurines, no doubt, also indicated a less pure religion of superstitious placating of earth gods instead of the Creator and Giver of fruits of the earth.

There is another source which has been drawn upon as evidence for the Fall. This is the myths of primitive peoples handed down orally from generation to generation, long before contact with Western civilisation. Many social anthropologists think this evidence is significant.

The World Views of Primitive People

Dr Zwemer in *Origin of Religions* (MMS, 1935) says:

> The evidence of anthropology therefore seems to be that of an almost universal tradition of a creation of the world by a High-God in which man occupies a special place as its culmination. Moreover, we find, together with this account of man's place in the universe and parallel to it, a widely-spread tradition of man's displacement, of a tragedy of disobedience and the loss of his former state of happiness. Who can resist the conclusion that these many and multiform creation myths, these constant memories of a lost 'age of innocence', point to a common human tradition and corroborate the scriptural data?

These myths are called the 'World Views' of primitive peoples. F. M. Savina reports in *Histoire des Miao*, published in Hong Kong in 1930, concerning the World View of original inhabitants of China called the Miao:

> The Miao hold an essentially monotheistic faith; they have never had a written language; they live in tribes and are an ancient people having inhabited China before the present Chinese and been pushed by them towards the mountains in the south. They believe in a Supreme Being, Creator of the world and of men. Death came as a consequence of man's sin. The woman had eaten white strawberries forbidden by the Lord of Heaven. They know of a deluge, followed by a dispersal of peoples.

J. A. MacCulloch reports on the Andamanese who are a preliterate and technologically simple people. Under 'The Fall', in *Encyclopaedia of Religion and Ethics*, Vol. 5, he says:

> The Andamanese, whose remarkable theology, according to the best authorities, is independent of Christian influence, believe that Puluga, the

creator, gave the first man, Tomo, various injunctions, especially concerning certain trees which grew only at one place (Paradise) in the jungle, and which he was not to touch at certain seasons during the rains, when Puluga himself visits them and partakes. Later, some of Tomo's descendants disobeyed and were severely punished. Others, disregarding Puluga's commands about murder, adultery, theft, etc. and becoming more and more wicked, were drowned in a deluge. Two men and two women survived and in revenge wished to kill Puluga, who, telling them their friends had been justly punished, disappeared from the earth.

Koestler in his symposium *Beyond Reductionism* (September 1969), says 'Man is an aberrant species, suffering from a biological malfunction, a specific disorder of behaviour which sets him apart from all other species, just as a language, science and art set him apart.'

Mistaken Scientists with no Experience of Fieldwork

In anthropology, the subject of religion is usually considered under the general heading of 'Religion, Magic, Ritual, Taboos and Witchcraft'. Until the 1930s, various attempts had been made to account for religion but most of them were subjective. Professor Evans-Pritchard, the renowned Oxford anthropologist, said that many such definitions were made by those least qualified to do so, as they lacked sympathy for and experience of religion themselves. Furthermore, their theories were not related to any fieldwork among primitive tribes. 'Many anthropologists had never been near a primitive people and so relied upon travellers' reports.' Among such was Sir J. Frazer, whose many volumes of *The Golden Bough* are still devoured eagerly. When asked if he had ever seen one of the primitive people about whose customs he had written, he replied, 'God forbid!'

L. H. Marett said that such empirical investigation was unnecessary. 'One need not live among these savages, as it was sufficient to experience the progression of thought in a university common room!'

Atheists Feel Need of Religion

Yet we have an insight into the innate instinct of religion from the number of atheists who eventually admit their need for it. Dr Mary Douglas of London University College Anthropological Department quotes Julian Huxley's *Religion without Revelation*. He admits that his growing need of religion caused him consternation, but describes his happiness and relief on realising that he did not need to believe in God in order to have religious comfort. Professor Haldane, the atheist, confessed in some of his last lectures that in response to an inner need, he was embracing religion. Professor Joad, Malcolm Muggeridge and others, who were aggressive atheists, have converted to a personal faith in God and, more recently, Dr Fred Hoyle, the Cambridge physicist. To what conclusion does this lead? It would seem that God has implanted within man the need to communicate with his Creator and personal presuppositions then became reversed.

Anthropology Supports the Bible

The theories of anthropology have also been reversed, largely through Professor Evans-Pritchard's insistence on fieldwork:

> Whereas before the 1930s, an evolutionary concept of religion was that it developed from animism and magic to polytheism and then finally to monotheism, fieldwork reversed this and anthropologists now realise that belief in one Creator God preceded all other religious concepts. This gradually corrupted to polytheism, and finally to the placating of an extensive array of nature spirits. Some popular lecturers in theology seem unaware of this change and continue to reshuffle the Old Testament documentary-wise, changing its story of one God revealing himself into an evolutionary process of man's groping from animism to monotheism. In this way many ordinands and clergy are being persuaded to forsake the claims of scripture that God has uniquely revealed himself through the Torah and the prophets and finally through the Christ.

The claims of fellowship between God and the patriarchs are often represented as folklore gathering colour by oral transmission and the statements that 'Yahweh used to speak to Moses face to face, as a man speaks to his friend' as a later development.

Fieldwork Evidence for Primitive Belief in One God

An example of fieldwork comes from New Guinea. As recently as 1956, in the mountain vastnesses of that largest of Melanesian islands, New Stone Age farmers were discovered whose techniques had changed little since the migration from the Garden of Eden. These and other tribes had been isolated from the rest of New Guinea and the world by a high rim of mountains rising 4,000 metres. They were not aware that there were any other people living in the outside world.

These people believed in a High God Creator. These 'World Views', as anthropologists call them, are quite abstract in their concepts. Dr Pospisil, living among the Kapauki in 1954 reported, 'This Stone Age tribe was not without its abstract philosophy. God is omniscient, omnipotent, and omnipresent, credited with the creation of all things and with having determined all events' (*The Kapauki of New Guinea*, Holt, 1963).

The Kapauki cosmogony consisted of a world which was a flat

block of stone and soil surrounded by water of unfathomable depth. The blue sky was a solid bowl in which the sun travelled from east to west on the inside and then slipped under the rim and travelled back above the bowl from west to east unseen. The stars were holes in the inverted bowl through which the returning sun gave pinpoints of light. Above the solid bowl existed another world which was the abode of the Creator.

When the first missionaries had committed the language of tribes near the Kapauki to writing, they were able to piece together the Dani story of creation. 'A long time ago, the very first people came out of the water that splashed down the mountain on the other side. It was quite natural that they appeared here, for one can easily see that this is very near the centre of the earth. Here the sky is high and the pillars that hold it up are nowhere visible. The people spread, clan paired with clan. Only later did attacks prompt war that separated the people into enemy groups.' Here perhaps was a hint at the Fall, a feature which appears more precisely in other primitive cosmogonies.

In another valley, the Uhundunis tribe sing traditional chants handed down from their forefathers. 'O Friend up in the sky in a large boat on a great lake, A-wai-wae. And to this wonderful place we want to go, A-wai-wae, A-wai-wae.'

Returning to God

In spite of such expressions, the effects of the Fall were evident. A youth named Hilittu was the first to realise the evil ways he and his tribe had followed. He prayed, 'O Jesus, I want you to treat my heart. I want you to take away all the bad things I have done. I have eaten people. I have stolen things. I have lied.' From then onwards, he began to pray for his enemies, even those who had killed his father. He said, 'I am not going to fight any more, and I am through with my fetishes.'

The hymnody of the Uhundanis developed along indigenous lines rather similar to the style of 'Old MacDonald had a Farm' and were composed around the camp fire. One man sings the developing story, a second man harmonises with a note, a fifth above, all others join in the chorus. A communion song is as follows:

Jesus took the sweet potatoes and returned thanks;
Jesus took the sweet potatoes and broke them;
Jesus' body was broken for us, like the sweet potatoes are broken;
His body was broken for you, His body was broken for me;
We love Jesus very much.

Jesus took the drinking gourd and then he returned thanks;
The contents of the drinking gourd are like Jesus' blood;

His blood was shed for me, His blood placed in payment for you;
His blood washed my sins, His blood took all your sins away;
Jesus died for us.

We are gathered together here;
We are thinking about the death of Christ;
We are thinking that Christ will come in the future;
We, who are Christians, will be taken to heaven by Christ;
We love Jesus very much;
He died for us.

The development of acculturation, of which the above is an example, is of interest to anthropologists who record aboriginal music.

Examples of an original and primitive belief in the High God or Great Spirit or Creator can be quoted from all over the world.

Professor Daryll Forde, Head of the Department of Anthropology in London University, speaks of the conception of Supreme God or High God, as being in a different category from earth gods. 'The Creator God concept is widespread, though attributes and doctrine vary from people to people. There is a strong identification with the sky and sun. There is a definite conception of God Creator who is the source of life of all living things.' (*Habitat, Economy and Society*, Methuan.)

To the findings of social anthropologists can be added those of prehistoric archaeologists. They are impressed by the fact that as soon as man is able to show some tangible record, he is seen at the outset to be thoroughly religious. At Çatal Hüyük, shrines worshipping the mystery of life abound. At Jericho before the first Neolithic city was built about 7400 BC, the Natufians were using the site as a shrine. The first city-states of Mesopotamia were centred around the temples. The first writing, invented 3400 BC, was for the purpose of recording the people's gifts and tenths to God or gods.

EXPULSION FROM EDEN

'To Adam he said, "Because you listened to your wife and ate from the tree . . . cursed is the ground because of you; through painful toil you will eat of it all the days of your life. It will produce thorns and thistles.' Adam named his wife Eve, because she would become the mother of all the living . . . So Yahweh Elohim banished him from the Garden of Eden to work the ground from which he had been taken' (Genesis 3:17).

It is perhaps significant that it was when Adam was expelled from these weed-free areas of the high plateau that he found he had to compete with voracious weed growth. Gone was the ease with which

Adam reaped and gathered the willing corn and crops. 'By the sweat of your brow shall you eat bread.' The ease experienced by Harland, the pre-historian, who reaped wild standing wheat on the plateau heights, was contrasted by the toil experienced by Maitland amidst the Hopi Indians:

It takes 2.5 acres to support one person, 40 to 60 acres to support a typical matrilineage. Transport alone was time consuming. Assuming that a man carries one bushel (56 lbs) of corn on each journey and does two journeys each day (one in the morning and one in the evening, 4 miles from the village) and his wife or son carries half that amount, they will bring in 20 bushels per week. At this rate it will take 6 weeks to bring in 3 tons of corn – an average yield of 10 acres. If the field lies 4 miles from the village, a single journey can hardly take less than four hours (one hour out, 20 minutes to load, one hour back to mesa foot, one hour to climb mesa cliff of 400 feet, 20 minutes to enter village to unload). Then there are other tasks to be done, such as picking the peach crop and weaving wedding garments, etc.

Farmers Migrate from Eden

The migrating farmers made their way through Europe as the centuries and millennia passed so that the cultural sequence of dates became more recent in ever-widening circles through the world, from the focal point of diffusion.

It is fascinating to study the various sites throughout Europe, as well as the sequence in Egypt, India and China.

Fossil pollen analysis also plays its part. It can tell us the actual succession of trees and crops which were grown in the field or clearing. We can trace the sequence of slash-and-burn farming as New Stone Age man made his way through Europe, making clearances in the forest with his sharp-ground stone axes and, when the soil was exhausted, passing on his way westward to make a new clearing.

The First Wave of Peaceful Farmers

By tracing the source of the igneous stone or flint used for such axes, we can trace their manufacture to five main factories which supplied farmers all over Europe, including the British Isles. The first 'wave' of farmers worked the lighter and easier loose soils of the wooded hills of Europe, mainly following the course of the Danube, hence they are called Danubians. The first Danubians reached Central Europe by 5000 BC.

They are noted for their long log houses built of split timbers. Some of these were as long as 120 to 150 feet. They would consist of a series of single rooms with a passage running the whole length of one side, rather like some army huts. Some show evidence of rooms being added as the family grew. The roofs were given an extremely steep pitch to give a quick run-off for the heavy rains of central Europe. This was an interesting adaptation to a cool temperate climate in contrast to the dry heat of the Mediterranean climate from which their forefathers migrated. The origin of their culture, however, was reflected in the shape of their pots. They were of gourd shape, typical of the Near East and incised with shell marks of East Mediterranean origin. This also showed that they were in trade contact with the Mediterranean.

They farmed in peace for a thousand years, on the slash-and-burn system. First they would make a clearing in the dense European forest of that time and plant their crops in the virgin soil, but after ten years the weeds which so cursed the exterior of the Garden of Eden, could be held back no longer and, as the new soil became exhausted, they would move to their new clearing. This would leave the old clearing to secondary growth, the evidence of which archaeologists of our time have been able to detect by pollen analysis.

The life led by the farmers of Borneo may be a good picture of that of the first Danubians. They lived in long rectangular wooden houses built on stilts. Each long house was divided into units for single families who were members of the greater family occupying the whole erection.

Every ten years or so they pulled down the erection and moved on to virgin forest. They cleared the new area by chopping down and burning the trees whose ashes they used to enrich the soil for the crops to follow. This was the typical slash-and-burn farming. The method caused soil erosion eventually and loss of good agricultural land for, once vegetation is removed, torrential rains wash away the soil.

In south-east Europe, the first farmers reached the Balkans over a thousand years before the first Danubians reached the central European loess hills, being nearer to the dispersal area of Turkey and Iran. This was from 7000 to 6000 BC. Their adaptation to the long deep valleys of Greece was to build round wattle huts on a stone base. Later they found that houses of a square shape better suited their needs.

It is astonishing to reflect that in these early times, 5000 BC, New Stone Age farmers sailed the length of the Mediterranean bringing with them their cattle, sheep and pigs. They would land to graze their domesticated animals as they migrated further and further along the northern shores of the Mediterranean. Their assemblage of implements was of the simplest. Indeed, they were noted only for possessing soup ladles and ear plugs. One can only imagine why the ear plugs were necessary. Perhaps their beat groups drummed far into the night!

Archaeologists had already worked out the dates for these peoples, when radio-carbon dating was invented by Libby in 1958, so it provided an independent check. The radio-carbon tests were done on the bones and crofts of migration throughout the world from the focal centre. Renfrew admits that the small later revision of C.14 dating by bristlecone-pine dating does not alter this general picture of diffusion.

Evidence of First Lamb Sacrifices for Fallen People

'Now Abel kept flocks and Cain worked the soil. In the course of time, Cain brought some of the fruits of the soil as an offering to Yahweh. But Abel brought fat portions from some of the firstlings of his flock. Yahweh looked with favour on Abel and his offering, but on Cain and his offering he did not look with favour' (Gen 4:2–5).

Abel kept flocks. The domestication of sheep and goats is traceable in development through the stratigraphical deposits in the Shanidar-Zarzi complex of caves of northern Iraq and Iran and around the area south of the Caspian Sea. Man commenced domestication while still dwelling in caves and open sites. The percentage of firstlings is a record of progress, for the cave-farmers killed an increasing number of lambs for food and sacrifice as they succeeded in controlled breeding. Consequently, the average kill of wild animals which were yearlings was not more than 25% judging by the bones in caves before farming.

By 8900 BC, the percentages of domesticated sheep remains were rising to 60% in the open site at the famous Shanidar cave in northern Iran. This is the earliest farming giving evidence of herding and slaughtering of up to 60% yearlings. In the cave strata itself, there were only 25% yearlings, mostly of sheep, which is the right percentage for a wild stock, so the yield of 60% on the adjoining open site indicated that some of the earliest breeding experiments were being made.

In a more backward area at Karim Shahir 8000 BC, there was a potential domestication of 50% of sheep, goats and pigs and also cattle and even horse remains. At Belt cave, the percentage of domestication of gazelle and sheep was rising steadily from 50% to 60% from the Lower Middle Stone Age to the New Stone Age until, at Jarmo, excavated by R. Braidwood, the percentage of domesticated animals had risen to 95% and included sheep, goats, pigs and oxen. At the pre-Flood sites of Hassuna and Halaf at the copper-stone stage, there was evidence of advanced development of domestication, also for cooking cereal products. There were husking bowls and saddle querns for grinding grain.

The Spread of Domesticated Animals from Eden

One was also able to detect how selective breeding had developed a woolly fleece from the coarse hair of the wild ancestor sheep which lived in the foothills and high plateaux stretching from Turkey through to the South Caspian. Remains of woollen cloth were found in carbonised form at the New Stone Age city of Çatal Hüyük on the Konya plateau of central Turkey. This shows that domesticated sheep were kept there very early, nine millennia ago. Woolly fleece must have replaced the coarse hair of wild ancestors in very early times, for artists in Mesopotamia at Ubaid depict this characteristic.

Early evidence of the spread from the nuclear area of domesticated animals came from the pre-pottery levels of Jericho, Jarimo and Ali Kosh.

Domesticated sheep were derived mainly from the Mouflon breed and goats from the Bezoar, *capra hircus aegagrus*. These species still live wild in the mountains of south-western Asia and are evidence that domestication commenced here in their native habitat before farmers migrated with them to other parts of the world.

A high percentage of young animals at certain times suggests that they were killed at certain seasons in winter and early spring. Later, of course, it was at this time of the year that the Israelites killed their Passover lambs.

One of the ways of tracing the progress of domestication is by the shape of the horn cores. The bony core runs two-thirds of the length of the horn sheath, but the horn sheath perishes in time. In primitive goats, the horns were scimitar-like in shape, but in more domesticated types they rise in a wide open spiral above the head. Those of early New Stone Age domesticated types are flatter in cross-section and sometimes have an incipient twist. Those of sheep differ with the sexes. The rams have horns which nearly always rise in a spiral, but those of the ewes have either short points or may be absent altogether.

European Farmers Follow in the Steps of Abel

We can trace the progress of the diffusion of sheep through Europe from the Near Eastern Garden of Eden. Some domesticated sheep of Western Europe, such as the Soay sheep of the Outer Hebrides, seem to be direct descendants of the true Mouflon and are very similar to the earliest domesticated sheep.

This should be expected, because it was the seafaring farmers who made their way from Turkey along the shores of the Mediterranean to Western Europe. As the centuries passed, they made their way through the Basque area of Spain and others through Gibraltar Straits to settle on either side of the Irish Sea and Scottish coasts, then over to Norway.

In New Stone Age times, a breed derived from the Urals was introduced into Europe from West Asia and is known as the Turbarg sheep. We find its goat-like horns at the Swiss lake-house dwellings of villages about 2500 BC and similar sheep have been identified in Britain at the Windmill Hill archaeological excavation of New Stone Age culture about 4000 BC. In Norfolk the black-faced sheep and Merino sheep probably have Ural ancestry. It should be an intriguing thought for Norfolk sheep farmers that they are following the husbandry of Adam's son Abel.

The Mystery of Cain's Rejection

It seems reasonable to assume that the worldwide primitive custom of propitiation by sacrifice had its origin in Adam's Fall. It would appear that the principle of forgiveness through the sacrifice of a lamb was revealed to Adam and Eve's family, for year by year the sin offering was offered. After many years had passed, however, their son Cain refused to acknowledge his need for atonement, so he offered a blood-less agricultural gift to God (Genesis 4:3–8).

Why did God refuse Cain's offering? This has puzzled many. It seemed unfair – he had done good work in food production. To put the answer simply, **Cain had refused God's atonement method and had offered instead his works as a sin offering**. In contrast, Abel had offered the required sin sacrifice of a lamb. God had shown them that only by a lamb sacrifice could sin be forgiven. This is evident in God's words to Cain: 'If you don't do right, there is a sin-offering close to hand!' Some translators have mistakenly put 'sin lies close at hand' in Genesis 4:7, but the Hebrew word here is *chatant*. This word is trans-lated elsewhere in Moses' work as *sin-offering* as many as 83 times, mostly in connection with the sin-offerings of the Tabernacle.

So what is God showing Cain? It is that the way to get forgiveness is not by one's own works (produce), but by trusting in the sin-offer-ing of the lamb slain for him. So to translate Genesis 4:7 as 'sin crouches at the door' misses the whole point: early in the Bible story, God is pointing to 'the Lamb of God who would come to take away the sin of the world' (John 1:29; see also Revelation 13:8 and Ephesians 2:8,9).

Origins of Primitive Sacrifice

Professor Zwemer says that 'We have in primitive sacrifice the three-fold idea of fellowship, gratitude and propitiation with a sense of sin or unworthiness. All of these are not found among all primitives, yet there are clear examples of each form in many far separate cultures, e.g. the Eskimos, the Pygmies, the Algonquins, the Bushmen and the Veddas.'

Professor Evans-Pritchard describes, from his experience of the primitive Nuer tribe in the Upper Nile, the form of their sacrifice. The supplicant presents the ox to be sacrificed to God, then consecrates it by spreading ashes upon the victim's back. This identifies the man with the ox. The supplicant then states the purpose of the sacrifice in the invocation and pours out in detail his sins and sense of guilt. This can sometimes last an hour. If the sacrifice is to be efficacious, everything he says must be true, because it is placed upon the back of the sacrificial substitute. When the supplicant has finished, he stands with upraised spear and with a tremendous thrust through the heart, slays the ox. In other parts of the world, animals appropriate to the ecology are chosen.

The Eastward Migration

'So Cain went out from Yahweh's presence and lived in the land of Nod, east of Eden' (Genesis 4:16).

When Cain fled from his homeland, he is said to have travelled 'eastward from Eden' (Genesis 4:16 RSV) and dwelt in the land of Nod. We do not know where the land of Nod was, but its name means 'wanderer'. Possibly it was on the Iranian plateau where preliminary excavation on city mounds reveals Neolithic origins. Although Cain himself may not have travelled a great distance, his move gave direction eastward to the momentum of the migration of his descendants. Other descendants of Adam would receive migratory momentum towards other points of the compass, e.g. westwards into Europe. (Helbaek states that farming came direct into Greece and Europe from Turkey.)

Still others would be impelled towards a southerly migration from Eden. For example, R. C. Kuttner in his *Race and Modern Science* says that 'the single district of origin of farming was on the northern side of the Near East in Anatolia, Turkey (i.e. Eden) and to have arrived much later on the southern side in Palestine'. Similarly, evidence for the early momentum of farming towards the east brings significance to the Genesis statement that Cain went 'eastward from Eden'.

Since stating the view that Asia and America received its farming from the Near East, evidence has been coming in to support this. Until fairly recently, it was thought that even India and China were places where an independent farming revolution arose. This was because rice and not wheat is the subsistence crop.

Worldwide Degeneration

The reality of the Fall is clear in both Old Testament history and in New Testament teaching. All tribes the world over strayed from the original revelation of God.

In the Old Testament, races which start with godliness degenerate into wickedness. This was the situation which led up to the judgment of the Flood. This was the situation even soon after the Flood, for the

Tower of Babel was a defiant erection to the sun and the moon.

This was the case with the descendants of Abraham's relatives. Lot's grandsons and descendants, the Ammonites and Moabites, were soon sacrificing their children to demon gods. It was the case eventually with Israel who forsook the Lord God and became as bad as the nations around them.

Even in Christian history, the Church has constantly adulterated the truth revealed in the Bible. Only revivals by God's Holy Spirit at various times has brought them back to truth and to Christ's salvation.

The first three chapters of Romans sum it all up. 'They did not like to retain God in their knowledge . . . degenerating into sexual immorality, wickedness, greed, murder . . . haters of God' (Romans 1:28).

'All have sinned and come short of God's standard.' The natural fallen nature is unwilling to believe this. 'By one man (Adam) sin entered into the world . . . for all have sinned' (Romans 5:12). 'But while we were still sinners, Christ died for us . . . God commends his love to us by this' (Romans 5:8).

Thus the story of man is 'Paradise lost and Paradise regained'. The Bible says that God is going to remake the world to be the happy place he intended. He can do it now for you and me. 'If any man be in Christ, he is a new creation' (2 Corinthians 5:17).

SUMMARY

EVIDENCE FOR FALL

Wickedness gradually increases:
* First pioneers along Danube needed no fortifications.
* Second Danubians fortified. Earth gods, sexy figurines.
* First Stone Age city had no sexy figurines (Gen 6:4) and no warfare.
* Oral tradition from primitives of age of innocence, e.g. China Miao, Andamanese, New Guinea Kapauki, Australian aboriginal folklore, First American Indians. Universal original belief in Creator, 'Sky God', before polytheism and animism.

Sin-offerings commence:
* Abel's sacrifice. Gen 4:2–5.
* Increase in lamb bones in Shanidar-Zarzi complex, Karim Shahir, Belt Cave, Jarmo, Ali Kosh.
* Worldwide primitive custom of propitiation.
* Prof. Zwemer: e.g. Eskimos, Pygmies, Algonguins Bushmen and Veddas.Prof. Evans-Pritchard: Nuer tribe, Upper Nile, confession over ox.
* Bible evidence. Tribes always degenerated from original revelation, e.g.
* Cain's violent descendants. Tower of Babel moon god.
* Abraham's relatives (Lot and Ammonites, Moabites)
* Jacob's descendants: Esau and Edomites, then Israel and Judah crucificed children to demon gods.
* Then idolatry into the medieval church as prophesied.

Rom 1:28. 'Did not retain God in their knowledge and degenerated into immorality, wickedness, greed, murder, hatred of God.'

Learn Rom 3:23; and 5:8.

11 CAIN'S CITY AND CULTURE
THE BIBLE AND CULTURAL EVIDENCE

For many years, prehistoric archaeologists sought to unravel the puzzle of where and how man had learned his horticulture. What had sparked off this sudden advance called the New Stone Age Revolution? From what source had he received his seed grain? In what locality or 'nuclear area' had the first farming experiments commenced?

Concerning the last question, each prehistorian favoured his pet area. The name 'prehistorian' is one used to combine anthropology with archaeology. Gordon Childe was one of the greatest prehistorians, but he was also an aggressive atheist, evidenced by his writings in *New Light on the Most Ancient East* in 1934. Childe wished to think that the agricultural revolution had commenced in Europe; then he shifted his attention to Egypt.

As more evidence came in, the search was taken to the Fertile Crescent of the Near East. Then Braidwood, at a hint from Seton Lloyd, investigated Jarmo village in the Iranian foothills. Meanwhile Kathleen Kenyon was excavating the city of Jericho down to the earliest New Stone Age and beyond.

A NEW STONE AGE CITY

The first urbanisation in the Middle East was thought to have commenced in Mesopotamia in the early Bronze Age, 4000 BC and then to have spread to Egypt. Who then was to believe the story of Cain – that recalcitrant son of Adam the farmer, that murderer who was supposed to have launched upon mankind the bane of city life?

At the time when this theory was prevalent, in 1963, I had written in the margin of my RSV Bible against Genesis 4:17 the exclamation, 'A New Stone Age city!' The text read, 'And Cain built a city and he called the name of the city after the name of his son Enoch'. The New Stone Age was referred to because the discovery of metals comes later in the text. This discovery was made by Tubal-Cain (Genesis 4:22).

Although farming in its early stages was present in these areas, it was later realised that the original culture was still to be found. When my remark was being written in the margin of my Bible, Professor James Mellaart had actually begun to excavate one of those New Stone

Age cities near the area described in that scripture. He startled the archaeological world by his articles. One appeared in the *Scientific American*, 1964, headed 'A Neolithic City in Turkey'.

He had discovered that Great New Stone Age city, Çatal Hüyük, on the Turkish Plateau, 5,000 feet up, far above the foothills, with its evidence of early farming. From the depth of excavations so far, its archaeological history stretches back at least to eight millennia BC and terminated 5000 BC. (Surveys have been hindered in recent years by government restrictions.) In this Neolithic city were the evidences that farming in the market gardens around was already well advanced. I worked under Mellaart's personal instructions. One of my photographs of the workings is shown in Figure 11.1.

Figure 11.1. One of the rooms in the Stone Age city of Çatal Hüyük

What has become evident is that the Bible was right in speaking about New Stone Age cities so soon after Adam's farming evolution.

It was no mean city either – far bigger than Jericho; it covered 23 acres and showed specialisation of trades, indicating a large market gardening area of villages to support the inhabitants.

Until this discovery, it was thought that New Stone Age social organisation was insufficiently advanced to support a city. To the surprise of all, Çatal Hüyük had a population of 8,000. They would have been supported by market gardening in the fields around the city. This would require the citizens to have specialised trades in order to pay the market gardeners for their food.

These trades soon became evident as the city was excavated. The weaver produced tapestries (Fig 11.2). This was revealed by the discovery of looms and the painting of woven designs in murals. The carpenter carved exquisite dishes, egg cups and boxes for domestic use. His products were distributed among the older and lower levels of the rooms, three stages before the making of pottery was invented.

Figure 11.2. (a) **Oldest example of a textile,** perhaps woollen, adhering to a fragment of human thigh bone. Level Vl, Çatal Hüyük, 6500 BC. *After J. Mellaart.* (b) **Berber woman spinning.** The spindle consists of a tapered stick weighed with a whorl. *After D. D. Duncan.*   *Courtesy: Sonia Cole, The Neolithic Revolution, British Museum, 1959*

Neolithic Refuse Collectors

In the burial director's house, there were black and white paintings on the walls of skeletons which were headless, accompanied by vultures. Mellaart puzzled over their significance. I suggested that headless skeletons would be found in the graveyards. You see, the skulls belonging to the skeletons were kept in the houses. I was right. The citizens liked to have grandpa's skull on the mantelpiece looking at them! The skeletons had been painted with red ochre.

That revealed the true purpose of the vultures which were painted on the walls. The undertakers must have regarded the vultures as a God-given utility for prevention of disease. After death, the body would be exposed in the open for vultures to clean off the flesh, thus preventing putrefaction. When the bones had whitened in the sun, they were painted red. This was to denote resurrection, if we are guided by other ancient customs. The detached head was then taken home!

A Great Trading City

The key to Çatal Hüyük's early success as a viable city may be the subject of another mural. On the wall, depicted in polychrome, a double-coned mountain stands behind the city. Looking out from the mound, one could see the actual mountain in the distance, now long since volcanically inactive, but when painted, it was in full eruption and viscous glass poured down its slopes. What could be the relevance of the picture? Finds in the city revealed stores of volcanic glass mined from that distant range. This black obsidian was ideal for Stone Age tools. Perhaps here was the source of Çatal Hüyük's prosperity. The flint-knappers' skill was evident in the blades of knives, spears and tools which were made from this volcanic glass called obsidian, much prized in the ancient world.

The manufacturing of flint tools and bone implements must have been a prosperous industry. The Neolithic farmers outside the city needed these, for extensive market gardening would be a 'must' in order to support the city. Flint sickles had to be made long enough by sticking rows of sharp flints with bitumen along a grooved reindeer's rib or in an ivory handle. All the carpenters' tools had to be produced in flint or obsidian, the equivalent to our planes, spoke-shaves, awls, drills, saws and the like.

Knives were in demand by housewives, agriculturists and shepherds. One knife particularly was a beautiful work of skill. Its transparent candy-coloured flint showed up the minute flaking to achieve its symmetrical shape. The pressure-flaking of the Mesolithic (Middle Stone Age and Neolithic) culture was a highly developed art from a long tradition. Professor Crabtree, the exponent of the method, told me that it took him 20 years to equal the excellency of such a difficult craft. The knife had a finely serrated edge – a very modern touch. The blade was bound and glued on to a bone handle bearing a twisted snake pattern. One wonders whether it was a knife like this which Cain plunged into his brother.

One began to piece together the evidence. This obsidian was traded along routes thousands of miles long, way along the Anatolian plateau to the east, also south to Jericho where obsidian tools have been found.

On another wall, hands had been dipped in colour and pressed on to the wall in a pattern. This brought reminiscences of cave designs in Provence, Southern France. Perhaps it was a briefer stage from cave dwelling to city building than one thought. After all, the first farmers started their horticulture when still living in caves.

Mellaart wrote (*Çatal Hüyük*, Thomas & Hudson, 1967):

> One cannot possibly be wrong in suggesting that it was a well-organised trade that produced the city's wealth. Moreover, it appears likely that the trade in obsidian was at the heart of this extensive commerce. This black volcanic glass, which first appeared in the preceding Mesolithic period, became the most widespread trading commodity during the Neolithic period in the Near East. It has been found in the 'proto-Neolithic' and pre-pottery Neolithic periods at Jericho. It occurs as far south as Beidha near Petra; it reached Cyprus in the sixth millennium. The origin of this obsidian, which was the best material of the time for cutting tools, was almost certainly central Anatolia, and it is extremely likely that the city of Çatal Hüyük controlled this source and organised the trade. The then active volcanoes of Hasban Dag, Karaca Dag, Mekke Dag and others lie on the edge of the Konya Plain. The nearest is some 50 miles east of Çatal Hüyük, and all are visible on a clear day. These sources of obsidian were well within the limits of the culture area of which Çatal Hüyük was the undisputed centre.

Such a discovery was a revelation. Earlier the Turkish plateau was regarded as no competitor for the distinction of being a centre for man's first great advance. It is unfortunate that in recent years severe restrictions have been imposed on further archaeological work.

Roof-top Highways

The culture which Mellaart revealed in the city was of even greater significance. The wall paintings and design of the city showed connections with former cave dwellers, for there were unmistakable similarities with those famous cave paintings around the Mediterranean and in the Sahara. Although the city was so elaborate, they did not enter rooms through doors but through holes in the wall – a rather cave-like conception. There were no streets. The dwellers walked over the flat roofs, for there were no alleys between the houses and sanctuaries.

To traverse the city, one climbed a ladder, walked across the roofs, and disappeared through a hole down a ladder into the desired house (Fig 11.3 and 11.4). It is interesting to know that the Pueblo maize-growing Indians have similar villages with roof-top access. Also, as we saw, they practise dry-farming similar to that described in Genesis 2

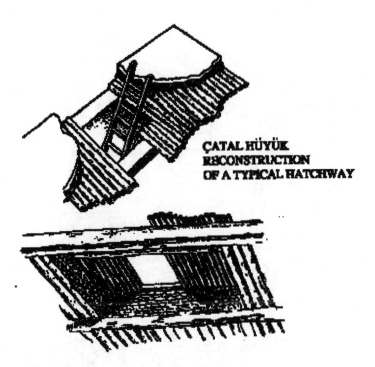

ÇATAL HÜYÜK
RECONSTRUCTION
OF A TYPICAL HATCHWAY

Figure 11.3. Hatchway design at Çatal Hüyük showing access from a homestead to pedestrianised area above.

(flood water seeps through porous strata to reach the crops).

It seemed to be a peaceful community. Throughout the earlier centuries of its long history, there were no signs of warfare. Although it was a very religious community, its offerings seemed to be Cain-like offerings of cereals without resort to animal sacrifices.

Early Farming Development

The beginnings of agriculture and sheep farming started while men were still in caves. This is shown through the Neolithic cave of Shanidar where an increasing percentage of sheep were firstlings. As well as proving that breeding was taking place, it also implied the use of lamb sacrifices, for we read that Abel brought some of the firstlings of his flock for sacrifice to the Lord God as an atonement for his sins. It was Cain's refusal to bring a sin offering which caused his rejection (Genesis 4:7).

We do not know whether Adam was sophisticated enough to build cities. It is unlikely and his descendants, Cain and his sons, are given the credit for this. So then Adam's initiation of farming would be in the proto-Neolithic stage when early farmers still lived in caves and rock

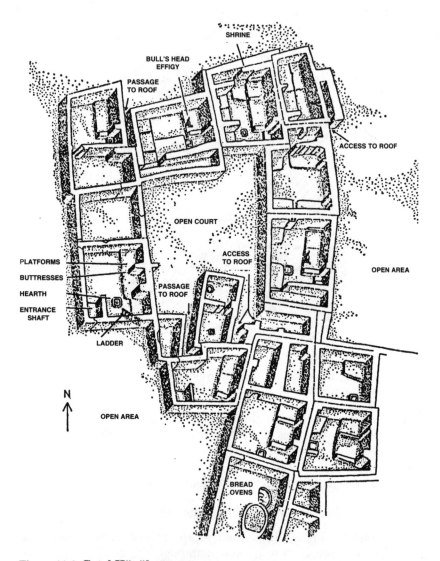

Figure 11.4. Çatal Hüyük: 5th Layer
Community Arrangements of 8,000 years ago in the Neolithic City, S. Turkey. Lower layers are much older than this. Note the access by ladders to the roof, from which all houses were entered.   *Courtesy J. Mellaart 'New Stone Age City'*

shelters, like the Natufians.

Mellaart says that the core of the mound remains to be sounded and may take the origins of Çatal Hüyük back to the end of the last continental glaciation (Ice Age).

It was at the termination of the Ice Age that farming developed. Prehistorians used to suggest that it was the post-glacial conditions which gave man the idea of farming. At the retreat of the ice caps on the Caucasian range and Ararat ranges in Turkey, a sparse tundra vegetation would be left which would later be succeeded by birch and pine wood. Meanwhile, melting ice would keep the plateau valleys supplied with water rather than through rain which might be scarce on account of the prevailing high pressure outward-blowing wind systems.

Adam is represented in Genesis 2 as being formed for the specific purpose of carrying out this New Stone Age gardening. The British Museum handbook by Sonia Cole, *The Neolithic Revolution* (1959) says, 'Corn was planted first in small plots, thus beginning as a garden rather than a field crop.'

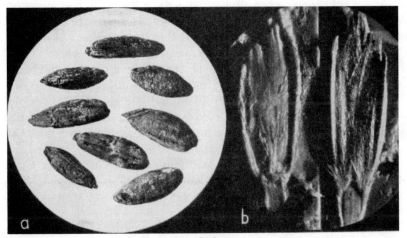

Figure 11.5. Archaeological remains of wheat.
(a) Carbonised grains of wheat from pre-pottery Neolithic, Jarmo, Iraq (upper three einkorn, the remainder emmer): (b) Cast of Jarmo wheat spikelet (left) compared with recent emmer. *After H. Helbaek.*

Courtesy: Sonia Cole, The Neolithic Revolution, British Museum, 1959

Carbonised grains and clay impressions of spikelets from the parching ovens of Jarmo in Iraq are archaeological records of the progress of man's horticultural development of wheat and barley (Fig 11.5). Until the discovery of carbonised grains at Çatal Hüyük, it was thought that the heavy crop producing six-rowed or hexaploid wheat had not developed until the Iron Age, but both hexaploid wheat and barley have been found at Çatal Hüyük on the Turkish Konya Plain. This should indicate that the process had a longer history or made more rapid progress in Turkey.

Many other crops were also developed and cattle, goats and pigs were bred in Eden's garden farms. Of Çatal Hüyük, Mellaart writes:

The zoological remains are no less interesting; they show the presence of domesticated sheep even below Level X and cows as early as Level VII.

Goats and dogs also appear to have been domesticated, but there is no indication that pigs were. Their absence may be due to religious considerations. Although the domesticated animals provided the community with wool, milk, meat and skins, the people had by no means abandoned hunting. Wild cattle and red deer were extensively hunted, as were wild asses, wild sheep, boars and leopards.

Cain's Wife

'Cain lay with his wife and she conceived and bare Enoch' (Genesis 4:17). 'After Seth was born (when Adam was 130 years old), Adam lived 800 years and had other sons and daughters' (Genesis 5:4).

As the reference comes after the statement that Cain had migrated eastward, some ask where did Cain find a wife? Cain's wife could have been one of his sisters – for Adam and Eve had daughters as well as sons (5:4) one of whom he may have married before he became a fugitive. Cain feared others when he said, 'I shall be a fugitive and wanderer in the earth and whosoever finds me will kill me.' Who would these other men be? By the time Adam and Eve were 130 years old (Genesis 5:3), they would have lived long enough for their children's descendants to have increased to a population as large as 3,000,000 and to have travelled some distance.

We should not suppose that Çatal Hüyük is the actual city Cain built, for, as we have seen, where Cain fled from his homeland, he is said to have travelled 'eastward from Eden' (Genesis 4:16 RSV) and dwelt in the land of Nod.

But the discovery of Çatal Hüyük does give us sound archaeological evidence that the Bible was right and that Cain and his contemporaries were capable of building cities, contrary to what many archaeologists had previously believed. Mellaart thinks we will be finding many Stone Age cities built farther east along this high plateau.

Wall Paintings and Women's Dress

Returning to Çatal Hüyük which, as we have said, is representative of the cities built in Cain's lifetime, the first citizens were not content with bare brick walls in their rooms. They had them plastered and it is well that they did because we have an insight into everyday life. On the plaster they painted frescoes in polychrome colours.

Have you been curious about what the women of Cain's day wore? The frescoes show them dressed surprisingly modestly. J. Mellaart writing in the Cambridge University *Ancient History* says:

As a source of information about Early Neolithic man's activities, appearance and dress, these frescoes are of unique importance. They show, for example, that the women wore long dresses and that the men wore loincloths of a white material, probably wool, which reached down to the knees or ankles, often combined with a leopard skin with tail. Caps of leopard skin are often worn.

Even portraits *en face* are on some walls.

The art of painting in water colours at the right time before the new plaster had dried out, indicates development in skills. 'Painted with a brush in a flat wash, these are the earliest paintings yet found on man-made walls,' wrote Mellaart. 'They show scenes of hunting and rejoicing including a deer hunt, an enormous wild bull surrounded by men, and several superimposed groups of hunters, dancers and acrobats . . . showing lively observation and naturalism.'

Jubal's Pipes and Harps

Slightly higher up in the city mound, levels 3 and 4, could well represent five generations after Cain. What do we find? Why – pictures of musicians playing their pipes and harps. Turn to Genesis 4:17–21 and at the end of five generations, we read, 'His brother's name was Jubal, the father of all those who play the harp and pipe.'

This was at the next stage of culture called the Copper Stone Age (Chalcolithic) because Jubal's half-brother (v 22) was Tubal-Cain who invented tools made from beaten copper and beaten iron. (This was before the secret of iron smelting, which was much later.)

The Technological Succession in Genesis

'Tubal-Cain, was a hammerer, a copper worker in copper and iron' (Genesis 4:22). The accuracy of technological succession in these early chapters and throughout Genesis is remarkable and could only be present in the text if its source of information was a contemporary one. Here the commencement of the Copper Stone Age is noted with the name of the inventor of this next step forward in technology.

I have given a literal translation of the Hebrew and Greek text because translators, not being technologists, have missed the significance of the root meanings of the original languages. The Greek Septuagint translation by Jews three centuries before Christ is often a good commentary upon the Hebrew, especially as *chalcos* in Greek means copper (not brass or bronze), as does also the Hebrew word *n'ghoh-sheth*.

It was during the New Stone Age that native copper was discovered to be malleable and responsive to hammering into various shapes and uses. This was before smelting and casting came as a further development. Hence the significance of the word 'hammerer', *sphurokopos* (not smelter as some translators have rendered it). *Chalkeus* means a worker in copper and *chalkou* means copper.

The word 'iron', which is *bar-zel* in Hebrew and *sideerou* in the Greek Septuagint, refers to native iron which was hammered but not smelted. Because it was so tough to beat out, it soon fell out of use until the Iron Age in 1500 BC when the Hittites learnt the secret of smelting. It is mentioned later in the Pentateuch in connection with these Hittites.

This Copper Stone Age commenced 7000 BC or earlier. Examples of drills or reamers from native copper and beads made from malachite have been found in Eastern Turkey at Cayonu Tepesi, which is upon the high plateau where farming commenced. The introduction of the full Bronze Age had to wait until 4000 BC when smelting and casting developed rapidly after a long stalemate. Archaeologists are puzzled by the stalemate in technical development – Genesis gives the reason. It was the Flood which caused the cultural hiatus.

The Genesis Cultural Succession

Before the Copper Stone Age, the cultural succession was first the Old Stone Age reflected in the hunter-gatherer milieu of Genesis 1:28–30, who gathered fruits and subdued animals. Then followed the Middle and New Stone Age of pressure-flake tools and ground tools of the first farmers spoken of in Genesis 2:8–15. Next comes the building of New Stone Age cities of Genesis 4:17, followed by the Copper Stone Age of Genesis 4:22.

This correct cultural and technological succession, which concerned pre-history from 12000 BC to 4000 BC, is truly remarkable, especially as it is incidental background material not essential to the story, also remembering that it was thousands of years even before Moses. So you see how accurate is the incidental background description that Genesis has, even of the progression of ancient culture.

What Lessons Can we Learn?

In the case of Cain, the biblical statement that he actually built a city looked unlikely to scientists for along time. Even archaeologists discountenanced it and treated it as folklore, but later the evidence of cities in Cain's time was found. Even before they were found, I wrote in my Bible margin opposite 4:17,22 – 'Neolithic City'.

You may never get to know the answer to some things in the Bible, but that should not prevent you from believing them. Why? Because the Bible says it is the Word of God. Don't be one who will not believe various items until they are proved. We are happy when evidence does come in our lifetime, especially as it is useful to evaporate the doubts of an enquirer, but stake your faith in God's wonderful revelation.

Entrenched doubt closes the mind even to evidence. It is a fact that those who started with faith were correct when the evidence came in. This is why a very high percentage of successful scientists were people who had personal faith in the Lord. Others with anti-biblical theories found themselves wrong in the end.

An attitude of faith in God's revelation in the Bible leads to accurate conclusions. Never be put off by what looks unlikely in the Bible.

It would be useful for you when you talk to others to make a list of things in the Bible which looked unlikely until evidence was discovered. What have we got so far? Following is **a list of 'unlikely' items in the Bible, which are proved later by science. Can you add other items?**

God's Word	*Evidence for Truth*
1. The universe has a beginning	World-wide radio telescopes
2. Creation was by God's speech	DNA code is a language
3. We all descended from one woman	Genetically correct from Mitochondrial DNA
4. All colours and cultures had one origin	Even agnostic scientists now agree
5. Religion degenerated instead of evolving	Anthropological theories corrected by field findings
6. Order of life as in Genesis 1	Same as the fossil records
7. Each species separately created	Fossil records favour a succession of creative acts
8. Eden at headwaters of four rivers	Farming began in Turkish plateau
9. New Stone Age cities built before Flood	Çatal Hüyük proves civilisation existed
10. Copper Stone Age came next	Çatal Hüyük and Cayonu Tepesi evidence

SUMMARY

CAIN'S CITY

1. New Stone Age City Gen 4:17 was before metals in 4:22.
Çatal Hüyük on Turkish Plateau discovered by Prof J. Mellaart.
Before this discovery, some thought Bible wrong to speak of cities
before Bronze age, because a city needed specialised trades to
support it and organisation.

2. Çatal Hüyük, 8,000 population had trades and market gardening outside.
Traded in volcanic glass tools for miles around, carpentry with
flint tools.
Weaving and dye-stamped cloth. Frescoes showed women in long
dresses and men in loincloth or skirt down to knees. Leopard
skin caps.

3. Levels 3 and 4 (five generations after Cain).
Pictures of *pipes and harps* (Gen 4:17–21).
Copper Stone Age arrives, but NOT smelting. 'Tubal-Cain was a
hammerer of copper and iron' (Gen 4:22). Hebrew means 'hammerer'. (Smelting of iron not until 1500 BC.)

4. Technological background to Bible 10000 to 1500 BC is
remarkable.
New Stone Age, Copper Stone Age, Bronze Age, Iron Age succession is correct.

5. Population explosion as in Gen 6. Other city mounds in sight.
In 130 years (Gen 5:3) computer estimates population at 3 million.

6. Religion: Çatal Hüyük was very religious, but astray from truth.
1 in 3 rooms were shrines to mother goddess.
Cain had refused sacrificial lamb method of atonement (Gen 4:5;
Heb. 11:4).

12 Noah's Flood

THE BIBLE AND SCIENCE AGREE

Various attempts have been made to account for the Flood; some which would not stand up to the scrutiny of scientific methods.

Here are some up-to-date scientific findings on the cause of the Flood which indicate that it was due to a change in the earth's axis. This is new evidence which the modern science of paleomagnetism brings. Later in this series, I will give you original information from archaeological digs in America and in the Middle East showing that the Flood was worldwide. It reveals also why the Old World animals of the horse, lion, elephant, camel, etc. disappeared from the continent of America and why they were replaced only in the continents of Africa, Europe and Asia but not in Australia. Much of this information is not widely known and will leave the reader asking how it is that the ancient documents in the Bible got it exactly right.

WHAT CAUSED THE FLOOD?

In the last few years, there have been dramatic discoveries on what caused the Flood. I am referring to the Flood of Noah in the Bible; that dramatic story from Genesis chapters 6–9, upon which the children's toy arks are modelled – the ark into which Noah collected all the animals – a story which is repeated around the world among over 200 ancient and primitive peoples, races and tribes who have never heard of the Bible.

Q What are these discoveries which throw light upon the world's best known story?

We start at a most unlikely point. It is a soup ladle made by the Chinese 100 years before Christ. Whatever has a soup ladle to do with discovering what caused the Flood? We shall see. This particular ladle was balanced upon a dish after serving the soup. To the amazement of all diners, the ladle moved round the dish and faced the opposite direction. It seemed to be moved by an unseen hand.

All the guests were startled. The server went over and moved the soup ladle back round the dish again to its original position. He had hardly let go when very deliberately it rotated back to its chosen position. The guests didn't know whether to fall down and worship it or tell fortunes with it.

Eventually they decided to do the latter. They drew signs on the dish so that when released, the ladle would turn to give an answer. Then they noticed that it always pointed in the same direction.

Yes, I expect you have guessed. The soup ladle had been made of magnetic material. The maker didn't know it, but he had accidentally made the first compass. By cutting the handle into a long shape, the lodestone material automatically became polarised with opposing magnetic poles, north and south, at opposite ends. Now, because the spoon end of the ladle was heavy and smooth, its weight kept it in the middle of the hollowed dish, leaving the handle end free to swivel around the edge of the plate.

The next episode of the story is by the ship's mariners. The sailors saw a marvellous use for it. They did not know what force this was but it was a God-given guide across the seas. Tradition dies hard in the Far East and it is amusing to see that for centuries, until recent times, they still kept the ladle spoon shape for their compass needle and it still revolved in a hollow dish shape. The markings on the dish retained the original fortune-telling signs (see Fig 12.1).

Figure 12.1. Ancient Chinese Compass A replica of a lodestone spoon or 'swivelling ladle' balanced upon a polished bronze plate, constructed several decades ago from an ancient Chinese pattern. This was the earliest form of the magnetic compass and is known from Chinese literature to have been in use by at least the first century BC. It works because a piece of lodestone cut into an elongated form automatically becomes polarised with opposing magnetic poles (N and S) at opposite ends. Because of its shape and fine point of balance, the spoon turns to align itself with the earth's magnetic field. The variety of signs on the base plate indicates its ancient use in geomancy (as a form of alignment or navigational aid).   *Courtesy: Hanley Central Library*

Q But what has this to do with the Flood of Noah?

No, you are wrong! Noah didn't guide the ark by a ladle-spoon compass! In fact, the ark was designed only to float and had no steering mechanism. Down the centuries, the compass came to be taken for granted, but the mystery why it always pointed in one particular direction was never understood. Then a further mystery was discovered: the 'north' to which the compass pointed was not the pole around which the earth turned.

The Earth's Inner Core

What was it that made the magnetic north different from the polar north of the globe? Various theories were put forward but it is only in recent years that the reason has been confirmed and only recently that it has been seen that it also gives a clue to what caused the Flood of Noah.

It all has to do with the inner structure of our planet. Modern implements and methods have now demonstrated that within the outer crust of our globe, there is an inner core. This core moves independently of the outer mantel because it is separated by fluid. Moreover, it is the inner core which makes the earth's magnetic field and as it revolves around its own axis it causes the north–south alignment of the magnetic poles to be offset a few degrees from true north.

The comparatively new science of paleomagnetics – the study of the earth's magnetic field throughout geologic time – has shown that at one time, both inner core and outer crust revolved together at the same angle.

Now, here's the crunch – if at some time in the recent past the outer crust suddenly started to turn at a different angle, **that could cause a worldwide flood!**

Science now acknowledges that there have been axis changes in the past, sometimes very slowly (as at present), but once at least, quite quickly. How could a fairly quick change of axis cause a flood? We shall look at the evidence for this, but first imagine the havoc which such a change would bring about.

If the outer crust began to rotate on a new north–south pole, the oceans near to the north pole would have to pick up speed to begin to travel around the new pole. Also at the equator, the oceans would have to change their angle of rotation.

Oceans Rush over Continents

The deep oceans would have rushed over the continents, swept animals into caves and even up mountains to beat their bones into broken bits and pieces.

Think of the volume of those oceans – three times deeper than the earth's mountains and covering nearly three times more of the globe than the area of the continents.

This immense volume of water would flood out of its ocean beds like water jerked out of a swirling wash basin. No wonder Genesis chapter 7 says, 'The fountains of the great deep were broken up'. No wonder the tablets found in the Middle East say, 'The Flood came up' – came up from the waters of the deep oceans or beneath the earth's crust. No wonder the Bible and the archaeological tablets say that, as a result, all flesh died. It was a catastrophe bigger than the world has ever known.

The Evidence of Paleomagnetism

Q What is this new evidence that sheds new light upon the cause of the Flood?

The comparatively new science of paleomagnetism is the study of magnetism which has been recorded in the rocks and which shows at what angle the poles were in the past. The angle of embedded magnetised particles shows that the earth has turned on a different pole in earlier times – probably where the magnetic pole is now. The geographic pole is now about 16 degrees away from the magnetic pole. Ships' compasses always point to the magnetic pole. They do not point at the pole around which the earth's crust turns. That is the geographic pole.

Q When did the geographic pole change from the magnetic pole? What effect would this have upon the world, upon the oceans, upon life on earth?

In examining the evidence, I shall draw upon information from the accepted realms of science, as well as my own research as a qualified anthropologist and geologist. There is no need to wander into way-out theories for there is plenty of evidence within the generally accepted disciplines.

We shall look at the evidence from all over the earth. The evidence in the caves inhabited by man, the succession of cultures, the redistribution of sea levels after the Flood and the magnetic evidence from the core of the earth.

Much of the information I shall give is not widely known. It comes from far afield, from Australia, from the Americas, from Europe, from Egypt, from China and of course from the Middle East. I bring it also from the earth sciences such as the record in the rocks of prehistoric magnetism of the earth's poles which, as I have said, is called paleomagnetism.

From all these sources, we find that the Flood was caused by a change of axis in the outer crust of the earth and that it happened between the Copper Stone Age and the Bronze Age. The Bible and archaeology agree on this.

In this chapter, I will give the evidence that the Flood of Noah was caused by a change in the earth's axis. In the following chapters I will use worldwide evidence to show that the Flood occurred between the Copper Stone Age and the Bronze Age, precisely when the Bible said it did.

The Old Axis

Let's start then with the evidence that the Flood was caused by a changing in the earth's axis. As many as 14 scientific types of investigation confirm this conclusion.

First is that we have records of the former axis of the earth's poles. I was glad to find that an old friend of mine, Professor Martin Bott of Durham University, had written a work on earth science using paleomagnetic evidence for axis deviation. I remember the times we had in geological fieldwork when I drove a group of geologists in a Transit around Anglesey and also the geological fieldwork centred on Fort Dale in Pembrokeshire. He was always thorough and impartial in his assessment of evidence.

In his work, *The Interior of the Earth* (Arnold, 1977), Professor Bott explains how it is that the rocks have recorded the changes in the earth's magnetic pole at various times in the remote past. Paleomagnetisation, the study of the geomagnetic field during the geological past, makes use of the permanent magnetisation which may be picked up by a rock when it is formed. The great advances in paleomagnetism over the past 20 years have been largely stimulated by Professors Runcorn and Blackett and scientists associated with them. There are also active Japanese, French and other groups working on rock magnetism.

I would also add that for the study of the deviation of the poles in more recent times, occurring in human history, at Oxford we were using pottery to find the direction of the poles at the time a vessel was baked, providing that the provenance of that pot was known.

When a pot is baked, it fixes in its atoms the direction of the poles at that time. The direction of the positive and negative magnetism within the pot is found out by spinning it around within coils of wire which create a magnetic field. This instrument is called a spinner magnetometer and is also used in the same way for rock samples.

This reveals that the poles have wandered and changed at various times down the geological ages, also in more recent times. In fact, the current change of the geographical pole away from the magnetic pole happened within the period of human history. Martin Bott writes on page 168 of *The Interior of the Earth:*

> Another important 'geomagnetic' result from paleomagnetism is that the field average over a few thousand years appears to have remained within a few degrees of the axis of rotation – the axis of the dipole field coincided with the axis of rotation rather than being ten or more degrees out of alignment as at present.

The Mysterious Core

Like most boys, I used to be fascinated by the mysterious influence of magnetism. We would put iron filings on a sheet of paper and then put a magnet underneath. The effect was dramatic. Immediately all the filings would jump into position, arranging themselves to radiate around the two ends of the magnet.

The magnet used was a horseshoe shape. The north pole and the south pole of the magnet were bent round so that both poles could attract, but we soon learned that like poles repelled each other. The south pole of the magnet attracted the north poles of the iron filings and the north pole of the magnet attracted the south poles of the iron filings. What was this mysterious unseen force?

Ancient sailors found that certain cigar-shaped stones could be hung on a string and would point northwards. They called them 'lodestones'. This was probably discovered by accident. We have already seen how someone made a soup ladle out of lodestone and they were surprised when the handle kept pointing in one direction when it was free to move and soon it became used as a compass.

Dr D. H Tarling writes in *Principles and Applications of Paleomagnetism* (Chapman and Hall, 1971): 'The geomagnetic field is generated by electric currents within the metallic core of the earth. These currents must be maintained by some form of dynamo action.'

It is the inner core which creates magnetism and consequently the magnetic pole is that to which our compasses point. The earth's core is like a huge dynamo generating the magnetic field and polarity (see Fig 12.2).

How the Earth's Crust Separated from the Core

Q Why then were both the magnetic poles and the geographic poles the same at one time in the past?

The answer is that, before the core had formed under pressure and cooling, there was no separate core. The whole mass of the earth turned together; then, in the process of time, the inner mass separated out into a nickel iron core which then became separated from the crust by liquid matter.

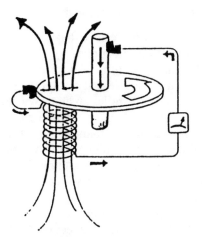

A mechanical model of the self-exciting dynamo. The copper disc is kept rotating about the vertical shaft. The shaft and the outer case of the disc are connected via brushes to make a complete circuit including a coil. As long as the disc is kept rotating in the direction shown, electric current will flow in the direction indicated by the straight arrows, producing a magnetic field in the coil as represented by the curved arrows.

Figure 12.2. The dynamo at the centre of the earth caused by the separate rotation of the core to the crust

The crust continued to turn in the same direction as the core; but, as it had no solid contact with the core, it was open to be disturbed to rotate away from the inner core's axis. The paleomagnetic evidence shows it began to rotate 18 degrees away from its original pole. The original pole continued to be kept by the inner core as the magnetic pole.

So does the distance between the magnetic pole and the geographic crustal pole indicate the amount by which the axis changed? It should be an indication, but only an approximate one, because the magnetic pole wanders slowly. Why?

If you take your tea cup, you can swill your tea round by holding the handle and making a circular movement with the cup. The tea then 'climbs' up around the edges of the cup and sinks in the middle. This same force causes the water at the equator to bulge out. It is caused by what is called centrifugal force. Consequently, the earth is not truly spherical. It bulges out all round the equator – land as well as water – and sinks or squashes flat at the poles. It is like this on the inside of the crust as well as the outside.

Another effect is that, after some thousands of years, this disjunction between the two revolving bodies separated by fluid causes what is called the procession of the equinoxes. The magnetic pole wanders slowly around the crustal pole in the opposite direction to its spin.

A spinning top or gyroscope gives a similar action. The top itself may spin in a clockwise direction, but the axis of the top gradually circles backwards at an angle in an anti-clockwise direction. But this gradual wandering of the poles is not what caused the big sudden change which brought about the Flood.

How the Axis Change Caused the Flood

The important question to consider now is the effect that a sudden change of axis would have upon the oceans of the globe.

With the crustal pole suddenly beginning to turn 18 degrees away from the old pole, calculations show that the icy seas at rest on the old pole would have to pick up a speed of about 300 miles an hour. We can imagine the deep oceans trying to do this. Their great volume would flood out over the mountains. We can liken it to rotating a cup of tea or a bowl full of water and suddenly changing the angle of rotation. The water would spill out backwards on to the floor. A contrary reaction would happen at the new pole. There, the oceans would have to break speed from 300 miles an hour to nil.

At the equator, the oceans are rotating with the earth's crust at a thousand miles an hour. They could not adjust their direction to the new angle of rotation all at once but would continue their thousand mile an hour dash in what had now become an east-north-east direction. Thus, the seas of the earth would move across from the old equator and fill up the northern hemisphere to cover the mountains. The top of Mount Ararat, 17,000 feet high was covered to a depth of 23 feet, according to Genesis chapter 7. Many have not realised what a tremendous amount of water there is in the seas or realised that the earth has nearly three times as much of its area covered by oceans as land. There is enough water in the oceans to cover the whole land mass to a depth of two miles.

Furthermore, *New Scientist* reported in 1997 the discovery that there were even more waters under the earth than in the oceans. A change of axis could well disrupt them, causing them to 'break out'.

Another edition of *New Scientist* reports that the waters of the Black Sea did experience a 'bursting out' about 5000 BC as evidenced by the sudden change of freshwater snails to seawater snails when the Black Sea was invaded by ocean water:

> The waters would have come thundering through with the force of 200 Niagaras and a roar which would have been heard 100 kilometres away.

So we can now understand the significance of Genesis 7 which says that the source of most of the Flood was from 'the great deep' and then speaks of the waters swirling to and fro. The Babylonian and Sumerian tablets also say that 'the Flood came up'. Rain, which came down, was only a minor result of atmospheric disturbance and lasted only 40 days, whereas the Flood was rising to mountain height for five months to reach peak altitude (Genesis 7:24). The seas took longer to recede – over seven months – making the Flood last for over a year in all. The starting date is given as the 17th day of the second month (Genesis

7:11) and the terminal date, over one year later, as the 27th day of the second month (Genesis 8:14).

Evidence of New Sea Levels

After the Flood, there would be a new distribution of sea levels because the equator bulge in sea depth would follow the new equator. This is evidenced by what are called fossil sea beaches throughout the world. Some of these can be accounted for by isostasy – that means the balance of a land mass upon the underlying supporting beds, but the rise would normally be too slow to leave a distinct elevated beach. The majority of fossil beaches are better accounted for by this readjustment of sea levels in relationship to the new equator (see Fig 12.3).

This must have happened relatively suddenly, otherwise there would not be a distinct beach left high and dry. If it had been a slow process of slowly rising land, the seas would have gradually eroded and deposited material down the mountainside and no distinct fossil beach would be left elevated above the new sea level. Sometimes these fossil beaches are just 60 feet above and sometimes hundreds and even thousands of feet above sea level. We shall examine some of these cases later.

How much deeper would the oceans be at the new equator? The seas would be deeper because of the equator bulge by some 12,000 feet and, at the old equator, land which was at sea level before the Flood, would be exposed up to 12,000 feet above the new sea level. Do we find this where the old equator was? We do. We find it in the Andes of South America. It solves the mystery of the former tropical culture of Lake Titicaca.

Q Why should there be a different sea level after the Flood?

Let us suppose that you have a bucket with water in it. You tie rope on to the handle. Then you begin to swing the bucket around your head. The bucket rises higher and higher as you whirl it faster until it is almost horizontal as you swing it around. The water keeps inside the bucket. The force keeping the water in is called centrifugal force.

The earth is turning on its axis at the equator. It is turning at over 1,000 miles per hour, but away from the equator the speed is less until, at the pole, there is no speed. This means that the vast oceans of water which are flung outwards by centrifugal force become deeper at the equator. The sea beaches mark the sea levels there.

Now a new pole or axis of rotation means a new equator and a new equator means that the oceans will become deeper along a line throughout the earth at an angle to the old equator. At the old equator, the original beaches will become stranded high up in the mountains.

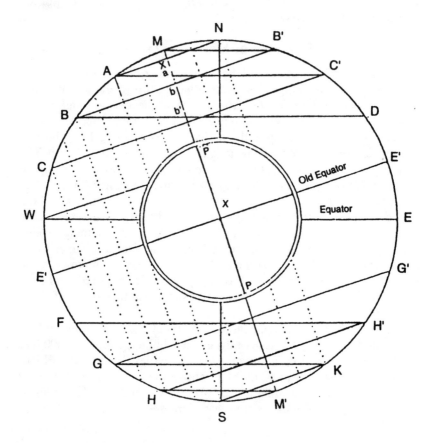

Figure 12.3. Diagram to illustrate the effects of the change of the magnetic axis in causing the submersion of certain lands

Let the large circle represent a section of the earth; the interior small circle a section of the earth's nucleus, in continuance.

NS and WE, the present axis and equator, marking the four points, North, South, West, and East.

M the magnetic north pole, 18½° from N; and MM¹ the former poles and axis of both the earth and nucleus before the deluge.

A, B, and C, points on the earth's surface; A, 18½° distant from M; and B and C at the same distance each from the other, on the same meridian arc.

AN, BB¹, CC¹, equidistant parallels of latitude upon the old axis; MB¹, AC¹, and BD¹, equidistant parallels of latitude on the new axis and post-diluvian globe.

E¹E¹ the old equator, before the deluge.

GG¹, HH¹, and SK parallels of latitude on the old axis; FH¹, GK, and HM¹, parallels of latitude on the new axis and present earth.

X the common centre; P and P the poles of the nucleus.

The dotted lines indicate the original polar parallelism acquired in the deposit of the strata, now changed to oblique.

Sea levels will change all over the world also – up in some places, down in others after the initial surge of water has subsided. So the question is – do we find new sea levels and old sea beaches after the Flood? The answer is yes, dramatically yes! Sea levels have changed throughout the globe.

Also, the old equator is featured by some of the highest mountain ranges of the world because they stand high, as part of the former equatorial land bulge. If one puts a line around the globe at right angles to the magnetic north pole to cross the present equator at latitude 0, this would represent the old equator. You will find that it crosses the Andes at the Bolivia–Peru border at Lake Titicaca. Then it stretches across the Atlantic to Abyssinia and on to the Everest mountains. If this was the original equator, we would expect this bulge like a tyre around the earth to be at these places. As I said, this is because of the action of centrifugal force of the earth's rotation which would deepen the seas and heighten the land mass wherever the original equator happened to be.

THE CHANGES IN GLOBAL FEATURES

The Angle of the Coral Beds

Our next evidence for axis change is that the coral beds through the globe are at an angle to the present equator. The habitat of certain corals is restricted to a certain temperature. It is significant that Dr Duncan discovered coral of the same age and species at Vienna, Bordeaux and Turin which have affinity to species now living in the South Seas, Indian Ocean and Red Sea. This indicates that before the axis change, they lived in a similar temperature and latitude in parallel with the former equator. The latitude now is 18 degrees in the West Indies and 48 degrees in Europe. If one stretches a line between these latitudes from Vienna to Jamaica, it will be seen that it is at an angle to the present equator and therefore shows that the earlier equator was at an angle to the present one and this is further evidence of a change of axis.

The Mountain Range Angle

Our next evidence for an axis change is the angle at which the mountain ranges incline NNW to SSE and also promontories, ridges and gulfs (see Fig 12.4) which are at 90 degrees to the old equator.

To list a few, we see it in the Pennine chain of Great Britain, the peninsulas of Italy and Greece, the Adriatic Sea, the Persian Gulf and the Red Sea and the corresponding Egyptian coastline of Egypt. Also, the general lie of the American continents and particularly the isthmus

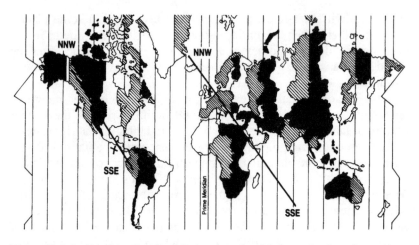

Figure 12.4. Inclination of natural features to the existing axis of earth rotation

(Source unknown)

of Panama, the peninsula of California and the chain of the Rocky Mountains.

Bible Clues

Does the Bible give clues to solve the mysteries? Are there indications in Scripture on what caused the Flood? A significant number of passages support the inference that it was caused by a change of axis.

Psalm 104:6–9 specifically speaks of the Flood and the rush of ocean waters. That the Flood is referred to is evident from verse 9 which refers to the promise of God that the earth will not be invaded by a flood again: 'You have set a boundary that the waters of the deep may not pass over them again; that they turn not again to cover the earth.'

Verse 6 tells us of these waters of the deep ocean: 'The waters came above the mountains. At God's rebuke they fled; at the voice of his thunder they rushed away. They go up the mountains, they go down the valleys into the place God has prepared for them . . . that they shall not cover the earth again.'

Frozen Mammoths

In Siberia, the freezing waters sweeping from the direction of the north pole engulfed mammoths feeding upon fresh grass. Now, being nearer the new pole, they were quickly frozen into solid blocks of ice, the food still in their mouths!

What are the mechanics for creating such chaos? At the old pole, the waters would have had no daily rotation but were at rest as on a pivot, simply turning round once every 24 hours; but their new position, 18 degrees from the pole, had the speed of rotation of the parallel of 71 degrees latitude. At this ,the measure around the earth would be 7,800 miles. This demands a rotational speed in 24 hours of 325 miles an hour. So the waters at rest on the old pole would have to pick up to this new velocity causing a backwards flood until gradual readjustment and levelling occurred.

Contrariwise, the waters which were 18 degrees from the old pole would have to slow down on the polar side of the globe, from that speed of 325 mph to nil. This oscillation of conflicting velocities would send miles-high cascades of water forwards in a south-eastward spiral around the globe to meet the contrary oceans rushing westwards.

Similar chaotic conditions would occur near the old and new equators. In fact, surging flood waters (from the depths of the planet) would move across the land masses around most if not all of the globe.

Different Sun Rise

No wonder another scripture, Job 38, describes the Flood as God's way of shaking the wicked out of the earth. If it were a giant meteor which struck the earth's crust to put the crust off balance into a new axis, this would certainly 'shake the earth'.

This passage accounts for the Flood as occurring when the sun rose in a different place on the horizon. This could result only from a changed axis of rotation. In Job 38:8–14, God describes the seas as bursting out of their beds, until in verse 11, he tells the oceans to return to their place. How did he cause this, he asks Job and then he explains it was by 'making the sun rise in a different place'. What makes the sun rise, he asks, and he explains that the earth is like a Babylonian seal cylinder turning on the clay to leave its imprint. Hundreds of these cylinder seals can be seen in the British Museum. On the rounded cylinder was the incised inscription. A stick was pushed down the hole through the cylinder and this enabled the owner to roll the seal over the clay, thus leaving the impression on the tablet. What makes the sun rise? God says it is because the earth turns like that seal as if on an axis (see Fig 12.5).

What caused the Flood? It was when the sun started to rise in a different place after the earth had turned on its axis. Thus the Bible corrects various theories which have been advanced to account for it.

Ancient Nations give Evidence

Traditions from ancient nations also indicate a change of axis. Such a change would make the sky look different. The dome of stars would appear to revolve around a different centre.

Figure 12.5. Twentieth-century BC example of Babylonian seal cylinder
The Babylonian Priest, 2000 BC, is rolling out a marriage certificate which is a clay tablet to receive the imprint left on it by the cylinder-shaped seal. A spindle is put through the hole in the centre so that the cylinder can revolve. God used this to illustrate to Job how the earth revolves to make the sun rise.

Courtesy: National Geographic Society

In about 470 BC, Anaxagorus recorded in his book of philosophy an old tradition of the appearance of the stars before the Flood: 'The stars were at first seen as if carried round within a vast dome in such a manner that the constant apparent revolution of the sphere was vertical to the earth and that the inclination, which it now has, was received afterwards.' To an observer on earth, a changed axis would make the heavens appear to rotate differently after the Flood.

St Peter gives a similar hint when he says that the heavens as well as the earth were different before the Flood. Here the word heavens refers to the appearance of the sky and the star arrangement. The observer would be surprised to find that after the Flood not a star or planet nor the sun and moon were found to be in their old places.

The world which was before the Flood was inundated by water and perished, but the present sky and earth by the same Word are preserved to be destroyed by fire, being kept for a day of judgment and destruction of impious men, according to 2 Peter 3:6–7.

Such a passage implies God's complete control of geology. In Genesis 9, he says that he will not allow a worldwide flood again, but that the next judgment will be, not by water, but by fire. 'The elements will melt with fervent heat.'

Conclusion: Science Vindicates Noah

Thus we have abundant scientific evidence to show that the Bible is absolutely right to give us the story of Noah's Ark. We also see how many other passages of the Bible shed light on events that are only now being explained scientifically. Again we can say that if scientists would only take the Bible more seriously, they would come to the right conclusions more quickly rather than later having to admit their errors.

In the next two chapters, we shall bring to bear further evidence from around the world and from the ancient tablets of the East.

A WORD OF CAUTION

Before giving you further evidence for the Flood of Noah, I have a word of caution.

There are those who say that the account in Genesis chapters 6 to 9 are two stories put together: One in which the word 'Lord' or Jehovah is used, the other in which the name 'God' or Elohim is used. This theory was formed by agnostics over a hundred years ago before anything was known about the writing methods of the ancient Middle East, a hundred years before archaeology began its report in the 1880s, but because unbelief clings on, this theory is still taught today.

The recent discovery of the Ebla tablets, 2500 BC, shows that both names were used on the same tablet for the one story, just as we use the word Lord and God alternately ourselves. Also Professor K. Kitchen shows that ancient Egyptians also combined more than one name for God in a single account.

By separating the parts in Genesis which have 'Lord' in them from the parts which have 'God', they change a harmonious account into two conflicting accounts; one account which says that the Flood lasted 40 days and another which says the Flood lasted over a year; one which says that only two of each kind of animal entered the ark, the other which says that seven of each entered.

Now the Hebrew word for two means 'pairs' – a male and a female, but of the 'clean' animals seven pairs entered. The clue is in Genesis 7:2.

Concerning the length of the Flood, 40 days was only one period of a number of periods, e.g. in chapter 7, 40 days rain, 150 days of the ocean waters rising to peak, then 40 days test period, followed by several weeks. The starting date and finishing date are also given with over a year between.

This accuracy comes from Noah himself and his sons. At the beginning of the account and at the end it tells you this, because Genesis 6:9

and 10:1 use the word *'Toledoth'*, sometimes translated 'generations' meaning 'record' or an account. It seems that the story in your Bible is Noah's own ship's log marking and dating each dramatic stage. Five progressive dates are given (7:6,11 and 8:4,13,14).

Down through the centuries, the account of the Flood has become corrupted by idolatry and by fantastic stories of quarrels between the gods. It is obvious that the media of those times, as in modern times, did not want to admit that the Flood was punishment for sin. Consequently, we have the Sumerian tablets and Babylonian tablets which say the cause was a quarrel among the gods and goddesses falling on top of each other in shock at the fierce elements. Then came typical media treatment of fantastic romanticisms. Scores of concubines and slaves.

There will be more information in Volume 2 about the critics of the Flood account; it is very sad how their theories have destroyed faith in the accuracy of much of God's Word, but this note will be sufficient at the moment to alert you!

S U M M A R Y

NOAH'S FLOOD

Flood caused by a change of axis
- Paleomagnetism of rocks proves it (alignment of magnetic particles in rock sediment).
- Magnetic poles caused by independent inner core and outer shell revolution.
- Outer crust geographical pole once aligned with the core.
- Sudden realignment caused huge surge of sea water sufficient to cover the land for many weeks.

Effect of change of axis would be a worldwide flood.
- Water stationary on old poles would have to speed up to 300 m.p.h.
- Oceans at old equator would swirl at an angle to new equator.
- Oceans are three times as deep as mountains.
- Oceans cover over twice as much of globe as land.
- Oceans would swirl out of the deep as in:
  - 'Fountains of the great deep burst out' (Gen 7:7).
  - 'The waters (from the deep) stood above the mountains . . .
  - They may not again cover the earth' (Ps 104:6–9).
- Sun rose in new place 'to shake the wicked out of the earth' (Job 38:12–15).
- Flood from around continents (2 Peter 3:5,6).
- 'Swept them all away' (Matt 24:39).
- God tells Job the earth is like a cylinder seal which turns on a spindle.

Evidence of axis change
- New sea levels throughout world. Fossil beaches high above present sea levels.
- Oceans were higher at old equator – centrifugal bulge. Fossil beach through Andes is 12,000 ft high.
- Coral beds at an angle confirming old axial alignment. Mountain ranges at an angle, too.
- Paleomagnetism indicates big change of magnetic poles in 'recent' human history.
- Nations testify to Flood and different pole star, i.e. Anaxagorus and St Peter (2 Pet 3:6, 7).

13 WORLDWIDE EVIDENCE OF THE FLOOD
SCIENTIFIC FACTS AGREE ON AN AXIS CHANGE

Now consider the evidence of fossil deposits. In the last century it was thought, mistakenly, that fossil sea shells on mountain tops, such as the Alps, were evidence of the Flood, even fossil shells on Mount Everest. Amateurs, untrained in geology still think this, but geology has since shown that they are the result of mountain building from an ocean trough. This is called a syncline. Into this ocean trough, the sea creatures dropped as they died and layer by layer built up under pressure into rock. Then two continental blocks of tectonic plates would push against each other and the sea trough would be squeezed as in a vice and push up into a mountain.

Some of these are the latest mountains to be found and are called the new fold mountains. They run through Southern Europe, through the Himalayas and around the Pacific Ocean. The fossil marine shells in them would have been laid down long ago when they were a sea bed around Jurassic times, if geological calculations are correct, then pushed up to become a mountain peak. In contrast, however, there are many other bone remains on mountains and in caves of more recent deposition. They appear to have been deposited there long after the mountain-building process just mentioned. In fact at the time of the Flood. Only the tremendous volume of water rushing up mountains as the result of an axis change could have carried them there.

Mystery of the Mammoths

The torrential volumes of ocean rushing over the heights would sweep along those huge whales, mammoths, rhinoceroses, hippopotamuses, all to be dashed into pieces. Fragments of teeth and fractured jaws and bits of skull of both animals and man mixed up with the teeth of a lion or hyena have been found embedded in the hard breccia of caves. Here would be a massive elephant's tusk and there would be bits of horns and bones of dismembered beasts.

These all help us to imagine the tremendous sudden nature of the worldwide catastrophe and the great force and violence of the invasion of the continents. Near the new pole, great mammoths would be engulfed in freezing seas and quickly frozen solid in blocks of ice.

Scores of these have been found when the melting ice in Siberia has disgorged remains, including a whole woolly elephant thousands of years old preserved fresh in the ice when it was suddenly overtaken by the freezing sea, with the grass it was eating still green in its mouth (see Fig 13.1). An Oxford anthropologist told me he had attended a mammoth-steak dinner made from these deep frozen mammoths. He said the meat was delicious!

Usually, as the block of ice melts, the trunk protrudes first and the

Figure 13.1. Mammoth from Beresovka, Siberia Note the attitude of the beast, as though endeavouring to extricate itself.

wolves would chew off the end, so it was a long time before one was found with a complete trunk, intact at the end It revealed that the cave-man's drawings of these mammoths were accurate in depicting a very much larger end to the trunk than in modern elephants.

The remarkable ice-caves of Oregon could have resulted from the swirling freezing waters from the old pole.

The phenomenon of animals escaping to higher ground is dramatically demonstrated in the New World also. Near Bogota, in Colombia, at 3,500 metres (about) above sea level, there is a broad plain covered with the bones of mastodons, the woolly elephant. It is called the 'Field of Giants'. All the evidence points to these mammoths being suddenly overtaken by a catastrophe.

About a thousand mammoths were found at the New Stone Age site of Predmost in Moravia. They were so numerous that their massive shoulder blades had been used to build tombs.

PRE-FLOOD ANIMALS IN NORTH AMERICA

Even more significant is the presence of whale skeletons in the midst of a continent. In Alabama, USA, the bones of the whale Zengledon were scattered over the fields on top of the ground in such numbers that they were a nuisance to the farmers so they were piled up at the sides of the fields to make fences. This could not be attributed to the Ice Age as glaciation did not reach to such latitudes at that time. In any case, slow-moving glaciers do not carry whales on to a continent! In Michigan, skeletons of whales have been found in post-glacial deposits and, on one of my visits to North America, the bones of whales were frequently being unearthed from recent deposits.

Mammoth bones uncovered at a construction site in West Richland are one of the best archaeological finds ever discovered in Mid-Colombia, researchers say (Fig 13.2)

The head of a University of Washington archaeology team was brought in to examine and excavate the huge bones. 'We can't say for sure how old they are until we get them back to the laboratory,' he said. 'This is one of the best finds we have had. The thing is very well preserved. I'm guessing it is a mammoth.' He called the site 'very productive'. 'The neat thing about this site is, besides the mammoth, we are finding rodents, frogs, birds, rabbits and other small mammals, all close together. Often a find is spread out all over.'

He said the area on Ironton Drive one mile from downtown West Richland, was once a flood plain of the Yakima or Columbia River. 'There is some reason that we are finding all these bones together,' he said. 'Somehow this area became a death trap for all of them, probably due to a flood.'

In America, huge mammoths perished and horses, lions, tigers and other wild beasts and even camels have drowned right across the continent. The waters retreated and the bones were covered in mud and debris. Never again did many of those animals return until thousands of years later when they were reintroduced by immigrants in the 17th century.

The disturbance caused volcanoes to erupt along the west coast. Mount Masmara sent out white ash for hundreds of miles around to cover the devastation and leave a useful time-marking layer for archaeologists. Human beings in these areas suffered similar fates. In other areas in the world where the waters were less violent, men of the Copper Stone Age clambered up trees to escape the rising waters or climbed up mountains, but were soon overcome.

Such an area would be the Turkish plateaux, 4,000 feet high and the rim of surrounding mountains. These mountains rose to 12,000 feet and 17,000 feet in the case of Mount Ararat. While great torrents of oceans would be sweeping around the world, the seas would flood into the Middle East more steadily to fill up the Mesopotamian plain and then rise to cover the high plateaux lands of Iran and Turkey and after five months to rise more gradually even above Mount Ararat.

Impelled by the angle of the new equator, the oceans of the south-

Regional Voice of the Mid-Columbia Empire   COPY 15¢

VOL. 70, NO. 36   Wednesday, February 8, 1978   Pasco, Kennewick, Richland, Washington

West Richland archaeologic

By BOB WYNNE
Herald Staff Writer

Mammal bones uncovered at a construction site in West Richland this week are one of the best archaeological finds ever discovered in Mid-Columbia, researchers say.

Martin, head of a University of Washington archaeology team brought in to examine and excavate the huge bones.

"We can't say for sure how old they are until we get them back to the laboratory," Martin said. "This is one of the best finds we've had. The thing is very well preserved. I'm guessing it's a mammoth."

Martin called the site "very productive."

"The neat thing about this site is besides the mammoth, we're finding rodents, frogs, birds, rabbits and other small mammals, all close together," Martin said. "Often a find is spread out all over."

He said the area on Ironton Drive one mile from downtown West Richland was once a flood plain of the Yakima or Columbia River.

"There is some reason why we are finding all these bones together," Martin said. "Somehow this area became a death trap for all of them, probably due to a flood."

Today's News Today

Tony Barnosky, a University of Washington researcher, painstakingly scraped dirt from the remains of a mammoth

Martin said the researchers have found no evidence of human life at the site so far. The large mammal skull was expected to be removed from

clay-like soil 10 feet below the surface this afternoon.

Once all the area has been excavated, the bones will be taken to the University of

Figure 13.2. Newspaper record of mass grave of mammoths and other creatures

ern hemisphere would be spiralling northwards, adding their volume to the oceans of the northern hemisphere. Such a volume of displacement would need the last seven months of the year for the seas to return to their new levels all around the world. They would leave old sea beaches at higher or lower levels to mark the former shores and the original sea caves.

Worldwide Disappearance of Life

I will now bring evidence from digs in the western states of the USA. I am indebted to the assistance I received from the Universities of Washington State, Oregon and Idaho.

My first clue that the Flood had affected America was when Dr David Cole of the University of Oregon showed me the stratigraphy of Wildcat Canyon archaeological site. These layers of culture showed that at about the same time as the Flood in the Middle East, all life had been wiped out in North America. This was about 5000 BC according to present dating. Then there was a long time gap of 3,000 years before life reappeared.

The significant feature was that, before what I believe was the Flood, the bones of the modern type of horse were there and all the Old World animals such as elephants, camels, lions and tigers.

When the first Europeans reached America in the 17th century, none of these animals inhabited America. The Spaniards re-introduced the horse to America and the inhabitants were terrified when they first saw them.

When Cortez and his steel-armoured soldiers arrived at the shores of America and rode their horses, which they had brought from Europe up to the fortress, the ruler and his retinue thought that the gods had come to their country. They had never seen a horse.

It has not occurred to the anthropologists to account for this disjunction by the universal Flood. They thought that the cause was the volcanic eruption of Mount Masmara which laid down the white volcanic ash, but soon it became evident that this gap was a widespread feature throughout the north-west and the Great Basin. It seems that the volcanic eruption was one of the minor features caused by continental readjustment to the axial centre.

Dr David Cole reported that he was curious about that 3,000-year blank in history and thought that an answer might be found in the materials taken from the 'Dirty Shame' site that remained to be analysed.

'Dirty Shame' Site Examined

When the 'Dirty Shame' site was further examined, the report was that it showed a similar hiatus when life had disappeared about 4,000 years BC and a changed selection of animals did not reappear until about 1000 BC (Fig 13.3).

Dr Stephen Bedwell comments in *Oregon University Notes* (1975), upon the finds of Haynes. 'Examination of all these areas reveals a hiatus of 1,300 years between 5100 BC and 3000 BC in the radio-active record, a hiatus which is real.'

It was at this time that North America became hotter in the altithermal climate. My comment is that, for North America, the new pole would be farther away and the equator would be nearer. This would cause a hotter environment and again it supports the axis change theory. Haynes adds that this climate change applied to all the areas of the south-west, Utah, Colorado, and Wyoming.

Fort Rock, Oregon

At Fort Rock, to the south of Oregon, Professor Richard D. Dougherty and others found the same hiatus and underneath it there were found the bones of the mammoth, camel, bison, deer and horse.

One could go on quoting reports which give the same picture from other sites, for example, a cave at Absaroka Mountains near Yellowstone Park Rock Mountains; also at the Paisley Caves, Comley Hills cave, Table Rock cave and Cougar Mountain cave, adjacent to the foothills of the Cascade Range. All these details feature in my archaeological notebook.

In a personal talk with Dr C. Melvin Aikens (Acting Head of Department of Anthropology, Oregon), he said that there was a general change of environment right across America after 5000 BC.

From what part of the world did the new inhabitants come after the Flood? Evidence that the re-occupation came via Asia to America was that the pottery brought by man was rather Japanese in style. In fact, he said some anthropologists think that they could have been brought by boat, borne along by the strong Black Current, as it is called.

I had a talk with Dr Randle Brown who spoke of the Horse Heaven Hills, Washington State, where I also had an archaeological excavation, but the disappearance of the horses and mammoths and bisons, he thought, was due to a food shortage factor.

So, in general, the fact of the hiatus was very evident, but anthropologists accounted for it by various causes. It never occurred to them that the universal Flood was the cause of this, because they had not linked it with Middle East archaeology.

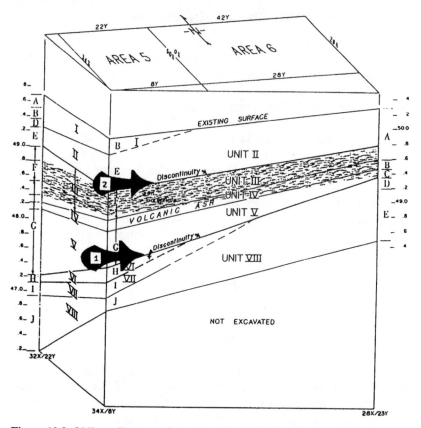

Figure 13.3. Oblique diagram of stratigraphy at Wildcat Canyon Site
35 GM 9, Areas 5 and 6 assessed by Dr David L. Cole and L R. Kittleman, Oregon University, USA.
I have reproduced the oblique diagram of Wildcat cane stratigraphy from the archaeological report. The thick line H to D records a break in time. The strata H to D had already been laid down and then eroded down to its present level by forces operating at a different horizon. When these forces had worn down the strata underneath, new sediments were brought by water and laid on top until a new discontinuity followed at E-A. The pre-Flood animals would appear below H-D. Life did not reappear between the two discontinuities at H and E, but an entirely different fauna appeared above E and A. The hiatus GF represents 2,000–3,000 years before life reappeared, but did not contain all the Old World animals which were there before the Flood.

Source: Oregon University

THE MYSTERIES OF SOUTH AMERICA

The changed equators solve the mysteries of the Andes and of Lake Titicaca. First is the mystery of an ancient city called Tiahuanaco. Although it is now in icy latitudes of 12,000 feet, it was built for a hot tropical climate. The surrounding remains of animals and agriculture were also those of a hot climate.

The second mystery is that Tiahuanaco was a harbour city with docks and quays built for ocean-going vessels, but which are now elevated 12,000 feet up above the sea (Fig 13.4).

The third mystery is that Lake Titicaca is filled with salt seawater. The surrounding catchment area could not supply it with salt water; indeed, the rainfall is unable to maintain its present level and the lake level has been decreasing from a former level of 12,900 feet to 12,031 feet and shrinking from 460 miles long into three lakes of 120 miles, 60 miles and 20 miles long, respectively.

The fourth mystery is that the fossil sea beach or 'strandline' stretches from Lake Titicaca for thousands of miles through the Andes. It does this with its peak at the lake at 12,900 feet and declines in a downward curve north and south until it reaches the present sea level hundreds of miles in each direction.

The fifth mystery is that the city of Tiahuanaco was built of huge monolithic blocks of stone which could have been transported from its quarries 30 miles away only by sea.

The sixth mystery is that this city is prehistoric and was suddenly overwhelmed by flood and prehistoric workings were covered by glacier ice until quite recently. Also, it appears that ships were suddenly wrecked, tools thrown down and broken bones of men, animals, pottery and beads were washed away together into a breccia (crushed fragments).

Tiahuanaco of the Andes

These mysteries show that the old equator passed through the Andes at this latitude, when the equatorial sea bulge made the ocean deeper by 12,000 feet.

The indications are that the climate was tropical when the city was built. The buildings of the city of Tiahuanaco were of great size and open to the sky in such a way as was out of keeping with the raw cold climate of the present altitude, but was typical of tropical climates. In size, they were comparable to the great amphitheatres of ancient Greece and Rome and were planned for thousands who would meet for sport, religion and politics.

For example, the sanctuary of the Sun Temple is equal to the area of Trafalgar Square in London; the Palace of the Sarcophagi was about the size of Waverley Square; Bloemfontein and the fortress of Akapana were about the area of the vast area of the Tower of London inside the moat. These splendid erections were made of monolithic building blocks of green-grey volcanic rock called Andesite. These were transported from across the valley 30 miles away. This was hardly possible unless there was a water route in between the sites for naval transport. Consider the size of these blocks. Some weighed up to 65 tons each.

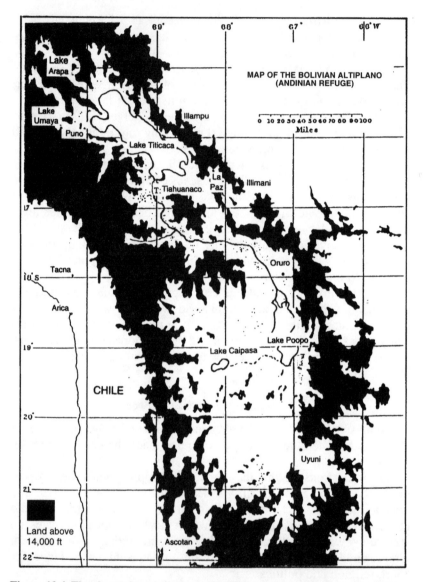

Figure 13.4. The elevated parts in the Andes The map above shows the present lakes in the Bolivian Altiplano: Titicaca and Poopo, connected by the Desaguadero, as well as marshy Coipasa which is seasonally replenished with water through the Lacahahuira. This state is practically the same as the Stage of the Lowest Level. The white space inside (and, of course, outside) the 14,000-foot mountain barrier, shown in black, is practically equal to the Stage of the Highest Level, when the waters inside the Altiplano were in connection with the girdle-tide. In between these two levels there was the Inter-Andean Sea of the intermediate level on whose shore Tiahuanaco was situated.   *Source: Stanford's Geographical Establishment*

Even the doorways were made of one block, not of three blocks such as two uprights and a lintel (see Fig 13.5), but one complete monolith cut from the rock. These doorway blocks measure nearly three metres long by two metres high by nearly one metre wide and weighed over eight tons. Designs on them were chiselled into the hard Andesite stone and grooves and tongues were also chiselled. The massive Calendar Gate, according to Bellamy, was even bigger. The single block was four metres long by three metres high and sculptured with elaborate symbols.

Those symbols also testify to a tropical climate. They consisted of stylised sculptured heads of men and animals, the latter being typical tropical species. There were flying fish, certain species of crustaceans, brachiopods and mussels. A frequent ornament was the fish-heads which indicates that the sea at this level must have teemed with tropical life. Moreover, in the area were the remains of giant turtles and other warmth-loving creatures. It was all such a contrast with the present snow-level environment of barren terrain.

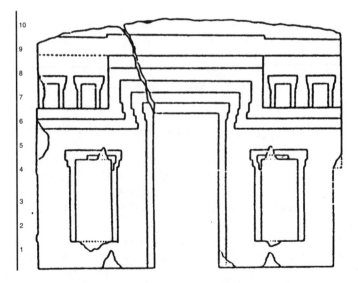

Figure 13.5 Elevation of the back of the monolithic gate
The two big shallow niches must have been closed by massive 'doors' or shutters of some sort, as is proved by the damage caused by the wrenching out of the pins or pivots on which they swung. The damage at the base of the gate was caused by the monolith being wrenched off the pins or cramps with which it was fastened to its foundation. Scale in feet.

Courtesy: H. S. Bellamy 'Before the Flood' Faber

Extensive Agriculture and a Sea Port

Under a layer of volcanic ash there was discovered the charred remains of a rich vegetation. In fact, ancient agricultural terraces rose up into the snows above Tiahuanaco from 13,000 feet to 18,000 feet. These extensive terraces upon which little now grows, would originally have grown food for the many thousands of citizens and would start only a little above sea level.

It was a means of using all available fertile land when much of the present continent was below water. Similar ancient terraces are seen in the highest parts of Abyssinia. These stepped terraces appear sculptured on the temple walls of Tiahuanaco as step motifs and symbolised the divine source of food and life.

When the Pacific Ocean was deeper and lapping the Bolivian Plateau, from Lake Titicaca southwards, it would feature as a sheltered tidal inlet protected by a peninsula. This would be similar to the Gulf of California, protected by the Californian peninsula and Tiahuanaco would be an entrepôt. The rectangular depressions near the ruins of the city were the docks and harbour basins with a canal connecting the city.

The strandline, which is now the fossil beach, declines in a slow curve at the rate of 1.4 metres per kilometre at first, then it decreases to 50 centimetres per kilometre further afield. This is what would be expected because the higher oceans around the belt of the old equator would decline in a curve to the present sea level hundreds of kilometres farther south in Patagonia.

CHANGES IN CLIMATE AND CALENDAR

We have examined the ancient records of old nations which inform us that it was a change of axis which caused the Flood and we have noted that the oldest documentary information about this is given in the Bible. We also have there an interesting remark about the changing seasons.

One of the effects of a change of axis would be a greater contrast of the seasons. The earth would now be tilted in its orbit around the sun. This would bring summer to a wider band of latitudes of the earth alternately – the Tropic of Cancer marking full summer heat in the northern hemisphere when the sun would appear to be directly overhead and the Tropic of Capricorn in the southern hemisphere. It is therefore significant that, after the Flood, the pronounced difference of winter and summer is mentioned in Genesis 9, when God promises that the seasons will not cease and that he will not destroy the world by flood again.

Before this climatic change, various parts of the globe would have either a permanent summer or permanent winter. There would be little seasonal change and so some latitudes would build up heat all the year round continuously. In contrast, ice and glaciers would build up and encroach in the higher latitudes.

Axis Change Adds more Days to the Year

Another change could well be the addition of more days to the year after the Flood. If the change of axis was caused by a cosmic collision, that same impact would not only shake the earth's crust, it could increase the speed of revolution if it struck the earth in the direction of revolution. A similar suggestion has been made recently by a scientist to explain why the axis of the planet Uranus has changed in contrast to other planets and why its moons have been affected.

However, Dr Martin Bott gives another source of variation of the earth's speed. He speaks about recorded changes in the speed of the earth's rate of rotation when it has increased and also decreased. He says:

> Of all the possible explanations of these irregular fluctuations in the length of day, the only adequate one is that angular momentum is periodically exchanged between the core and the mantle. If the crust and mantle speed up, then the core must slow down so as to maintain constancy of angular momentum, and vice versa. The only feasible known mechanism for the transfer of the angular momentum is electromagnetic coupling between the outermost core and the mantle. This theory seems to be able to explain both the changes in length of day and the westward drift.

It will be remembered that the angular momentum was caused by the outer crust changing its axis to rotate in a direction at an angle to the core.

Now there is universal data to show that the earth's surface speeded up after the Flood so that 360 days in the year before the Flood became 365 and a quarter after it. The crust managed to turn five and a quarter more times in the year than formerly.

Post-Flood Mathematicians

Our first evidence comes from archaeological discovery in the Middle East of the remarkable mathematical culture of the Sumerians. They lived soon after the Flood about 4000 BC. It is from them that we still divide up our circle into 360 degrees and it is the reason that there are 360 degrees on our compasses. It is also from the Sumerians, all that time ago, that we have our hours divided into 60 minutes and our minutes into 60 seconds. This is because, as all mathematicians know, they added up in columns of 60. They were the first to make mathematics possible by giving place value to columns of figures.

Now why did the Sumerians divide the circle into 360? It seems that it was because the earth encircled the sun in 360 days. In fact, all the ancient nations which are descended from this time continued for some time to use a year of 360 days and reluctantly came to add another five and a quarter days at the end. Man's adjustment to change is usually very conservative!

Noah's Calendar

The interesting thing is that when we turn to Noah's account of the Flood in Genesis 7, we find that his years consist of 360 days and all his 12 months consist of an equal 30 days, so that 12 × 30 equalled 360. Thus, when we are told that the Flood waters took 150 days to rise to their full height of over 17,000 feet, we are shown that this equalled five months: 5 × 30 = 150.

Now we look at those nations which migrated after the Flood to see if they have supporting information.

Archaeology has shown that the migration of civilisation after the Flood was from Mesopotamia to the Indus Valley to the east and to Egypt in the south-west. So, although they do not have exact written records as old as the Bible, we would expect some information from their ancient traditions. Do we have such information? Yes, we do.

Calendars throughout the World

In Thibant's *Astronomie*, we find that the Hindu year consists of 360 days which are divided into 12 months of 30 days each.

Also, the Brahmin texts from the Veda, speak of a year of 360 days. F. K. Ginzel, in his *Chronologie*, is surprised that it took so long for the Hindus to readjust to the longer year and thinks that it was because the Hindus were pledged to the tradition of the 360-day Savana year which appears in the ancient Veda literature. In the *Aryabhatiya*, an ancient Indian work, there is a chapter on the reckoning of time. In it we are not surprised to find that the Sumerian measurements in 60s are applied to the day which is divided up into 60 and each of these 'nadi' as they are called, is divided into another 60 'vinadikas'. We are not surprised, therefore, to find that they also observed the same 360-day year. Not until later did the Hindu year have the five and a quarter days added.

Beyond India, the Chinese also had a year of 360 days of 12 months of 30 days long. This is recorded in W. D. Medhurst's translation of *The Shoo King*. Eventually, the Chinese added five and a quarter days as a separate period which they called Khe-ying and to show the connection of the degrees in a circle, they began to divide it up into 365 and a quarter degrees! They also used the Sumerian coefficient of 60.

They even retained their 'moons' of 30 days each even though now the lunar months had become shorter.

On then, even farther east to America. What do we find there? We find that the Incas of Peru and the Mayas of Yucan had the calendar of 360 days.

Now let us trace the migration from Ararat south-eastwards to Persia. Did the ancient Persian year show the same features? It did, but later, a period called the Gatha days, five in number, were added to the calendar. The old Babylonian year of their cuneiform script used a 360-day year also and later Ctesias wrote about the measurement of the walls of Babylon. 'They were 360 furlongs in compass,' he said, 'as many as there had been days in the year.'

For the Greeks, the story is the same. Herodotus wrote his classic work and referred to the same traditional calendar reckoning. As for the Romans, Plutarch gave similar information.

Now down into Egypt and we find that at the time when Joseph of Genesis chapter 37 was Prime Minister in Egypt in the days of the Hyksos pharaohs, the calendar was divided into 360 days. Later dynasties always used such terms as 'The year and five days' and the year was always considered to have ended on the 360th day for celebrations. The five days were an extra period. Herodotus says, 'The Egyptians reckon 30 days to each month and add five days in every year over and above the number.' So tradition dies hard, but it gives valuable support to our claim that originally, before the change of axis, the year was 360 days long.

Conclusive Evidence

Thus there is a mass of evidence that the Flood was caused by a change in the earth's axis. Paleomagnetism supports it, the nature of the earth's core supports it, the former line of equatorial land and sea bulges bear testimony and the traditions of the ancient peoples add their support.

Credible evidence also exists of a related change of speed of rotation, affecting the number of solar days in the year and the number of lunar days in the month.

We can therefore safely conclude that the Bible's account of Noah's Flood, together with all the circumstantial details it gives, has the full weight of scientific evidence in its favour.

SUMMARY

WORLDWIDE EVIDENCE OF THE FLOOD

1. Skeletal
* Animal bones on mountain tops. Not syncline fossils.
* Mammoths of Siberia frozen whole in ice blocks.
* Mammoth bones frequently uncovered in USA.
* Whales in Alabama (mid-continent) bones used for fences.
* Pre-Flood animals under stratum in USA (horses, lions, etc.) but not above

2. USA sites with Flood disjunction
* Wildcat Cave (Dr D. Cole).
* 'Dirty Shame' site.
* Fort Rock, Oregon.
* Lake Titicaca in Andes: equatorial agricultural ridges now frozen at 12,000 feet above today's sea level.

3. Calendar changes after Flood
* Greater angle made bigger seasonal contrasts (Gen 8:22).
* Only 360 days in year before Flood. Dr M. Bott's reason.
* Reason for 360 degrees in circle and compass.

Ancient Calendars had 360 days and 12 months of 30, e.g.:
Noah's Calendar. 5 mths = 150 days to flood peak (Gen 7:11; 8:3, 4).
Hindu Calendar. 360 with 12 × 30 (Thibant's *Astronomie*).
Chinese Calendar. 360 with 12 × 30 (as per Medhurst).
Greek Calendar. The same (as per Heroditus).
Babylon cuneiform script had 360. Same for Romans (Plutarch) and Incas of Peru and Mayas, Persia and Egypt (total 10 nations).
Proves major planetary disturbance.

4. Main source of water
* From oceans or under earth's shell: 'great deep' (Gen 7:11).
* Rushed over mountains (Ps 104:6–9).
* By axis change (Job 38:11–14).
* From water in which continents stood (2 Pet 3:5–7).

14 UNRAVELLING THE ANCIENT RECORDS
TABLETS AND CULTURAL CLUES GIVE EVIDENCE

Guess where this next story is from! Here we have the fantastic Babylonian version of the Great Flood.

A terrible quarrel broke out among the gods. Some wanted to wipe out the whole of mankind; others argued against it. They were led by the goddess Ea. After fierce argument, it was decided to annihilate the human race by a gigantic flood. The flood was then worked up into a fury by the gods who controlled the wind, the water, the clouds, the canals, the deep oceans and the god of lightning. Each god worked up the fury of his element to the highest pitch. The resultant fury was so great that all the gods were thrown together in a heap.

When the flood was at its height, the god Enlil arrived from on high and burst into anger when he saw a great ship floating on the waters with survivors. The survivors were Uta-napishtim who had taken on board 70 concubines. 'No one was intended to survive!' he shouted. The other gods blamed the goddess Ea. She warned Uta-napishtim to build a boat.

At the end of the flood, Uta-napishtim made sacrificial offerings and the supreme goddess, Ishtar, descended to stop the angry Enlil approaching the offering, because he intended to destroy her people by the flood.

Such is the fantastic Babylonian story of the Great Flood.

THE FLOOD BEYOND DOUBT

In the Near East, archaeologists have unearthed tablets of various ancient peoples which give a very full account of the Flood. They come from the Sumerians of south Mesopotamia, a culture which came into being soon after the Flood. There are tablets also from the migrant Eblaite Society in Syria and also from the Babylonians who were much later, c. 1900 BC. The biblical account also appears to be based on tablets and, apparently, as we shall see, older than any of the others (see Fig 14.1). In addition, there are Hindu, Persian, Chinese, Japanese and Tibetan records of the same event.

As André Parrot, the famous French archaeologist, points out, it is difficult to doubt that such detailed and persistent records have a factual basis. 'There can be no question that the Flood marked a clear break in history,' he writes. 'The memory of it remained vividly in

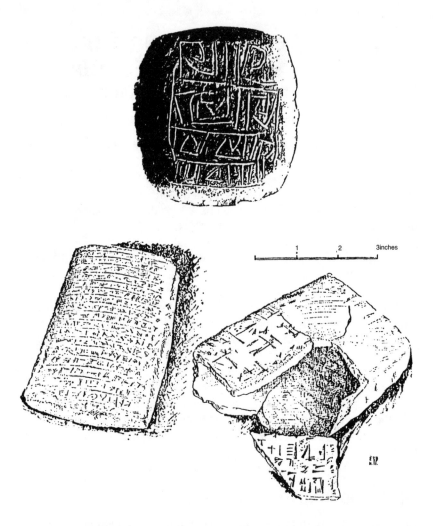

Figure 14.1. Record-keeping over 5,000 years ago Clay tablet recording legal proceedings, with its clay envelope upon which is summarised the contents. The Toledoths of Genesis may have had a similar source. Baked clay envelopes were made soon after 3000 BC. This outer envelope, protecting and identifying the enclosure, was usually limited to an excerpt.

men's minds as well in Mesopotamia as in Palestine.' And again, 'The cataclysm was accompanied by destruction on such a scale and made such an impression that it became one of the themes of cuneiform literature.'

It is significant that the further away from the dispersal point, the more primitive ethnic stories are to be found and the vaguer they become in detail. This we would expect as the descendants of Noah migrated to the four points of the compass. However, most of these stories have reference to a boat and that there was a refuge centre. We learn from the Bible and from many ancient tablets in the Near East that the refuge centre was artificially provided by the building of a huge boat called the 'ark'.

The Sumerian tablet WB62 consists of eighteen lines and gives the names of the ten kings who reigned before the Flood. An interesting factor is the great length of life credited to these individuals, as it is in the Bible.

It is strange that at Hacilar, Turkey, which is a pre-Flood site and at Al Ubaid, which is immediately post-Flood, there are skulls in which the teeth are worn right down to the gums. It seems hardly possible that a grain diet could explain such rapid wear, as the teeth are hard and undecayed. Longevity may well be the cause.

Among the names on the tablet are included individuals known from other tablets. The names of the five pre-Flood cities are also given.

Tablet WB444 then takes up the story. As is common in such tablets, there is a recapitulatory note to link up the preceding tablet with the sequel (Fig 14.1). It mentions the name of the last king and that there were eight others and names the five pre-Flood cities. Then appear the words: 'The Flood came up. After the Flood had come up, kingship descended from heaven. The kingship was at Kish.' A list of post-Flood cities and kings follows.

The words 'The Flood came up' correlate with the expression in Genesis 7. 'The fountains of the great deep were broken up.' It confirms that the greater volume of water came up from the oceans, rather than as rain coming down from the clouds. The rain was probably due to the atmospheric disturbances accompanying the cataclysm.

These post-Flood cities are in south Mesopotamia and accord with the biblical statement that, a considerable time after the Flood, the descendants of Noah moved from the East, from the mountain plateau of Iran, to settle on the mud-flats of Mesopotamia. This means that the dispersion must have first migrated slowly along the plateau heights south-eastwards from Armenia. There is evidence of grapevine-growing starting in Iran at this time, as reflected in Genesis 9:20. 'Noah the farmer was the first man to plant a vineyard. He drank some of the wine and became drunk.' Elam, the son of Shem (Noah's son), gives his name to that part of Iran (Genesis 10:22).

At Susa, the capital of Elam (Iran), traces of a cuneiform script on the oldest bricks was found to be in Semitic language (i.e. the language of Shem, Noah's son).

The Ubaidian settlement of the marshes immediately after the Flood, is regarded as an important phase in Near Eastern archaeology.

Later, the population increased and city states were founded as mentioned in Genesis and on the Flood tablets.

The cities mentioned in Genesis 10:10 are in south Iraq (Mesopotamia) and have been correlated with archaeology as follows:

Bible	Tablets
Shinar	Sumer of the Sumerians
Erech	Uruk or Warka, whose king was Gilgamesh of the Gilgamesh epic.
Babel	Babylon
Calneh	Nippur

Accad gives its name to the Akkadian empire and language.

From south Mesopotamia, one of the kings went to the north to rebuild the pre-Flood Nineveh. This is where excavation reveals a hiatus break in culture followed by a stratum of Ubaidian culture.

The Akkadian Tablets

The Babylonian account of the Flood is recorded in various tablets found in a number of the old city-states of Mesopotamia. They should be referred to as the Akkadian accounts. They vary in their versions, indicating that, as regards the Akkadian accounts, the Flood stories were told and re-told in their localities long before being recorded on the Babylonian tablets.

It is evident that, relative to the original story, these tablets contain many deviations, accretions and omissions, whilst a number of the historical personalities have become gods in the conception of their narrators. Thus Nimrod of Genesis 10:8–12, who features upon the hunter-palette (Fig 16.4) has become Ni-mur-rud, the god to whom the Lagash temple is dedicated. He is also featured upon a mace-head.

In all the tablets, the majestic monotheism of the Genesis tablets has become grossly polytheistic. In anthropology, we see that monotheism is the more primitive conception, the supply of more and more intermediary gods or spirits between the High God and human beings being a later development. Even in Christianity, this trend of human nature to add intermediaries, is seen in the addition of more and more saints and angels who are credited with controlling the various departments of natural phenomena.

Let us take, for example, the Akkadian tablets dated 2000 BC. The highly poetic description and romancing is typical of literary development rather than of an original account. There is a graphic description of the storm which is brought about by agency of the gods of wind, water, clouds, canals, the deep and of lightning. According to these tablets, as we see at the opening of this chapter, the bringing of the deluge was an outcome of much quarrelling among the gods. Some opposed it, others wished it to wipe out mankind and the god Enlil was particularly angry that the goddess Ea had warned Uta-napishtim (Noah) to build a ship in order to escape. It continues:

> As soon as Enlil arrived from on high, he saw the ship and was wrath. The god Enlil was filled with fury against the gods. 'Who then has escaped when no man was to live through the destruction?' Nimerth opened his mouth and spoke. He said to warlike Enlil, 'Who but the god Ea can imagine such schemes?' When the supreme goddess, Ishtar, arrived from on high, she forbade Enlil to approach the sacrificial offering made by Uta-napishtim (Noah) when the Flood was ended. 'Let the gods approach the offering, but let not Enlil approach the offering because he did not consider, and brought on the deluge, because he consigned my people to destruction!'

GENESIS: THE ORIGINAL VERSION

There is, in all these accounts, little conception of God's grief at the sin of mankind as in Genesis 6:5–14. These are the type of details which would be unpopular and get left out of later secular accounts.

> The Lord saw that the wickedness of man was great in the earth and that every imagination of the thoughts of his heart was only evil continually. And the Lord was sorry that he had made man on the earth and it grieved him to his heart. So the Lord said, 'I will blot out man whom I have created from the face of the ground, man and beast and creeping things and birds of the air, for I am sorry that I have made them.' But Noah found favour in the eyes of the Lord. Noah was a righteous man, blameless in his generation; Noah walked with God. And Noah had three sons, Shem, Ham and Japheth. Now the earth was corrupt in God's sight and the earth was filled with violence. And God saw the earth, and behold it was corrupt; for all flesh had corrupted their way upon the earth. And God said to Noah, 'I have determined to make an end of all flesh; for the earth is filled with violence through them; behold, I will destroy them with the earth. Make yourself an ark of gopher wood; make rooms in the ark and cover it inside and out with pitch.' (Genesis 6:5–14).

The deluge, according to the Akkadian tablet, was so terrible that even the gods trembled and sought refuge. They crowded in a heap like a dog in his kennel and the gods and goddess wept for pity: 'The gods were afraid at the deluge and they fled. They ascended the heaven of Anu. The gods cower like dogs and lie down in the open. The goddess Ishtar cries out like a woman in travail . . . The Anunnaki-gods weep with her, the gods howl, they sit down in tears.'

Mythology versus Reality

The description of details such as the shape of the ark is more mythological in the Akkadian account than in Genesis. In the Akkadian epic, the ark is cube-shaped, 200 × 200 × 200 feet (using 20.6 inches = 1 cubit) and is divided into seven storeys. Food in the form of bran in the morning and wheat in the evening was rained down from heaven and was brought into the ship with beer and wine. Slaves and concubines were also brought on board.

The dimensions of the ark given in Genesis 6:15 are more realistic – 500 × 85 × 50 feet (150 × 25 × 15 m). These figures have a similar ratio of length to breadth of the most seaworthy vessels in the 19th century when large liners began to be built. In contrast, the Akkadian cubic vessel would spin around constantly. Again, the Akkadian account says that Uta-napishtim sent out a dove, a swallow and then a raven. This order is rather pointless; the non-return of the raven, which might feed upon the corpses, would prove nothing. In the Genesis account, the dove, with its homing instincts, was sent last and returned with an olive branch. This indicated that the Flood had receded from the lower slopes of hills which are the habitat of the olive tree.

Thus, the evidence points strongly to the priority of the Old Testament account over the Akkadian version. Here, the normally sceptical F. H. Woods admitted that 'some few particulars in the Bible story may be actually more original than in the Akkadian version', while K. A. Kitchen, of the School of Oriental Studies, Liverpool University, comments as follows in *The Bible in its World* (Paternoster Press, 1977):

> The contrast between the monotheism and simplicity of the Hebrew account and the polytheism and elaboration of the Mesopotamian epic, is obvious to any reader. The common assumption that the Hebrew account is simply a purged and simplified version of the Babylonian legend (applied also to the Flood stories), is fallacious on methodological grounds. In the Ancient Near East, the rule is that simple accounts or traditions may give rise (by accretion and embellishment) to elaborate legends, but not vice versa. In the Ancient Orient, legends were not simplified or turned into pseudo history (historicised) as had been assumed for earlier Genesis records.

The Danger of Subjective Theories

Modern anthropology has learnt to be cautious of subjective theories which are founded in isolation from empirical investigation. It has learnt how easy it is for the best minds to become so impressed by plausible theories simply because they sound good to Western ears. When fieldwork has revealed the theory to be contrary to fact, there has often been a reluctance to think again.

A case in point is the readiness to accept that the story of the Flood in Genesis chapters 6–9 is a compilation from two separate sources, sometimes contradictory, called 'J' and 'P'. This theory was completely subjective. It was framed without reference to archaeological investigation and has for some time resisted correction. Theological colleges and schools should abandon it in the face of what is now known of the literary methods of the Ancient Near East. It is a fact that, among all the thousands of tablets, there is no known example of several accounts having been carved up and pieced together to make one record.

Moses, the compiler of Genesis, is obviously anxious to preserve all the words of the tablet as they are too sacred to be lost and so includes the recapitulation of the colophon which might be separated from the body of the text either by a line, or on the edge of the tablet or on its baked clay envelope. (Colophon = toledoth, the linking sentence between tablets, usually in the form of a summary; see Fig 14.1.)

Words Uncover the Truth

Further evidence that the tablets which the compiler of Genesis included were more archaic or original than the Akkadian tablets or even those of the Sumerians comes from the archaic nature of words in these sections, and also of the description of the topography when they were written.

The word translated 'ark' in the Hebrew is *Tebah*. Its original meaning has been lost. It can only be guessed that it meant something like 'chest' or 'box'. After the Flood accounts of Genesis chapters 6–10, it does not appear anywhere else in the Bible. As the Babylonian accounts do not use the word, but use the ordinary word for ship, we conclude that the latter were written long after the Genesis account. Even the word in Exodus 25:10 for the Ark of the Covenant is the different word *Aron*. In contrast, the word *Tebah* occurs in the Genesis Flood tablets 26 times. Very significantly, it appears equally in the supposed 'J' and 'P' section (eleven times in 'J' and 15 times in 'P'), yet it never occurs again even in those passages of the Old Testament which are supposed to belong to the 'P' document.

In Genesis, the ark is said to have been made of gopher wood. This word is never again used in the Old Testament, so that no one knows its meaning. The word was old even by Moses' time. Similarly, the meaning of *tsohar* (Genesis 6:16) has to be guessed at. Commonly translated 'windows', it probably means 'ventilator' judging from related words, the word for 'windows' in Genesis 7:11 is a different one.

Incidental topographical remarks are sometimes revealing. The territory of the Canaanites is described as extending to Sodom and Gomorrah. Genesis 10 reads like an antique travel guide. It says, 'That's as you go through Sodom and Gomorrah.' Hence we know that the writer of that lived long before Abraham in whose day these wicked cities were destroyed. Again, by the time Genesis 10:13 was written, Mizraim is still the name of the ancestor who later migrated from Mesopotamia to found the land of Mizraim, later still renamed Egypt.

A Ship's Log Book and Ancient Song Writers

A unique feature of the Genesis account is its succession of dates and periods with repeat phrases. It is as if they were copied from original diary entries or ship's log, perhaps recorded by a primitive mnemonic system of symbols.

We have thus raised the question of whether there was writing **before** the Flood.

How writing developed soon **after** the Flood has long been discovered by archaeologists. Writing was first invented 3400 BC in Mesopotamia and then spread to north-west India and to Egypt 200 years later. Its origins were simple. They consisted of small tablets with simple signs to record the tenths (tithes) given to the temples. We have some of these in the Oxford Ashmolean museum.

But Colin Renfrew reveals that simple proto-writing existed long before the Flood. Tablets round about 6000 BC exist. They are the Tartaria tablets of the Sinca Copper Stone period (see Fig 14.2). These three baked tablets were found in Romania, but some scholars think that their style shows links with the Middle East. Renfrew also refers to the mesolithic village of Lepenski Vir in the Balkans, 5500 BC. These religious symbols indicate an economy based upon fishing in the Danube and are therefore a diffusion of the Danubians from the Near East. Their symbols serve as aids to prompt the memory for a chant which probably constituted an oral tradition.

As I have said, the record in Genesis chapters 7 and 8 would appear to be a record of events noted as in a ship's log during more than a whole year's length of the duration. It is recorded day by day, week by week and month by month. The way in which the tremendous experiences are listed against dates and time periods does indeed look like a ship's log. It would seem that the entries were made as they occurred. One can almost relive the experiences entered as the days go on.

A Complete Record of Events

There are seven 'open door' days of the ark when the animals entered in pairs, male and female, seven pairs of clean animals and only one

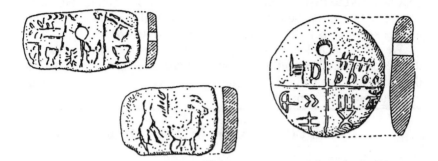

Figure 14.2. The Tartaria tablets Three baked clay tablets from Tartaria in Romania. The signs have been interpreted by some scholars as showing early Near Eastern influence. The round tablet has a diameter of about 6 cms.

Courtesy: C. Renfrew 'Before Civilisation' Cape

pair of each unclean species. On Noah's birthday, the door was shut. From then on, no one was able to see out of the ark. Ventilation and light probably came from a long fanlight which stretched along both sides of the whole 450 feet of the roof.

They were completely shielded from the sight of the fury of the elements until they felt the ark bump upon the top of one of the mountains of the Ararat range. Noah 'opened the window' to look out. As clear glass was not yet invented, this must have been just a solid panel of wood. At first they could see nothing. It was water, water, everywhere. It still covered the mountain range. This must mean that the ark had rested on the highest mountain. That would be Mount Ararat itself, 17,000 feet high. Otherwise, as they looked out, they would at least have seen this peak towering above them, because it would be another 5,000 feet above the range which was itself a mere 12,000 feet high.

At the height of the Flood, the seas had risen 32 feet above the highest mountain which was Mount Ararat. It had taken 150 days or five months to rise to this climax and then over seven months for these swirling waters to recede.

Five dates or periods are given. These mark the beginning, the date of resting on Ararat, the date when the waters had disappeared and the date when Noah left the ark. Interspersed between these dates were the first week, the 40 days rain, the 40 days invasion of the continents by the oceans which reached the ark on its Turkish plateau 4,000 feet up and bore it up. The total of 150 to peak, then 40 days before Noah began to send out the birds each week.

It is obvious that, until Noah removed some of the fabric of the ark in Genesis 8:13 after eleven months, that he was unable to have a clear view of the earth below. Genesis 8:13 says: 'And it came to pass in the year 601, in the first month and the first day of the month, the waters were dried up from the earth and Noah removed the fabric of the ark and looked and, behold, the face of the ground was dry.'

We may conclude, therefore, that Noah was able to keep a day-to-day record of events and that present evidence points increasingly to the view that the Genesis account of these early times pre-dates all other accounts known to us.

THE CHRONOLOGY OF THE FLOOD

There were 40 days during which the rain fell (Gen 7:12)	40 days
Throughout another 110 days the waters continued to rise, making 150 days in all for their 'prevailing' (7:24)	110 days
The waters occupied 74 days in their 'going and decreasing' (AV margin). This was from the 17th of the seventh month to the 1st of the tenth month (8:5). There being 30 days to a month at that time, the figures in days are 13 plus 30 plus 30 plus 1	74 days
Forty days elapsed before Noah sent out the raven (7:6,7)	40 days
Seven days elapsed before Noah sent out the dove for the first time (8:8). This period is necessary for reaching the total and is given by implication from the phrase 'other seven days' in verse 10	7 days
Seven days passed before sending out the dove for the second time (8:10)	7 days
Seven more days passed before the third sending of the dove (8:12)	7 days
Up to this point 285 days are accounted for, but the next episode is dated the 1st of the first month in the 601st year. From the date in 7:11 to this point in 8:13 is a period of 314 days; therefore an interval of 29 days elapses.	29 days
From the removal of the covering of the ark to the very end of the experience was a further 57 days	<u>57 days</u>
TOTAL	<u>371 days</u>

With acknowledgement to the New Bible Commentary, IVF.

Agatha Christie Clue at Nineveh

There is an unexpected Agatha Christie clue to the Flood, as Agatha herself went there to investigate with her husband.

Agatha's real name was Mrs Mallowan and her husband was Professor Mallowan, the archaeologist who excavated the old mighty city of Nineveh. This site is in northern Iraq.

To discover at what point in Nineveh's long history the Flood occurred needed better clues than at some of the other sites. The reason is that here there were several layers of clay laid by floods, so which one was the Flood of Noah? This is where the cultural clue is important. A mistake which some archaeologists make in identifying the Flood is by looking for clay deposits, but such a surging flood would erode as well as deposit. A more accurate way is to be guided by the Bible series of cultures. In the Bible, the Flood comes **between the Copper Stone Age and the Bronze Age**. It is followed by the survivors migrating along the Iranian plateau and then descending into the Mesopotamian plane.

Another clue is that pots have spouts like teapots in all the cities. Before the Flood, the pots are quite different.

Isn't it exciting that all those city states described in Genesis 10 have been excavated and that this chapter is literally factual in prehistoric times? This passage could not have been written later when separate autonomous city states had been combined into one Assyrian and Babylonian empire.

The Flood stratum, originally dated at 4000 BC (now redated at 5000 BC), was discovered by Professor Mallowan at Nineveh; he dug a shaft 100 feet deep. Mallowan numbered his stratigraphy from the bottom upwards as geologists and anthropologists do. This has the advantage of numbering the oldest and first to be laid as level I. The same method was followed by Seton Lloyd at Hassuna. Other archaeologists have numbered from the top down which is a little confusing.

Nineveh level I, then, commences at the Neolithic of 6000 BC (which classes as Pre-Pottery Neolithic B in its lower reaches). There are saddle querns for grinding flour and flint sickles and – a feature of this area – the shallow pottery husking trays containing multiple divisions to be shaken rather like a sieve to free the husks from the grain. The pottery is plain and unburnished. This gives place to Nineveh II with red or black monochrome pots. Flinting becomes poorer as the culture is shading off to Chalcolithic or copper-stone, which is the culture before the Flood.

At a depth of 60 feet come the Flood strata of 13 bands, alternating mud and riverine sand, in which a copper pin was found typically Chalcolithic and then at 51 feet a layer of black mud and pebbles. The excavators describe this as 'the accumulation of a well-defined pluvial

The Strata of a Typical Cave.

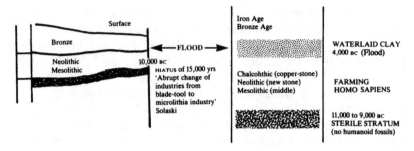

Figure 14.3. Cave strata in the Middle East

1) Caves with a hiatus before the Mesolithic	2) Caves commencing with the Mesolithic	3) Open Sites
Shanidar cave	Zawi Chemi	Karim Shahir
Hazarmerd	Zarzi	M'Lefaat
Babkhal	Palegawra	Giro Chai
Kebara	Hotu	
Ksar'Akil	Belt	
Yabrud		
Warwasi		
Kara Kamar		
Havah Fteah		
Mt Carmel (revised)		

period indicating an important climatic change'.

Above this occurs Nineveh III and a late arrival of Ubaidian culture, followed by Jemdet Nasr proto-literate of 27 feet. The pottery styles are now entirely different in form. The teapot shapes and spouts are much more elaborate, but the colours are dull and unconnected with the Hassuna-Halaf type. We are in the Early Bronze Age. This position in cultural succession is more important than the evidence which any Flood strata may give, for it marks a cultural hiatus. The early Bronze Age is above the 'pluvial interval' and the copper-stone artefacts are below it. This Copper Stone Age is also represented at Sialk in Iran, Hacilar and Çatal Hüyük in Turkey, at Fayum and Merinde in Egypt. It is the failure of some archaeologists to recognise the significance of this cultural hiatus between Chalcolithic (copper-stone) and the Bronze Age, which has confused some archaeologists.

After the Flood, Mesopotamia would be hardly above river or sea level and for many centuries was liable to flooding, sometimes on a large scale.

This disappearance of the Chalcolithic red on cream pottery is a common feature of the other north Mesopotamian sites – Arpachiya,

Gawra, Samarra and Hassuna. The dull Ubaidian pottery above this cultural hiatus is unconnected with the Chalcolithic pottery below. In archaeologists' notes, the phrase keeps appearing: 'Pottery entirely different'; 'Break in pottery succession and culture'. New elements appear, such as painted eggshell ware and the peculiar lentoid tortoise-shaped vase which is diagnostic on all these sites of the Early Bronze Ubaidian period with its baked clay sickles and milking vessels.

To account for the disappearance of the Chalcolithic culture, the theory of some archaeologists is that it was wiped out by the Ubaidians. In view of the collective evidence, it would seem more likely that it was the Flood which obliterated it, so that the Ubaidians occupied a vacant land. Such evidence correlates with sites in Turkey, the Balkans, the Aegean and in Europe, where archaeology confirms a hiatus of over a millennium between copper-stone and bronze. This harmonises with Genesis which places the Flood between these two eras.

In south Mesopotamia, where the migrants first descended to the mud flats of Sumer, most of the cities were post-Flood in date, except Eridu which is mentioned in the Babylonian epic as existing before the Flood. It is significant, then, that at Eridu there is again a break in culture below the Ubaidian. The Ubaidian phase at Eridu displays the same diagnostic artefacts as in north Mesopotamia such as painted egg shell pottery, lentoid tortoise vases, etc. Below it was a Chalcolithic culture unconnected with that above. It was featured by what Seton Lloyd calls Eridu ware, which is quite unlike any other (see Fig 15.2).

Conclusion: a Perfect Correlation

Thus we have a perfect correlation of Scripture with the findings of archaeology. The tablet records are evidence of the existence of a simple proto-writing before the Flood which would enable these accounts to be kept, while there is growing support for the view that the Bible's account precedes all the others. The cultural succession of the Copper Stone Age, followed by no progress in metallurgical techniques for a thousand years, mystified archaeologists and is reasonably explained by the Flood; and after it, the Bronze Age and city states of Mesopotamia.

The Bronze Age, with its invention of writing and literacy, is usually regarded as the beginning of civilisation and it spread within 200 years to Egypt and the Indus valley of West Pakistan and beyond. This correlates with Genesis 10:13,14 and 26–30.

SUMMARY

ANCIENT RECORDS, TABLETS AND CULTURE

Fantastic idolatrous tablets
- Babylonian: Flood caused by 'quarrel among many gods'. Fury of Flood so great that 'they all fell together in a heap'. Uta-napishtim (Noah?) with 70 concubines warned by goddess Ea to build ship. Enlil angered to see ship. Sacrifice to goddess Ishtar after flood.
- Sumerian Tablet WB62: List of kings **before** Flood. 'Flood **came up**'. Tablet WB444. After Flood kingship 'descended from heaven' to Kish first, then list of post-Flood cities and kings. At Susa, Iran a Semitic cuneiform script (Shem).
- Akkadian Tablets: (Babylonian) many variants showing it was told and retold. 'The gods trembled.' Slaves and concubines.
- Others: Eblaite, Hindu, Persian, Chinese, Japanese, Tibetan and 200 primitives.

André Parrot, French Archaeologist says worldwide evidence proves reality of Flood. Long lives of pre-Flood people proved from teeth evidence at Hacilar and El Ubaid.

Genesis the original tablets
Sin judged, not excused.
Ships logging method of progressive events 7 days, 40 days, 150 days, 371 days with five dates interspersed proves Genesis to be an original account of Ark voyage. Prof. Kitchen says 'original' higher critical divisions of Genesis are erroneous; *'tebah'* found equally in 'J' and 'P' versions.

Jesus said the Flood 'swept them all away' (Matt 24:39).

15 REPOPULATION OF THE EARTH AFTER THE FLOOD
EVIDENCE IN THE MIDDLE EAST

Noah's sons and their descendants had the task of repopulating the earth after the Flood. The sons of Japheth went west into Turkey, towards the Mediterranean, then on into Europe; the sons of Ham moved south into Mesopotamia, Canaan and towards Egypt, while the sons of Shem moved in a southerly, then easterly direction, into the land of Caldea, where Abraham later lived – and beyond.

> Then God blessed Noah and his sons, saying to them, 'Be fruitful and increase in number and fill the earth' . . . This is the account of Shem, Ham and Japheth, Noah's sons, who themselves had sons after the flood . . . These are the clans of Noah's sons, according to their lines of descent, within their nations. From these the nations spread out over the earth after the flood (Genesis 9:1; 10:1, 32 NIV).

The evidence supports the Bible by showing that the earth was repopulated from a common ancestry (see Fig 15.1) and from a common geographical area, from which we can trace the spread of mankind after the cultural hiatus of the Flood incident.

Migration from Ararat to Iraq and Babel

With the passing of years, the survivors of the Flood made their way along the Iranian mountain plateau south-eastwards. Some of them then descended into the Indus valley towards the east, where their culture has been excavated at Harappi. Others descended westwards into the Mesopotamian valley. 'Now the whole world had one language and a common speech. As men migrated from the east they found a plain in Shinar and settled there' (Genesis 11:1). Here they are called Ubaidians, from their type site at al'Ubaid. In the totally different environment of Mesopotamia, they were forced to use new materials for the buildings and crafts.

According to Genesis 11, it was here in south Mesopotamia that the Ubaidian settlements of pise huts were first followed by the founding of post-Flood cities and their temples. This is confirmed by the succession at the various sites of the Early Bronze Age city states. These include al'Ubaid, Ur, Uruk, Uqair and Eridu.

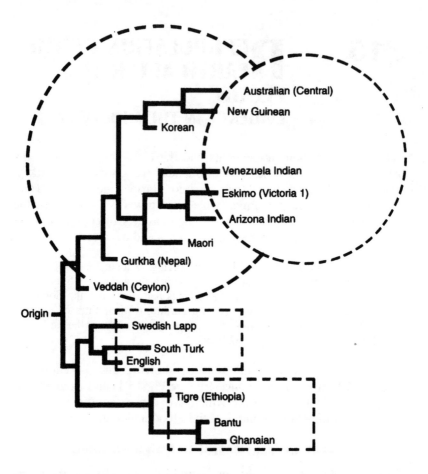

Figure 15.1. Racial family tree computed from blood group gene frequencies
From Cavalli-Sforza and Edwards 1963. It demonstrates one origin of all races and
separates clearly:
(1) the three African groups from
(2) the three European groups with
(3) Asiatic, American Indian and Oceanic representatives occupying the other end of
the tree and forming a more heterogeneous group.
Notice the three main overall groupings. These could be from Noah's three sons.

Based on information from: Royal Anthropological Institute

The first four cities are founded upon what has been regarded as
virgin soil, but which is more likely to mark the Flood, because above
it is the typical Ubaidian Bronze Age culture with its painted eggshell
pottery, lentoid tortoise vases and clay sickles. At Eridu, the site with
strata older than the Ubaidians, there is a different culture beneath this
break, that immediately before the break (level VIII) being
Chalcolithic (copper-stone).

UBAIDIANS AFTER THE FLOOD

Pottery, after the Flood, was, as mentioned briefly before, entirely different from the pots before the Flood. For the first time, we see pots and kettles with spouts. This indicates that there was a complete break in cultures. The people before the Flood were wiped out and those after the Flood were people who had migrated from Ararat after a long time and had reoccupied the site with a new culture with developed styles.

In my charts (see Fig 15.2), you will notice that I have drawn the pottery styles found at five sites in north Mesopotamia and five sites in south Mesopotamia. It is thought that the idea of spouts came first from spouts they made to put on bellows to blow the furnaces to make them hot enough to melt the copper alloys in their Early Bronze Age new techniques.

Post-Flood Pottery

A list of cities is given on the Sumerian tablet accounts of the happenings before and after the Flood. Genesis 10:11 tells us that it was from these newly established cities in the south that migrants went north to re-establish ancient Nineveh and other cities.

A similar picture is seen in Egyptian archaeology, except that the Early Bronze Age Gerzian culture has a time lag of about 200 years relative to the post-Flood eras in Mesopotamia. This is a reasonable time to allow for migration to reach Egypt.

We have seen that the first cities must have been Neolithic according to Genesis 4:17, followed by the copper-stone era, because, in verse 22, the use of copper came in later through the ingenuity of Tubal-Cain. The Flood of Genesis 6 must therefore have followed this copper-stone era.

We have seen that the culture which followed the Copper Stone Age was the Ubaidian. But what is the evidence that this culture was of early bronze character? As it had descended into a topography so devoid of minerals that even the sickles had to be of clay, this might not be immediately apparent, yet surprisingly the evidence appears. Evidence comes from the unearthing of nozzles and leather bellows for inducing draught for the forges and this evidence is supported by the finding of crucibles, open moulds and then closed moulds. The clay nozzles made for bellows introduce a new feature into pottery, for teapot-shaped spouts, like the nozzles, appear on pots from the Ubaidian onwards into Uruk and Jemdet Nasr phases.

Analysis of copper tools by Tylecote and Coghlan shows that tools were first hardened by arsenic and antimony, but the temperature required for melting copper containing these elements was 1083 degrees centigrade. Even malachite copper ore, which was often used,

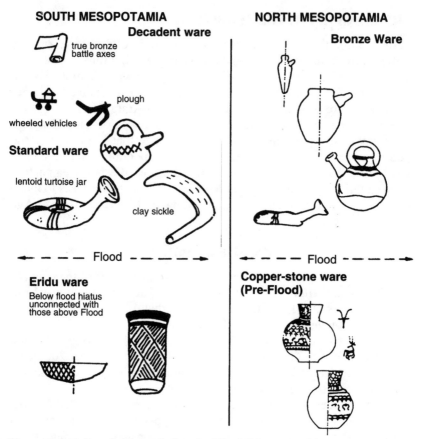

Figure 15.2. Pottery before and after the Flood (Mesopotamia)

requires 800 degrees centigrade.

Induced draught by leather bellows with baked clay nozzles helped to raise fire temperatures. The Ubaidians discovered that by alloying copper with lead, the melting point occurred at a lower temperature. This, however, softened the metal and later the alloy tin was found not only to reduce the temperature required, but also produced bronze which was harder.

Early Ubaidian pictograms also bring evidence of post-Flood tools and materials. They show splayed blades which must therefore have been cast and indeed these tools and weapons have been unearthed – hoes, pickaxes, trident flesh-hooks, spearheads, daggers with convex hilts. The extraordinary thing is that, from the first, the pickaxes, etc. are cast with holes for handles. Two-leaved moulds soon developed into three-leaved moulds.

The clever method of casting works of art by the *cire perdu* or lost

PRE- AND POST-FLOOD SOUNDINGS IN MESOPOTAMIA

SOUTH MESOPOTAMIA (Shinar – Gen. 10:10 & 11:2)					
Archaeological Period	*al-Ubaid*	*Ur*	*Uruk (Warka)*	*Uqair*	*Eridu*
Sumerian Dynasties **Decadent ware** 2800 BC Prolo-Illerate Jemdel Nasr Late Uruk Early Uruk 3500 BC		Gold helmet end of plano-con-vex bricks	Erech of Gen. 10:10		
					I to V
	Pictographs. Controlled irrigation. Plough. Pot-ter's wheel Great advances	III	Warka mask XI to XIII Painted pot-tery disappears	Temple abandoned but con-tinuity	
Standard ware Ubaidian Gen. 11:3 4000 BC	Heraldic Arms Black painted green clay pots 1st architec-ture Mass pro-duced bricks Vitrified pots spouted	I and II Aeolian dep. Present valley floor	XIV to XVIII	Public buildings 3 ft walls Pise huts	Sailing boats 1000 bricked graves Painted egg-shell pottery
BRONZE AGE COMMENCES					
Flood	Green clay (flood)				Flood
	COPPER STONE AGE				
Eridu ware	Virgin soil				VIII to XVIII

wax method was quickly invented. First the figure is carved in beeswax, then clay is pressed around it; then, when the clay is baked, the wax is melted, which runs away to leave a mould ready to fill with molten metal.

The contribution to civilisation of these early post-Flood descendants is seen in that all these types and patterns make their way through to Europe, Egypt and the East.

The early experiments of the Bronze Age were made before the Ubaidians descended from the Iranian heights. At al'Ubaid, in the Mesopotamian valley, they made baked clay copies of copper tools which included the shaft holes and expanded blades, thus showing

NORTH MESOPOTAMIAN SITES (Gen. 10:11, 12)

Archaeological Period	Nineveh site	Arpachlya site	Gawra site	Samarra site	Hassuna site
Early Dynastic	V		VII		
3400 BC Proto-literate	IV		VIII to XI		
Ubaid Early bronze Appearance of spouted pottery, diagnostic tortoise vases, dull colours unconnected with Halai and Hassuma. Milking.	III	I to IV Advanced agriculture Graves V	XII to XIX (XIII Acropolis)		XI to XIII
		Nineveh refounded by Nimrod. Gen. 10:11	Pottery different	Buttressed temples. Formal Architecture. Eggshell and Tortoise ware		BRONZE AGE
4000 BC	Flood Clay		GAP		Break in pottery and culture
					COPPER-STONE
Copper-stone Disappearance of Halai & Hassuna type of Chalcolithic red on cream pottery	V. hot kilns over 1000°C	Polychrome Tholol	Copper, rosettas, gold studs, large beaker		
Halai	II Red and black monochrome pots	VI to X	XX Impressed lamp seals. Pin-prick shards.		VI to X Burnished pots Flint sickles
Hassuna 6000 BC Pre-pottery Neolithic 'B'	Plain pottery, unburnished I Husking trays Flinting poor developing to W. chalcolithic			Samarran unburnished pots	Husking trays Chart hoes II to V Obsidian arrows Pre-pottery Neolithic 'B'
					I Camp sites

their earlier contacts in Iran. In Mesopotamia and up into the plateau of Armenia and the Caucasus, the hiatus between Chalcolithic and Bronze Age is shorter in terms of time because they were nearer the new point of dispersion. The gap widens as one goes westwards through Europe.

EVIDENCE OF METALLURGICAL PROGRESS

Another line of analysis which reveals the chronology of Mesopotamian metallurgy is that at first copper oxide ore was mined, as this was nearer the earth's surface. Later, azurite, malachite and chalcopyrite were used. Dr Pickard says, 'Absence of sulphur in prehistoric copper proves that it was smelted from native metal or from ores thoroughly oxidised and therefore free from sulphides.' Professor Desch says in *Oxford Lectures*, 'Early Mesopotamian objects are usually free from sulphur . . . in favour of oxidised outcrop ores, such as malachite – but early dynastic and Akkadian copper contain 1.0% sulphur.' By protoliterate and early dynastic times, soon after the early Ubaidians, sulphur ores were being used. This reveals that mines were penetrating deeper into the hills where the copper was present as sulphide.

Sulphur copper ores are more difficult to reduce during smelting and need preliminary firing and hammering to separate the slag. Consequently, hammer stones, found in association with smelting, add to the evidence for this progression.

Thus the development of metallurgy from the Ubaidian period onwards has the following succession – arsenic copper, lead alloyed copper, oxide bronze, sulphur bronze and finally with 6% to 10% tin by the end of the early dynastic period, by which time the techniques of riveting and soldering had also been mastered.

This succession of alloys and techniques was diffused from Mesopotamia to Europe with a time lag of many hundreds of years between each coincidence of development. It proves a useful addition to the identification of tools by their shape.

Cultural Succession and the Hiatus: the Real Clues

Thus, it is the cultural succession and hiatus which are the true clues to when the Flood occurred, not water silt layers. Why is this?

Small floods occur frequently in Mesopotamia and each one leaves a silt layer, so it is important to follow the right clue to find which is the Flood stratum. What is the clue? It is to be guided by the culture layer rather than any particular layer of clay. In other words, to look for the break in culture between the Copper Stone Age and the Bronze Age.

What do I mean by culture? It refers to the pattern and method seen in vases and tools, called artefacts. We have seen that, in other parts of the world, the Flood hiatus came between the Copper Stone Age and the Bronze Age. In Mesopotamia it does the same. This correlates with Genesis. If we follow this guideline, it serves to unravel many an archaeological puzzle.

In Mesopotamia, many of the cities excavated are mentioned in Genesis 10 and 11. It is a reading of Genesis that shows that the Flood occurred between the Copper Stone Age and the Bronze Age. The new Bristlecone-pine dating has corrected Carbon 14 dating and adds clarification. We know that Neolithic and Copper Stone Ages apply to the era before the Flood from the note in Genesis 4:22. The Hebrew word here means copper.

Do not be misled by the mention of iron there. It refers to native iron. Iron was discovered as early as this, but never smelted, only hammered into shape. The full Iron Age of the Hittites did not arrive until 1500 BC. Archaeology harmonises by finding a cultural hiatus between these areas. This hiatus between the Copper Stone Age and Bronze Age has been widened significantly by the Bristlecone-pine dating. The correct methodology, therefore, is to correlate the Bible and archaeology on the basis of culture.

The temptation to correlate on the basis of dating should be avoided because, on the one hand, archaeological dates are open to correction and, on the other hand, the genealogical tables of the Bible do not give unbroken succession. Even the existence or non-existence of a clay stratum is secondary evidence, owing to those frequent floods in Mesopotamia. Also, in many places, rushing flood waters can erode rather than deposit.

Building Sites Before and After the Flood

If we have to choose a clay stratum for dating, however, the culture alignment would guide us to choose the Flood stratum dated at 4800 BC because it is after this that the Bronze Age city states of archaeology are founded. This new burst of building activity using new techniques in the founding of city states is accurately described in the eleventh chapter of Genesis and is placed as coming after the Flood of Noah.

In south Mesopotamia, only one site existed before the Flood. This is at Eridu, called Erech in Genesis 10:10 and occurs about 5000 BC. This is characteristically Copper Stone Age. Its pots are quite different from those which come after the Flood in the clay stratum higher up. They are unburnished and are patterned with angular geometrical incisions. The tools are stone and copper.

Up in north Mesopotamia, there are two sites which have artefacts before this Flood hiatus. They are Nineveh and Samara. Here again, the culture is Copper Stone Age. Moreover, the artefacts are the same as sites in Turkey, high up on the plateau which are also pre-Flood copper-stone. In fact, the pre-Flood culture in Mesopotamia is named after sites farther north. They are called Halaf and Hassuna ware. The pottery again is unburnished with angular patterns. Also, they have characteristic husking trays. These are trays in which the husks were shaken off the grains of wheat. They were baked clay trays with multiple divisions. The grain was put in and then shaken to and fro. The husks were knocked off from the grains by the divisions.

There were also copper rosettes and arrowheads made of volcanic glass.

Above this, there is gap in culture. Life disappeared and in some sites there is Flood clay. This marks the Flood.

After the Flood hiatus in south Mesopotamia, five sites are excavated. One is the city of Ur where Abraham lived. They show a fresh start. The pottery is quite different above the Flood level. One important difference is that, after the Flood, many vessels have spouts. There is a kettle shape with a spout and also what looks like a bedpan with a spout. There are also sickles made of hard baked clay. These characteristics occur also in north Mesopotamia where there are four sites, Nineveh, Arpachiya, Gawra and Samara. All are characterised by these spouted vessels and also thousands of bricks as mentioned in Genesis 11:3. Now this all correlates in all details with the cities of Genesis chapters 10 and 11.

Egypt After the Flood

The table of the nations of Genesis 10 is a very remarkable document. Archaeology of ancient times has confirmed the details.

Notice that Egypt is mentioned in verse 13 in the Revised Standard Version. This was the Greek LXX name for the Hebrew 'Mizraim' who founded Egypt. The most famous Egyptologists have confirmed the identity of those who returned to Egypt after the Flood. These Egyptologists are Frankfort, Petre, Aldred, Baumgartel and Caton-Thompson. Here I will sum up the findings, leaving out technicalities.

The Flood made a remarkable change to the climate, topography and people of Egypt. Before it, the inhabitants used flint tools and copper-stone tools and dwelt on the higher hills. This was because Egypt's valleys were wet marshlands. The whole area was well wooded and what is now the Sahara Desert was very fertile with lush green growth.

These people also farmed. They were the original migrants from the Garden of Eden. Many animals roamed the woods and the people before the Flood hunted them and left their rock drawings of the animals still to be seen today. All had suddenly disappeared and a very fertile area had become the desert which we know today.

A millennium later, the new migration repopulated the earth and the Gerzians, as they were called, built low down on the mud flats of the Nile valley. The whole topography had changed. The game animals depicted in Sahara cave drawings had disappeared. The sites upon the hills' spurs were now barren and dry and only the flats down near the Nile were able to support life and agriculture. The redistribution of sea levels caused by the changed axis had lowered the water table throughout the Sahara so that now only oases and low depressions like the Fayum were in contact with that lowered artesian supply. Also, Baumgartel speaks of the rejuvenation of the Nile at this time. A river is rejuvenated when the sea level is lowered.

The new migrants from Mesopotamia and Ararat are known as the Gerzians by archaeologists. Their tools and pottery were quite different. They were Early Bronze Age in culture. Also, their skulls are rounder, not long like those before the Flood.

They lived in grass-reed huts of beehive shape. They had learnt to write by 3400 BC in Mesopotamia (the modern Iraq) and wrote from the right side to the left. Having reached Egypt, they start to write from

---

SEQUENCE OF CULTURAL PHASES IN EGYPT

Neolithic to Chalcolithic and predynastic
   Kartoum artefacts (Uko argues for their being mesolithic contrary to others)

Tasian in Upper Egypt	Fayum in Lower Egypt
Badarian in Upper Egypt	Merinde in Lower Egypt
Amratian in Upper Egypt	Omari, etc. in Lower Egypt

Hiatus at about 5,000 BC = *THE FLOOD*?

Bronze Age
Gerzian (Nakada or Naggada II, Pre-dynastic) 3400 BC
Unification of Upper and Lower Egypt 3200 BC
Archaid Dynasties I and II of the Old Kingdom

the left to the right and made more picturesque signs in their hiero-glyphics.

When hunting animals, they shot arrows which had a wedge shape at the tip. Then they used lassos to throw over the heads of the wounded animals before they could get away. They learnt this from Nimrod who is mentioned in Genesis 10:8 – 'Nimrod was a mighty hunter before the Lord.' His style of hunting is carved on a lady's beauty palette (Fig 16.4) which they used for their cosmetics. He must have been a great hero for the ladies.

His hunting style was also carved on an ivory knife handle, which they had brought with them to Egypt from Mesopotamia.

A Fundamental and Abrupt Change

Baumgartel, whose work of excavation is well known, had written in 1955 in *Proc. Archaeological Society*, of a 'fundamental and abrupt change' between the Amratian and Gerzian civilisations in Egypt. Her reply to Arkell and Ucko in 1964 is that 'the changes which come in with Naggada II (Gerzian) are too vital to be explained by development only. As the imported pieces show, there was a connection with Western Asia which had not existed before.'

The Gerzian post-Flood culture replaces what was largely a hunter-gatherer complex with some agriculture, although Caton-Thompson brings evidence that these pre-Flood Neolithic and Chalcolithic peoples of Egypt were more serious farmers than they were hunter-gatherers. However, these communities were comparatively simple and small and they lived in reed and grass huts of 'beehive' and rectangular shapes. James Mellaart reminds Arkell and Ucko that even this early farming is a derived culture from the Near East (the Garden of Eden): 'Neither the wild ancestors of wheat, barley, etc. nor those of sheep and goat are native to North Africa and their presence in Egypt is artificial and man-made' (*Anatovia Before 4000 BC,* CUP, 1994*).*

The Chalcolithic Amratians lived, as has been said, when all the Sahara was covered with forest and grassland, inhabited with a full complement of roaming game. According to Myers, there are tree trunks where it is now desert and the reason that the Badarians and Amratians built on spurs was to be out of reach of the marshes. The change from forest to desert had taken place before the Gerzians arrived with their new culture and built towns on the lower mud flats of the Nile banks. It was in exploiting this new ecology that by 3200 BC, the large-scale organised irrigation and hoe and plough agriculture were introduced.

This important epoch is depicted upon the famous mace-head of the Scorpion King, now in Ashmolean Museum, Oxford. The Scorpion wears the skittle-shaped White Crown of Upper Egypt and is offically opening the excavation of a canal amidst a scene of rejoicing. Organised agriculture is indicative of the growing towns whose populations need to be fed.

Mesopotamian Influence and Egyptian Ingenuity

There is a problem, however, with the rise of civilisation, of architecture and writing. Why is it that this Mesopotamian style of culture has in it much that is exclusively Egyptian?

In explanation, Aldred says that the Egyptians were quick to adopt new styles in all spheres, but only as a rapid transition into a typical Egyptian milieu. The marks of origin rapidly became assimilated into a Nilotic application.

This is illustrated by the advent of writing in Egypt. The Egyptians soon changed the Mesopotamian symbols in writing to those figures which are typically their own and, although they wrote from right to left at first as the Mesopotamians did, they soon changed to left to right. The story of the advent of writing is as follows.

It may have been the idea of writing which was first communicated to Egypt. The earliest step is thought to be shown upon the mace-head of King Scorpion mentioned above. The king's name is pictographically shown by the Horus. Similarly, there are two signs on the Hunter's Palette. Pictographic writing made its first appearance on small limestone tablets in Mesopotamia used in recording the tithes paid in gifts to the temple in 3500 BC.

There are a number of pointers to Mesopotamia as being the source of Egypt's development of writing. First the Carbon 14 date places it at 200 years later than its appearance in Mesopotamia. Secondly, writing itself suddenly appears in Egypt without much preparation. The Egyptian system of hieroglyphic writing in ideograms and phonograms appears in fully developed style and in complete sentences in contrast to the brief tallies in Mesopotamia.

This indicates that Egypt received the invention of well-developed writing from elsewhere. That source is certainly Mesopotamia because there we have the record of the development of writing. Further, the system of writing which arrives in Egypt is from right to left which is that of Mesopotamia. Later, this is reversed by the Egyptian development of left to right writing.

Moreover, Aldred contends that the system of writing in origin had been devised to record Semitic manner of speech in spite of the fact that it is mixed with Hamitic words. This supports Frankfort's reply to the problem of why the symbols are not Mesopotamian. He says that Egyptians always liked the pictorial and concrete rather than the Mesopotamian abstract, so they assist understanding by clothing the hieroglyph with their own figures and meaning. This is, of course, in keeping with Egyptian treatment of art and architecture where the subjects are clearly Mesopotamian in origin, but the application is indigenised by the local environment.

The Flood Solves Scientists' Problems

Professor Colin Renfrew asks why there should have been so long a stalemate in cultural development between the early spread of farming in the New Copper Stone Age and the Bronze Age, in Europe as well as in Egypt. The Flood catastrophe would explain this for Renfrew and would solve his problems about the gap in culture and stratigraphical record.

It all fits in to the Flood occurring after the Copper Stone Age as a result of the change of axis. Such a change could not be the result of ice-melt because that would heighten the ocean and water table and it would not cause Egypt to be further from the equator. In actuality, the water table was lowered. This was because Egypt was further away from the new equator than it was from the old equator. Also ice-melt would raise sea levels and the Nile would not be rejuvenated.

Skulls Change in Egypt

The comparison of skulls of human beings in Egypt before and after that hiatus shows them to be an entirely different people unconnected with each other. The Amratians would be descendants from the earlier migration from Adam and Eve's family. They lived before the Flood and were long headed, but after the Flood the Gerzians, descendents of Ham, son of Noah, were broad-headed and long-faced. Emery says that the graves of the Gerzians 'were found to contain the anatomical remains of a people whose skulls are of greater size and whose bodies were larger than those of the earlier natives, the difference being so marked that any suggestion that these people derived from the earlier stock is impossible.' It should be remembered also that the graves of these people are in different areas and that no mixed types are found in them.

Not only was there a geological and anthropological change in Egypt, we shall see that the difference in the post-Flood era is witnessed to in culture, pottery, art, architecture, palettes, writing and boats.

FLOOD HIATUS IN EUROPE AND ELSEWHERE

Scientists have been at a loss to account for the disappearance of culture and life in the Old World between the Copper Stone Age and the Bronze Age. If they accepted the Flood as an explanation, it would solve their enigma. Some have described this in various terms. It has been called 'the hiatus', 'the gap', 'the sterile period' and 'the yawning millennium' .

This hiatus, as we call it, occurs in Egypt, around the Mediterranean and in the Middle East and India and probably in China. The inhabitants of Europe were also wiped out by the Flood. It was one thousand years before new peoples repopulated it, by the new migration from Ararat. They are called by archaeologists, the second Danubians, because they migrated along the River Danube, as had the first Danubians before the Flood.

If we examine the cultural background to Genesis chapters 4–11 and correlate it to the archaeological succession of the Old World, we see that this is the very time in which the Bible places the Flood. It is therefore the Flood which caused this break in the cultural history of mankind. The culture stopped at the Copper Stone Age and then an entirely different culture began with the Bronze Age and many other inventions such as writing and the invention of the wheel quickly followed.

Karl Butzer says that the hiatus between the New Stone Age and the Gerzian Bronze registered great changes which 'coincided with the European Atlantic phase', when England was cut off from the continent.

In a lecture I gave to scientists at Chelsea College, London University, I was asked by the well-known zoologist, G. E. Barnes: 'Would it be true to say that your paper demonstrates that over a large part of the Old World there was a simultaneous cultural hiatus at a period that partially coincides with a possible biblical dating of Noah's Flood, but does not in itself demonstrate that the cause of that hiatus, except in Mesopotamia, was flooding?'

My reply was: 'There are indications outside Mesopotamia that the cause of the hiatus was a flood and also that populations vanished.'

Deposits at Shippea Hill, Cambridgeshire

To mention some, in England at Shippea Hill, Cambridgeshire, a clay stratum indicates a flood occurring between the Neolithic and Bronze ages (see Fig 15.3). At that time also, the British Isles separated from the continent, marking the Atlantic phase. In North Africa, according to the geologist, J. Prestwick, the rubble drift was caused by flood erosion and not by Ice Age glaciation. Also, the isostatic readjustment resulting from the Flood would explain the lowered water table which caused the Sahara to become a desert at that time. It is significant that this occurred between the Copper Stone Age and the Bronze Age.

In south-east Asia, the Woakwine submergence indicates that a flood was the cause. There are indications in China, but details of site and cave stratigraphy are sparse. There are also genetic and ethnic data

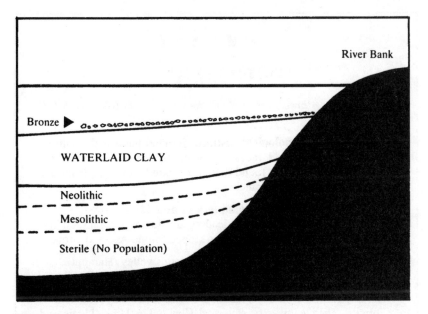

Figure 15.3. Deposits at Shippea Hill, Cambridgeshire

which indicate a disappearance of population, a fresh dispersion and repopulation of the Old World.

Conclusion

I have given you a lot of facts in order to demonstrate that the Bible is accurate even in the smallest detail. But don't forget the main points of the Flood account. What are they? That God rules in science as well as theology and that, when man resists God, corruption and judgment follow.

SUMMARY

POST-FLOOD CLUES

'From these three sons of Noah the whole earth was populated' (Gen 9:19).

The Royal Anthropological Institute Journal published results of samples from world races computed by Cavali S. Forza and Edwards 1963. They found that all mankind had come from one origin, in three main branches.

The migrations of Genesis chapters 11 and 12
Accuracy proved by world's leading archaeologists. Cultural hiatus caused by flood was between Copper Stone Age and Bronze.

Route: Along Iran. Some descended to Indus valley (Harappi).
Some westward to Europe, others into Mesopotamia (Ubaidians).

S. Mesopotamia Ubaidians had houses and baked clay tools and bricks. Then came city states: al'Ubaid, Ur, Uruk, Ugais and Eridu (Gen 10:10).

N. Mesopotamia Nimrod founded Nineveh (Agatha Christie's husband excavated there).
Clue – Copper Stone Age pottery quite different from Bronze Age.
Other sites: Arpachiya, Gawra, Sammarra, Hassava.
These Genesis cities are all documented.

Egypt Man's name in Gen 10:13 as translated by Greek LXX from 'Misraim' (Heb) who founded Egypt. Migration to Nile proved by 1st step pyramid (designed from Tower of Babel and buttressed temple at Hierapollis and Nimrod's palette).
Semitic style from Mesopotamia underlay Egyptian hieroglyphs.

Europe Mysterious culture gap throughout Egypt and Europe (C. Renfrew) solved by the Flood.
Evidence of Flood at Shippea Hill, England.

16 THE TOWER OF BABEL AND NIMROD
FURTHER EVIDENCE IN MESOPOTAMIA

'They said to each other, "Come, let us make bricks and bake them thoroughly." They used brick instead of stone and tar instead of mortar. Then they said, "Come let us build ourselves a city with a tower that reaches to the heavens . . ." But the Lord God came down to see the city and the tower' (Genesis 11:3–5).

We have seen how the survivors of the Flood dispersed from the Iranian mountain plateau. Some of these made their way south-westwards into the Mesopotamian valley, where they are called Ubaidians, from their type site at al'Ubaid.

In the mountains they had used stone; now they had to make their own artificial stone – in other words, they had to bake bricks. Mass-produced bricks made in moulds were produced by the Ubaidians on a large scale. This prehistoric archaeology correlates with Genesis 11:3, 'Let us make bricks and burn them thoroughly. And they had bricks for stone and bitumen they had for mortar.'

In the mountains, they mined copper for nails. But here in the lowlands, they had to devise some other artefact to hold down their house roofs, so they baked fat clay nails slightly hooked to hold down the reeds with which they thatched their houses.

When in the mountains, they had flint or obsidian for sickles. Now even their reaping sickles were made of baked clay. The cutting edge of these Ubaidian sickles is surprisingly sharp; one is easily tempted to doubt it and run one's finger along the edge and get a cut!

For mortar, they used bitumen which was plentiful and, to enable them to walk over marshy areas, they wove thick reed mats. The challenge of this inhospitable though fertile environment was answered by a response of technology by which they surpassed all previous development. These later phases are called Sumerian from 'Sumer'. (In Genesis 11:2 it is spelt Shinar.)

Ambitious Building Projects

Their building projects became larger and more ambitious until in each city the Sumerians built huge towers or artificial mountains called ziggurats. These great works of solid brickwork, jointed with bitumen (Genesis 11:3), had facades of rebated buttresses and were terraced with trees and plants, while the summits were crowned with temples (Fig 16.1). The whole conception reflected the former mountain environment of the builders. Thus, in the archaeological strata above the early Ubaidian period, there is a remarkable development of architecture on most sites.

Figure 16.1. Ziggurat in Mesopotamia
Source: Sir Leonard Woolley 'Ur of Chaldees', Pelican Books, 1952

We have the well-known ziggurat at Ur excavated by Woolley and the sensational religious acropolis at level XIII at Tepe Gawra described by Spicer – which corresponds to Genesis 11:3–4. Its plans commenced the formal architecture which later spread to Egypt, for in Egypt similar styles of buttressing were repeated in the Temple of Saqqara and the step pyramid. The latter are the earliest type of pyramid in Egypt and owe their inspiration to the terraced ziggurats in Mesopotamia (see Fig 16.2 and 16.3).

Mysterious Destruction of the Tower of Babel

The most remarkable erection was at Babel or Babylon. Its mysterious destruction is described by Seton Lloyd, University of London archaeologist:

> The heat had been so great that, in many cases, the brickwork had actually melted and survived in the form of huge vitrified lumps. This, in fact, is a phenomenon which one has seen before in Iraq, on the summit of the ziggurat at Birs Nimrod (Borsippa) which is traditionally considered to be

Figure 16.2. King Djoser of Egypt (2780–2782 BC) with his architect I-em-hotep. Showing the Mesopotamian influence on pyramid design in the background. King Djoser built the earliest pyramids: the stepped form indicates the Egyptian ancestors migrated from present-day Iraq after the Flood, because its design reflects the Tower of Babel (Genesis 11:1–9).

Painting by H. M. Herget. Courtesy: National Geographic Society

Figure 16.3. The stepped pyramid of Saqqara, northern Egypt
The oldest free-standing stone structure in the world (excluding the partially destroyed Tower of Babel)

Source: I. E. S. Edward, The Pyramids of Egypt, Pelican Books, 1947.

the ruins of the biblical Tower of Babel. But there, one is compelled to assume that the 'tower' must have been repeatedly struck by lightning in some tremendous electric storm. For the solid brickwork has vitrified like glass and great masses as big as icebergs are split off and tumbled at all angles.

Genesis 11:2–4 describes this stage: 'And as men migrated from the East (descending from the Iranian plateau) they found a swampy plain in the Land of Shinar (Sumer, Mesopotamia) and settled down there. And they said to one another, "Go, let us bake bricks thoroughly . . . and let us build a city and a tower whose top may reach into heaven." '

Cities and population explosion usually indicate a flourishing economy. At Arpachiya, we get an insight into the advanced agriculture which has developed into field cultivation to feed the swelling numbers.

Below the ziggurat at Uruk (Erech of Genesis 10:10), we have a stratified record of earlier and smaller temples before it, including the famous White Temple, bringing us to the first days of the migrant Ubaidian settlers after the Flood. Filby is thus quite right in identifying the Flood stratum as being almost on the alluvial valley floor. In Woolley's excavations at Ur, the supposed virgin soil which he struck at the bottom of his shaft, must be the Flood stratum, as the Ubaidian pise huts were above it. The bank of clay higher up which he thought was the Flood stratum, is now thought to be of aeolian (air-blown) origin.

Reed Boat and Basket Builders

The stratum of mud upon which the Ubaidians had settled, was formed of decayed vegetable matter which appears to be water-laid. In it, potsherds were all lying horizontally as if swept there by a flood from some neighbouring site. The pottery below this stratum is a culture quite unconnected with that above the stratum. It is known as Hassuna-Halaf or Chalcolithic and is mostly cream coloured on which red geometric patterns with stylised bulls' horns are painted (bucrania motif). Below this, 'three feet below modern sea level, there was stiff green clay pierced by sinuous brown stains which had been the roots of reeds. Here all traces of human activity ceased and we were at the bottom of Mesopotamia,' wrote Woolley.

This, then, was the deposit of the earlier Flood which had swept pots and potsherds from a neighbouring site. The Flood had withdrawn and an adjustment of sea level taken place perhaps due to a rise in the level of the land.

Then, after enough time had elapsed for the new dispersion to make its way along the mountains of Iran from Ararat, the mud had hardened, but the area was still marshy, according to Sumerian testimony, so that reed mattresses had to be woven and stamped down to make a building raft upon which the reed and clay pise huts could be erected (see Fig 16.4).

Even the Ubaidian boats had to be made of reeds. They were bound together into elegant shapes to set the new style of boat, which was eventually to reach Egypt with the commencement of the new post-Flood Gerzian culture. The making of reed boats was to continue for many centuries. Even the baby Moses was later laid in a small reed boat to be hidden from the assassins.

The Greatest Sports Hero of Old

The latest sports news of the day 3500 BC makes a headline in Genesis 10:8. Featured large is the hero – Nimrod – a name which has fascinated mankind ever since. He was one of those charismatic pioneers, not only of sport, but also in the founding and building of several city states. This was after the devastation of the Flood. What a list of achievements he had to his name, Nimrod.

First, consider his sport. His name was proverbial. 'Nimrod, the mighty hunter before the Lord.' In addition, he planned and built separate autonomous communities. They became known as city states. The planning was to avoid a centralised despotic empire. Each city state would have the local interests of the community at heart. The ruins of each city are, today, the prime interest of archaeologists and

EXCAVATION OF THE ZIGGURAT SITE

The famous archaeologist Sir L. Woolley who excavated the area wrote in his book *Ur of the Chaldees* (Pelican, 1929, 1952):

The Ziggurat is a peculiar feature of Sumerian architecture and as such calls for explanation. I have already said that we do not quite know who the Sumerians are; tradition would make them come from the East.

People living in a mountainous land nearly always associate their religion with the outstanding natural features of that land and worship their gods on 'high places', and this would seem to have been true of the Sumerians. When they moved down into the alluvial plain of the Euphrates they found themselves in a country where there were no hills meet (fit) for the service of God, a country so flat that even a private house, if it was to be safe from the periodic inundations (floods), had to be raised on an artificial platform. The latter fact supplied a hint as to how the former difficulty could be solved: the platform had only to be built high enough, and there, made by man, was the high place which nature had failed to provide; and so the Sumerians set to work to build – using **'bricks instead of stone, and slime (bitumen) had they for mortar'** – a 'ziggurat' whose name might be called 'the Hill of Heaven' or 'the Mountain of God'. In every important city there was at least one such tower crowned by a sanctuary, the tower itself forming part of a larger temple complex; of them all the biggest and the most famous was the Ziggurat of Babylon, which in Hebrew tradition became the Tower of Babel.

Such a tower had become a temple to worship the sun or moon. 'So the Lord scattered them from there over all the earth' (Genesis 11:8).

The material used for this tower was accurately described in Genesis 11:3. 'They said to each other "Come let us make bricks and bake them thoroughly".' So they used brick instead of stone (which was available in their mountain environment before they descended to the plain) and bitumen they used for mortar.

anthropologists. Genesis 10:8–12 is a running commentary upon their discoveries:

Figure 16.4. The Ubaidians after the Flood descended to the swamps of Mesopotamia
Here they are stamping down their reed mats (Gen 11:2) – Fourth millennium BC.

Painting by H. M. Herget. Courtesy: National Geographic Society

And Cush (grandson of Noah) begat Nimrod: he began to be a mighty one in the earth. He was a mighty hunter before the Lord; wherefore it is said: even as Nimrod the mighty hunter before the Lord. And the beginning of his kingdom was Babel and Erech and Accad and Calneh, in the land of Shinar. Out of that land went forth Asshur, and builded Nineveh, and the city Rehoboth and Calah, and Resen between Nineveh and Calah: the same is a great city.

The most famous of those city states is Babylon. This was called Babel at first. To my mind, the fact that things went wrong at Babylon centuries later is not the fault of Nimrod. Late in history, Babylon became all that is typical of false religion. Also, ambitious despots forsook Nimrod's ideology of local government and created for the area an empire which was to impose its errors and rule all over the then known world.

'Chariots of Fire'

Long before this, however, the Bible records Nimrod as the great sports hero. It would seem that his sport was dedicated to the Lord. He was rather like Eric Liddell about whom the film *Chariots of Fire* was made. It is surprising that the film was so widely approved and received the top film prize of the year. It shows that the general public likes a sports hero who stands up for his godly principles.

As regards Nimrod, a great archaeological find was made. It was the famous 'Hunter Palette'. A copy of it is in the British Museum (see Fig 16.5). The palette is a beautifully carved dish made for some favoured lady to hold her beauty preparations. It is in low relief and shows a lively scene of Nimrod hunting animals. A lion is being hunted by bows and arrows and lassos. The bows are of a peculiar stylish shape. They have a deep curve at either end for the attachment of the bow-string and the arrowheads have a wedge-shaped point.

This is completely accurate according to the artefacts that have been found in the archaeology of this time. But, can a lion hunt be dedicated to God especially if it involved killing as a sport? Perhaps, however, with Nimrod, it was a necessity. I remember one hunter in Africa in Victorian times saying that he had killed a lion which had been responsible for the deaths of as many as 80 villagers from time to time.

The particular interest in this palette is that it was found in Egypt although Nimrod's domain was Mesopotamia. This indicates that the migrants came from Mesopotamia and that Egypt's culture originated from Mesopotamia.

Mesopotamian Town Planning

As I have said, Nimrod was a great organiser and builder as well as a

Figure 16.5. 'Nimrod's Palette' was found in Egypt
The bows and wedge-shaped flint arrow heads are similar to the grave weaponry of
Nimrod's time. His fame had migrated to Egypt from Mesopotamia. Three pieces of
this ancient 'vanity' are treasured in Paris and London.

sportsman. He built the post-Flood cities and states named in Genesis
10:10–12. Today, they are renowned archaeological sites. The first city
he founded – Babel – was in south Mesopotamia (called Shinar in
Genesis 10:10 and 11:2), which archaeologists call Sumer and the population, the Sumerians. We know them to have been superb mathematicians.

Erech was the next city which Nimrod founded (which has been
excavated) and then Accad. Archaeologists have found these to be the
first city states as the Bible says. Then, for some reason, Nimrod
moved to north Mesopotamia and began building there. He built
Nineveh as Genesis 10:11–12 says (NKJV; RSV; NIV). That was excavated in modern times by Professor Mallowan. Calnah and Resen were
next founded by this remarkable pioneer Nimrod.

In my stratigraphical diagrams (Fig 14.3) I have shown how in all
these sites the Flood hiatus comes between the copper-stone culture
and the bronze culture. Also, notice how the pottery shapes, motifs and
art are quite different above the Flood hiatus from the artefacts below
the hiatus (Fig 15.2).

At first, archaeologists thought that these Bronze Age cities in
Mesopotamia were the earliest built by mankind. But they were built
after the Flood. They ignored the statement in Genesis 4 that there
were cities built before the Flood and the Bronze Age. It was later on
that cities before the Flood were discovered by my tutor, Professor
James Mellaart, as we have already seen. Kathleen Kenyon unearthed
the Neolithic stage in the city of Jericho, but Mellaart's city was earli-

er and it was high up on the Turkish plateau.

To cover those elevated cities, the Flood had to be more than just a local one. Now this is important because it corrects those who thought that the Flood was confined to Mesopotamia. A flood vast enough to cover the Turkish plateau 4,000 feet up and also the ring of mountains around must have involved the oceans. As the Sumerian tablets say, 'The Flood came up'. Came up from where? From the great deeps, the seas and oceans.

So it was from these first cities on the Turkish plateau that men migrated down from the mountains and built a few New Stone Age cities before the Flood in the fertile crescent. This was in Palestine and in Mesopotamia. Then it is because of the cultural differences between buildings before the Flood and buildings after it that we are able to identify the time when the Flood came.

A Trader Sends his Delivery Bill to Sodom

Ancient and accurate and precious are the records which we have in Genesis and which were preserved by Moses when he incorporated them into his work. For example, in chapter 10 verse 19, Sodom and Gomorrah are mentioned in a manner which shows that they were not only in existence, but that the writer of the original records had no idea that they would be overthrown in Abraham's day.

The Ebla tablets, discovered recently, dated 400 years before Abraham, actually have a merchant's delivery bill of goods sent to Sodom. The delivery bill was a clay tablet. The deciphering of this was actually made public just as a sceptic was saying on television that Sodom was a myth! Would hard-headed business men send their goods to a mythical city? Once again we see that the Bible was correct and that it was being discredited by people who didn't have the facts. It is surprising that doubting scientists don't think twice before writing off the biblical account now that there is so much evidence for truth to support its reliability.

The Copper Stone Age Ice Man

What an exciting find that was in the Alps – a frozen man over 5,000 years old! His frozen body had been conserved all that time. The radio carbon date makes him 5,309 years old, but whether you accept radio carbon dates or not, his tools show that he lived in the Copper Stone Age and that suits the archaeological dating very well.

It is thrilling to me, as an archaeologist, to see the man whose tools we have so often dug up. You might have thought his tools were crude because he still used a copper axe and flint arrow heads. The axe was mounted into a bone antler collar fixed to an angle-branched stick and

the arrows had triple flight feathers. They were very typical of technological progress at that stage.

His clothes revealed professional skill in their making, and his
leather shoes were tied with shoe laces. It was not just an animal skin
thrown over his shoulders; his leather suit was tailor-made, with the fur
inside to keep him warm and his boots were stuffed with grass to keep
his feet warm.

Where does this Copper Ice Man fit into the Bible's history of
mankind?

Well, it was after the Flood and after the Tower of Babel and 300
years after the invention of writing, so this man could probably write.
It was many generations before Abraham. In his list of forebears, in
Genesis 11, it would be around the lifetime of Reu, in verse 20.

A New Start in Europe

Probably this Ice Man would belong to the migration mentioned in
Genesis 10:3 and descended from the branch which migrated through
central Europe – they were called the Danubians. One branch settled in
Switzerland, where their lake houses have been discovered built upon
stilts on the lakeside. All these people were given a fresh start by God,
according to the Bible. So perhaps this snowman knew God.

But why was this man caught up there travelling through the Alpine
snow? The answer is that he was near one of the passes between
Austria and Italy. This was a trade route. In Austria the mountains were
rich in copper. We are able to see the tunnels that early Bronze Age
man made to get at the copper veins. They would light a fire against
the tunnel wall and, when the rock was hot, they would throw water at
it so that the sudden contraction would split open the copper veins so
that they could dig out the copper ore.

Then their travels would take them through Europe to Cornwall.
There they would mine for tin. The tin was mixed with copper in the
smelting to make bronze. Then the trader would journey north into
Derbyshire to find amber. This amber was fossilised resin. They
thought it was magic, because when rubbed, static electricity attracted
things to it.

A Five-Thousand-Year-Old Haircut

I was surprised to read that this Ice Man had recently had a haircut. It
was evident from the more than one hundred hairs on his leather suit.
Unfortunately, we cannot tell what his hair style was because, after a
person dies, the hair continues to grow. But, if his clothes are anything
to go by, he would have neat and tidy hair.

The importance of this find in the Alps is that it provides us with a clear time-link between the cultural succession described in the Bible and the date which has been ascribed to this Ice Man, as determined by the carbon method.

His age of 5,309 years (c. 3300 BC) would place him between the Flood and Abraham. His tools, weapons and artefacts place him in the correct technological stage which is described in the Bible for his time: the Copper Stone Age.

THE IMPORTANCE OF INCIDENTALS

Having now completed our study of the period between creation and repopulation of the earth after the Flood (Genesis: 1–11), the Bible then sets the scene for Abraham and his descendants, thuswe are in a position to look back and take stock to see just how perfectly the Bible correlates with up-to-date archaeological discovery.

This archaeological and scientific accuracy of the first 11 chapters of the Bible is all the more extraordinary when one considers that the scientific information given is only incidental to the unfolding story of God's grace. None of these details are given as a record for scientific purposes, but are merely statements of fact – almost as passing comments – in connection with the activity or achievements of the Bible's personalities.

The following chart gives the correlation between archaeological discovery and what the Bible says about the cultural and technological development of each period. This striking correlation is food for thought for any doubter.

CORRELATION OF GENESIS WITH ARCHAEOLOGY AND CULTURE SEQUENCES

Before the Flood: Gen 2:8 to 6:13.
- Shanidar-Zarzi complex of caves and earliest farming experiments 10,000 BC.
- First city-building era:
- New Stone Age and Chalcolithic: Çatal Hüyük, Hacilar.
- Natufian and New Stone Age: Jericho.
- North Mesopotamian villages of Hassuna and Halaf type.

Continued

The Flood: Gen 6:14 to 9:17.
Post-diluvial dispersion, Gen. 9:18 to 10:32.

After the Flood
Commencement of second city-building era in South Mesopotamia:

- Gen. 11:2. Migration from Ararat along Iranian plateau (Zagros Mountains) south-eastwards, then descent from the east on to the flood-plain of Sumer (Shinar) of South Mesopotamia. Ubaidian colonisation of the marshes (c. 3900 BC); reed huts; irrigation; an important step forward. Some hundreds of years represented by the word 'settled' (RSV).
- Gen. 11:3. Mud bricks appear first in the Ubaidian phase, as there was no mountain stone available on the mud flats. Even sickles and roof nails were made of baked clay. Warka phase follows.
- Gen 11 :4. Protoliterate phase of city states with temples, 'Come let us build a city' (c. 3500 BC).Ziggurat building commences with heaven-temples at the apex. A ziggurat was a man-made mountain reflecting the mountain origin of the immigrants. Writing commences 3400 BC.
- Gen 11:7–9. Babel and Erech (Uruk). Confusion and dispersion. This passage correlates with the stage in the table of the nations recorded in Gen 10:10–14. The relationship of Sumerian and Akkadian languages on tablets at this time are an archaeological puzzle. Akkadian (Accad, Gen 10:10) migration from the south to North Mesopotamia; then farther northwards to found Assyria and Nineveh, Gen 10:11.
- Literate civilisation reaches Egypt 200 years later (Gen 10:13) and reaches the Indus Valley 400 years later (Gen 10:29,30).

Correlation of technology
We find the alignment is correct also as regards the history of the use of stone and the development of metallurgy, i.e.:

- *New Stone Age* followed by 'copper-stone' (Chalcolithic) and the use of native copper and haematite in Turkey and copper smelting at Cayonu. Gen 4:22.
- *Bronze Age* – 4000 BC onwards. Gen 10–11.
- *Iron Age* – Commenced with the Hittites, 1500 BC, Deut 3:11. They held a monopoly of the secret of iron smelting until the eleventh century BC, cf. Judges 4:3. The Philistines acquire it, 1100 BC. 1 Sam 13:19. Then the Hebrews acquire it, 1000 BC, 2 Sam 12:31.

THE RELIGIOUS SIGNIFICANCE OF SUCH REMARKABLE RECORDS

We must not miss the purpose of all these wonderful and ancient records. Why were they preserved for us and faithfully handed on to us when all secular writings were allowed to perish?

It was to prepare us for the coming of the Saviour through Shem's descendants. This is why the descendants of Shem are given last in Genesis chapter 11. It leads us to Abraham, the descendant of Shem, whom God chose to be the ancestor of the Lord Jesus Christ. From then on the story of the Bible unfolds.

God preserved all this remarkable record for you and me so that we can rejoice in his glorious salvation. That rebellious human nature, which so easily forsakes our good God, can be changed for the better. That rebellious nature also affects our thinking and our theories.

Theories about the science of man have undergone great changes in the second half of the 20th century. One important one for us is the origin of religion. For many years it was taken for granted that religious ideas evolved and were the product of man's reasoning. It was taught that the worship of sticks and stones came first; then that there were many gods and, finally, that man believed in one God and Creator.

Many still insist on this to justify their atheism, but it was founded entirely on theory. However, Professor E. E. Evans-Pritchard of Oxford insisted that anthropologists went to various tribes throughout the world to test their theories. The fieldwork reports revealed that the exact opposite actually happened. The earliest idea of God was that he was a supreme Creator, then religion degenerated to the worship of many idol gods and, finally, to animism.

In the other two volumes in this series, I shall be dealing with these issues in detail. Many theories about religion, how the Bible was written, who its writers were and so on and so forth, have been put forward. Most have sought to undermine the credibility of the Bible. In the next chapters, we shall see how these, too, fall into disrepute when tested against the evidence for truth.

Agonising Questions

To sum up, the opening chapters of the Bible answer questions which have agonised mankind. Why is our race so cursed with violence, greed, cruelty and perversity? What is the purpose of it all?

The taking of the forbidden fruit gives an answer which science cannot give. Man was made innocent and with all the possibilities of right dealing in a wonderful planet, a planet like no other which God had endowed with oxygen, seas, continents, gravity, plants and abundant food and beauty. He also provided eyes to see the beauty.

The first fossil record of life shows that the earliest marine animals had perfect eyes (e.g. the trilobite). The eye is an advanced mechanism, yet the very first animals to appear had them at the outset; furthermore, all different orders of life have eyes and unrelated kingdoms of animals have eyes.

Adam hid from God and our fallen nature has implanted that trend to run from God ever since. 'He gave us eyes to see them' – the beauties of creation – as the hymn says. God wants our eyes opened to the truth, for our fallen nature has blinded us to it until we turn to God.

In spite of God's gift of eyes to us, we are unable to understand God's plan of redemption while we are spiritually blind. That same Satan who caused spiritual blindness in the Garden of Eden has blinded eyes ever since.

The Supreme Demonstration

But the Bible account demonstrates how God, in his love, repeatedly calls man back to himself to have spiritual insight, to see and understand the workings of his creation and his plan of redemption. The supreme demonstration of this is that the Second Adam, the Son of God, came to win us back. As a representative of our fallen race and having no sin of his own, he atoned for sin.

Even as Adam and his sons were shown that the way back was by atonement, so the Lord Jesus Christ atoned for us on the Cross. Genesis 11 ends with the descent line which leads to Abraham. This line reveals the purpose of God. He promised Abraham that the redeemer of the world would come through him. He sent Abraham to Palestine because this was the Promised Land in which the promised Saviour would come.

SUMMARY

BABEL'S SPORTING HERO IN MESOPOTAMIA

All that Gen 11 says has been proved accurate in every detail by archaeology of events 5,000 years ago. After the Ubaidians the Sumerians began building with hard-baked bricks and tar for mortar (Gen 11:3).

Nimrod the sports hero made headlines. His palette showing him hunting has been found. He was a great builder also. Five sites built by him have been excavated (Gen 10:8–10). Tower of Babel (ziggurat) is still standing, but split and burnt by lightning.

Second city building era in south Mesopotamia
- Gen 11:2. Migration from Ararat along Iranian plateau (Zagros Mountains) south-eastwards, then descent from the east on to the flood plain of Sumer (Shinar) of south Mesopotamia. Ubaidian colonisation of the marshes (c. 3900 BC); reed huts; irrigation; an important step forward. Some hundreds of years represented by the word 'settled' (RSV).

- Gen 11:3. 'Let us bake bricks thoroughly'. Mud bricks appear first in the Ubaidian phase, as there was no mountain-stone available on the mud flats. Even sickles and roof nails were made of baked clay. Warka phase follows.

- Gen 11:4. Protoliterate phase of city states with temples, 'Come let us build a city' (c. 3500 BC).

- Ziggurat building commences with Tower of Babel heaven-temples at the apex. A ziggurat was a man-made mountain reflecting the mountain origin of the immigrants. Writing commences 3400 BC.

- Gen 11:7–9. Babel and Erech (Uruk). Confusion and dispersion correlates with Gen 10:10–14. Sumerian and Akkadian (Accad, Gen 10:10) migration from the south to north to Nineveh, Gen 10:11.

- Literate civilisation reaches Egypt 200 years later (Gen. 10:13) and reaches the Indus Valley 400 years later (Gen 10:29,30).

17 THE BIBLE SPEAKS FOR ITSELF (1)
UNDERSTANDING THE TORAH

Before we look at more evidence for biblical truth which I give in my second volume of this series (Archaeology), we must consider further the influence of religious attitudes and scientific assumptions which have blinded believers and non-believers through this century.

When a person wishes to become better acquainted with Christian evidence, he usually wants to know when and how the Bible was written and what evidence there is to support the Bible's claim to be God's message to man.

It may be that the only commentary to hand is of a sceptical nature or that a course of study undertaken ignores books written by the highly qualified scholars who believe all that the prophets have written. (There are many professing disciples today whom the Lord would still have to rebuke 'for their unbelief and hardness of heart'.)

The Influence of Attitudes

It is this **reductionist attitude** which blinds people to accepting evidence. They ignore the Bible's own statements on its origin and regard the Scriptures as largely the ideas and folklore of man. Such ideas were founded upon the lack of knowledge which prevailed 100 years ago. In spite of the fact that such theories are no longer valid, they are often called 'modern' and are widely taught. They ignore the actual literary methods of the ancient Orient and are thought-conditioned by Western concepts.

'How does this appear to my Western mind?' is asked, instead of the right question, which should be, 'What literary methods did the ancient scribes use, as revealed by the tablets and documents which archaeology has discovered?' For any brought up on such modernist theories, some of the statements in this chapter may come as a surprise.

As a working basis, we shall take seriously what the Bible says of its origins and writers, then examine the supporting evidence.

The Five Books of Moses

The first section of Scripture is the Pentateuch or the five books of Moses: Genesis, Exodus, Leviticus, Numbers, Deuteronomy. It tells us of creation, man's rebellion against God, the Flood, God's choice of a nation through which the Saviour of mankind would come, the

THE OLD TESTAMENT WRITINGS

These three sections of the canon of Scripture reflect the three occasions in history when the Scriptures existing up to that time were brought together.

Section (Order as in Hebrew Bible)	Theme	Time completed (according to Scripture)
1. THE TORAH Genesis to Deuteronomy (the Pentateuch)	Creation, man's rebellion against God, judgement by Flood, Israel chosen to produce the Saviour, Israel delivered from slavery, God's Laws and the Way of Atonement, 40 years pilgrimage.	Written by Moses with epilogue by Phinehas. Up to the time of Joshua: 14th cent. BC. Copy made at Gerizim by Abisha, grandson of Aaron.
2. THE PROPHETS a. The Former Prophets (Joshua to 2 Kings) b. The Latter Prophets (Isaiah to Malachi)	a. Entry into promised land, rule under Judges, rise of monarchy and divided monarchy (2 tribes and 10 tribes), invasion and exile to Assyria and Babylon. b. Calls to repentance to avert God's judgement by exile. Detailed prophecies of the birth, life, and atonement by the Messiah.	a. Book of Joshua by Phinehas, son of Aaron, 13th cent. BC. Judges to 2 Kings compiled by Jeremiah 7th to 6th cent. BC using the contemporary accounts of Samuel, Nathan, Gad, etc. and School of the prophets. Baruch appends the Epilogue in Babylon. b. Remaining books written by the prophets named.
3. THE SACRED WRITINGS a. 1 Chronicles to Esther with Daniel b. Wisdom Literature (Job to Song of Solomon)	a. Recap of history from Adam to the return from exile as affecting David and the messianic line. b. Poetry, Psalms, and Wisdom from time of Moses to exile.	a. Compiled by Ezra and Nehemiah: 5th cent. BC using contemporary records of Shemiah, Iddo, Isaiah, Nathan, Ahijah and priest's records. b. Remaining books written by those named.

deliverance of that nation from slavery, the giving of God's laws and the way of atonement. The whole section was and still is called the Torah or law; in fact that is Scripture's name for it. From the first synagogues even to today, the Torah is kept in scroll form in a beautifully made cabinet in the holiest place of the synagogue which is called the Ark.

Jesus referred to it when he said that Moses wrote of him, 'O foolish men and slow of heart to believe all that the prophets have spoken!' . . . and beginning with Moses and all the prophets he explained to them in all the Scriptures the things concerning himself (Luke 24:25 and 27). 'Everything written about me in the Torah of Moses and the prophets and the psalms must be fulfilled' (v 44).

When Jesus referred to the Torah, the Prophets, and the Psalms, he was referring to the three main divisions of the Old Testament as being 'all the Scriptures'. Notice that he did not include the Apocrypha. When he was speaking, of course, the New Testament had not been written. He found himself prophesied and depicted in all the three sections of the Old Testament.

The Authorship of Moses

Sceptical theologians have long since come up with theories which deny that Moses was the writer of the Torah, so what indications have we, in the text of the Torah itself, that it was Moses who wrote of Jesus?

We must remember that Moses lived in the greatest period of Israelite history. He it was who led Israel out of the slavery of Egypt. It would have been strange if he had made no record of such events, especially as every monument of Egypt in his time depicted scribes recording every event, even routine daily agricultural processes. That Moses also had the habit of recording current history is seen in Deuteronomy 31:22, 'Moses wrote this song the same day'. Other references to Moses' writing are in Exodus 17:8–14; 24:4,7; 34:4; Numbers 33:2; Deuteronomy 31:9–12,24–26. Moreover, Numbers 33:2 tells us that Moses methodically recorded all the travels of his 40 years' leadership.

That a regular account was kept seems to be the point of the remark in Exodus 17:14, 'Write this for a memorial in **the Book**', as though there was a regular account kept in a well-known book. A similar inference comes from Deuteronomy 17:18, 'Let the king write him a copy of this Torah in a book out of that which is before the priests and Levites'. Moses had been brought up in the palace of Pharaoh as the Queen's adopted son. 'Moses was learned in all the wisdom of the Egyptians' (Acts 7:22). The occurrence of Egyptian words and customs unknown to a later age occur frequently in Moses' writings.

Josephus, writing about AD 70, says, 'We have not an innumerable multitude of books among us, disagreeing and contradicting one another, as the Greeks have, but only 22 books which contain the records of all the past times; which are justly believed to be divine and of them five belong to Moses which contain his laws and the tradition of the origins of mankind till his death' (*Against Apion*, Book 1, sec. 8)

Figure 17.1. Egyptian murals at the time of Moses, fifteen centuries BC
It depicts scribes writing down all details given by captured Philistines. (It was recorded in hieroglyphic form on papyrus pads as found in the tombs of the Valley of the Kings, Egypt.) This supports the statements in the writings of Moses that he practised the same routine of recording everything. The Egyptian method of repeating the same details again under each item is seen in Numbers 7:12–83 and elsewhere. Sometimes the audible voice of God was heard, as in Numbers 12:1–8.

Source unknown

Q Why then has the authorship of Moses been so widely denied?

First, because in the last century it was thought – wrongly – that writing was not invented until the eighth century BC. Therefore, it was contended that all the Bible history of events before this must have been handed down orally. Second, it was thought that the sources of this oral tradition could be traced by the use of the divine names

Yahweh (Lord) and Elohim (God) or by the nature of the material, e.g. it was thought instructions on ritual would come from the priests and so they called this the Priestly Code.

A similar suggestion was made in 1770 by Astruc, who was a Paris physician noted for his loose morals, but his theory was largely ignored until Wellhausen's day, a hundred years later.

Professor G. Herbert Livingston, in *The Pentateuch – its Cultural Environment*, sums up the attitude towards God's Word which is behind these assumptions of what is called the 'Documentary Theory':

> A thorough-going rejection of a concept of a living God who can speak to individuals and independently act in history, a view that holds that all ideas are purely the result of human thinking processes express themselves in evolving institutions. Consequently:
>
> a) Moses' authorship is rejected as a fraud;
> b) The hero Patriarchs are regarded as fiction and not real;
> c) The Pentateuch is said not to give a true picture of ancient times, but the early post-exilic period, 500 BC;
> d) None of the Patriarchs worshipped the One God Creator, but they were animists;
> e) God did not reveal himself to them as represented in holy scripture;
> f) The Israelites never had a tabernacle in the wilderness and no exodus or entry into the Promised Land.

Form criticism since 1960 has modified Wellhausen, but only watered down the attitudes.

Archaeologists Teach Wayward Theologians a Lesson

Archaeology has contradicted these assumptions by revealing that all the culture background and customs of 2,000 to 1,500 years BC are faithfully portrayed in the Pentateuch. A later writing or writer could not know of them. As Dr G. Wenham says, 'The Pentateuch has long been recognised as having some of the most archaic material in the book. Albright, Cross and Freedman have argued that the spelling and style of poems, for example, show that they must have been written relatively soon after the events they describe' ('Religion of the Patriarchs' in *Essays on the Patriarchal Narratives*, eds. Mullard and Wiseman, IVP, 1980).

The Bible presents that God revealed himself at the outset as the one true Creator and that belief in many gods was a corruption which came later. The rise of evolution, however, persuaded many that religion evolved from animism, polytheism to belief in one God (a theory now denied by anthropologists). To change the Bible story, it was therefore necessary to develop Astruc's suggestion.

Theories of Primitive Religion

Earlier anthropological theories now being built upon by Professor John Hicks and others have long since been abandoned by anthropologists, Professor E. E. Evans-Pritchard tells us.

It is ironic how some theologians are busy abandoning the basics of Christianity in favour of Victorian theoretical anthropology.

As Evans-Pritchard says, 'For the most part, the theories we have been discussing are, for anthropologists, as dead as mutton.'

Under the title of *Theories of Primitive Religion*, (OUP, 1965) Evans-Pritchard, Professor of Social Anthropology in the University of Oxford, delivered lectures at the University College of Wales and then at Oxford. (I took down these lectures at Oxford before they were actually published.)

The reason for abandonment is that, when these theories began to be tested in field research by anthropologists, they were found useless and contrary to empirical facts. The trend of these theories was that religion evolved in the primitive mind from man, animism, dreams, magic, to religion via polytheism to monotheism. Field research from 1920s onward revealed that the development of religion went in the opposite direction. First came belief in one Creator High God, then fragmentation into the placating of many intermediary gods and nature spirits.

Q How did it come about that early theorists were so off the beam and theologians so determined to follow them long after they were discredited?

Evans-Pritchard says that 'the impassioned rationalism of the last century coloured their assessment of primitive religion. Wild surmise followed on wild surmise. The simplest rules of inductive logic were ignored.'

This mode of reasoning was followed by Tylor, Frazer in *The Golden Bough* (1890, 1922) along with Marett, Levy-Bruhl, etc. Its method was whether a theory sounded convincing to Western ears. 'To understand primitive mentality,' said Marett, 'there was no need to go to live among savages, the experience of an Oxford Common Room being sufficient'(!) These armchair philosophers are long since dead, but sadly not so their methods.

Wide of the Mark

No wonder anthropologists found this completely subjective method had reached conclusions which were wide of the facts. But the method has not been abandoned by textual critics. People are still asked to form their own opinion and impression by comparing sections of the text. That opinion may be untrained in the knowledge of ancient Eastern documents where repetition is normal and where set styles are changed according to whether the subject matter is legal, political or theological. The appeal is thus not made to discover facts, but to impress Western-conditioned attitudes.

When asked if he had ever lived among the natives of whom he had written, Frazer replied, 'God forbid'. Evans-Pritchard says, 'One sometimes sighs, if only Tylor, Marett, Durkheim and all the rest of them could have spent a few weeks among the peoples about whom they so freely wrote!'

Baker said of the Nuer tribes that they were without belief in a Supreme Being. Evans-Pritchard went to live among them and found that this was not true. Likewise, Dr A. Butt found belief in a Supreme Being in Guyana. This supports the findings of such as Schmidt, Lang and Zwemer, who found that original beliefs all over the world were in a Supreme Being often called the Sky God or High God. They thought this indicated that God revealed himself to earlier peoples who had handed it down to present day primitives. Polytheism came later as a corruption of the original purer revelation.

Q What modern knowledge have we which makes Astruc's documentary theory impossible?

First is the knowledge that writing has been in regular use since 3400 BC. Second, that among the thousands of tablets and documents found written since then, there is not a single example of such a practice imagined by the documentary theory, as it is called. Third, belief in one supreme God is found to have been held earlier than the belief in a multiplicity of gods. Fourth, all the styles of writing, i.e. J, E, D, P, were in use in the Hittite legal code method of recording covenants at the time of Moses in the 14th and 13th centuries BC.

J, E, D, P, stand for Jehovah, Elohim, Deuteronomy and Priestly; they were the names given to various supposed sections. They cut up all the accounts into hundreds of these sections, then reassembled them to give an evolutionary picture of religion as a development of man's ideas. Belief in one supreme God, instead of being first (by revelation) was regarded as late. The Priests' ritual and sacrificial system was regarded as late – a production of the exile. The critics thought that all the documents were more or less pieced together. They applied this method not only to the Torah, but also to all the history from Joshua to 2 Kings.

A passage, Exodus 3–6, is referred to where God tells Moses that he did not reveal himself to Abraham, Isaac and Jacob by his name Jehovah but as **El Shaddai**. If we look at passages where God revealed himself to these patriarchs, we find that Moses is quite correct. God revealed himself in the name of El Shaddai 'God Almighty' (Genesis 17:1; 28:3; 35:11; 43:14; 48:3; 49:25). This does not mean that the name Jehovah was unknown to them, but that God revealed himself as the Almighty One, even as today he reveals himself to individuals as 'Saviour'. 'El Shaddai' was the name in which he sealed his covenant with the patriarchs, but that with which he sealed his covenant with the Israelites was Jehovah 'The Eternal One' or the one for whom all time is present.

An Israeli Scholar Points to the Truth

Professor U. Cassuto, who is an Israeli scholar of the Hebrew University of Jerusalem, says that the use of different divine names was not an indication that they came from different sources, but followed certain principles. These principles are shown by archaeology to have existed in ancient times and also in our Lord's time by scribal writings and continue among Jews even to this day.

The principles are these: Elohim (God) and the shorter name El, was an international name for God, a common noun. It is used when foreigners are involved or when reference to him is made as Creator who is outside and above the physical universe, as, for example, in Genesis chapter 1. The deity here is eluded to as a Transcendental Being who exists completely outside and above the physical universe. It appears in the Wisdom literature of the Bible and in hieroglyphics of Babylon, Accad and the recently discovered Ebla Tablets 2400 BC.

The name Jehovah (Yahweh) is employed when God is presented to us in his personal character and direct relationship to people and nature. It is God's name – a proper noun. Thus it is used in Genesis 2:4, where a personal relationship is established with Adam as an individual. (This section is a sequel to chapter 1, not another creation story.)

Thus the Israelites from Moses' time to the present day use the various names as suited to the context, both in the Old Testament and in their worship.

A full treatment is to be found in Professor Cassuto's book, *The Documentary Hypothesis* published by the Jerusalem and Oxford Universities.

Exciting Discoveries of the Ebla Tablets

The recently discovered Ebla Tablets unearthed in Syria have fully justified the contentions of this Israeli Hebrew scholar.

This exciting discovery, which was released to the world in 1977, was made by Professor Pettinato. Ebla was a city of a quarter of a million inhabitants. Before this great city mound of Ebla was unearthed, this empire was unknown apart from some references to it in Egyptian and Sumerian texts. The Eblate empire commenced about 3500 BC and the Tablets which Pettinato has been translating date at 2300 BC. There are 17,000 Tablets, each one about one foot square (35 × 30 centimetres). Each Tablet contains about 6,000 words. As K. A. Kitchen of Liverpool University points out, the names of God (El) and Jehovah (Yaw) alternate as names of God in the work of the same scribe. (Yaw is an abbreviated form of Yahweh.)

So, as Arthur Gibson of Manchester University points out, the use of these two names is not an indication of different authorship or of later sources. The one author, Moses, would quite naturally follow the literary methods of his time and use both names in their related texts.

Moreover, archaeology reveals that legal covenants had to be drawn up in Moses' time on the Hittite Code principle. This included the various styles including 'P' present in the full Torah (i.e. Genesis to Deuteronomy), so the Torah could not have been written at varying times at later dates.

It is strange, in the light of evidence for truth, that some think that Deuteronomy was a book written separately in King Josiah's time, 632 BC, for it is mentioned two or three times in earlier reigns before it was rediscovered in the temple, in Josiah's day. Josiah's reformation followed a period of neglect of the Word of God. The scripture says it was the Torah which was found, not Deuteronomy only. The discovery of Deuteronomy would be unlikely to cause a reformation, as most of its contents were already in Exodus, Leviticus and Numbers.

The name Torah has always been used for the whole five books. Indeed, originally they were one work and the evidence is that they were divided into five for the Greek translation at Alexandria 288 BC and called the Septuagint. The titles of the five books in the Septuagint are not really titles, they arise from the opening words of each section.

So then, when Moses finished writing all the words of this Torah and placed it in the safe keeping of the Ark of the Covenant, it was the complete Torah scroll (Genesis to Deuteronomy). It is this one scroll containing Genesis to Deuteronomy which the Jews still keep today in the Arks of their synagogues all over the world. Deuteronomy was written after the defeat of Og recorded in Numbers 21 and Deuteronomy 1:3,4 near the end of Moses' life.

After Moses gave the Torah into the custody of the Ark, a copy was to be made of it and read to the Israelites on entering the Promised Land. This was done (Joshua 8:31–35) as commanded by Moses. Those who think that Deuteronomy was not in existence until six centuries later should note that the command to read the Torah on entry is contained only in Deuteronomy itself, so it must have existed in Joshua's time for that instruction to be observed.

Rulers were also to make a copy and read it daily. As Israel was surrounded by petty kings, this was an obvious anticipation. King David did this, Psalm 119:11–18; 19:7–14; and King Amaziah, 2 Kings 14:6. In the ungodly times which followed, these copies must have perished, for Josiah's priest discovered the original copy of the Torah when cleaning out the neglected temple, 2 Kings 22:8.

After the return from exile under Nehemiah in 530 BC, the Torah was read again to the people. It took seven days to do so. It is unlikely that Deuteronomy alone would need to take that long.

God's Direct Message to Moses

It should not be overlooked that almost two thirds of the Torah is represented as a direct record of what God actually said to Moses. In Numbers 12, God rebukes the brother and sister of Moses for thinking that they had as direct an access to him as Moses did. 'Moses will I speak to face to face' (literally mouth to mouth) said God, 'with words which he can hear . . . With others I speak in visions and dreams' (Numbers 12:6–8).

The methods God adopted to convey his message to others varied considerably. As Hebrews 1:1 says, 'God at various times past spoke in a variety of ways . . . but has in these last days spoken unto us by his Son.'

The book of Genesis records events before the life of Moses. The author appears to indicate his sources by reference to the patriarchs whose names the sections bear. Archaeology has demonstrated that the events and cultures depicted are accurate.

It would seem that the scribe Moses used, namely Phinehas, was also used by Joshua and it would be he who added the postscript to the Torah after Moses' death. His son would also write Joshua's history of the occupation of the Promised Land (Joshua 24:26). This Torah remained the 'Bible' of Israel until 722 BC when the Samaritans had it copied for themselves. It must be the origin of the Samaritan Torah, a copy of which is still preserved by them today, 2 Kings 17:28. It is written in a pre-exilic Hebrew (see Dr J. W. Wenham, *Christ and the Bible,* Tyndale) and is similar to the Siloam inscription which was engraved a few years later in 701 BC. It was discovered in recent times in the water conduit which King Hezekiah had excavated to bring water into the city so that they could survive a siege (2 Kings 20:20).

The Siloam Inscription

The Siloam inscription was discovered when an Arab boy fell into the pool of Siloam. He swam frantically to the wrong side of the rock barrier. As he came up inside in the darkness, he groped about anxiously and found it led into a tunnel 6 feet high and 2 feet wide.

He had found the conduit bored by King Hezekiah in 701 BC (2 Kings 20:20) to bring water into the city of Jerusalem in preparation for the forthcoming siege by the Assyrians. The conduit was an engineering feat over half a mile long linking up with the spring of Gihon, and also with the older vertical shaft up which David's men climbed to capture the city above (2 Samuel 5:8).

Inside the conduit, the Siloam tablet was found recording the engineer's proud accomplishment. It was written in the older Hebrew of the time and is now in the Istanbul Museum. It told how they tunnelled from both ends to meet in the middle, and heard each other's voices before their pick-axes broke through. When I walked through, waist high in water, my torch showed up the very pick-axe marks referred to on the tablet.

But what connection has this with the Samaritan scroll?

Hezekiah, king of Judah, survived the siege, as admitted by the Assyrian monuments; but the Israelite northern kingdom was destroyed and resettled by foreigners who became the Samaritans (2 Kings 17). They sent for a Jewish priest to bring his textbook *The Law* to teach them 'the way of the God of the land'.

To the Jew, the Law has always meant the work of Moses called the *Pentateuch*. This scroll was then one complete work, Genesis to Deuteronomy without break and is still so regarded today in Jewish synagogues.

Samaritan Clue Supports Authorship of Moses

This time of Hezekiah would be the obvious time for the Samaritans to acquire their copy, certainly not after they had quarrelled with the Jews in Ezra's time, 400 BC. The descendant Samaritans today claim that their ancient scroll is either that copy or a copy of it made soon after.

But, as we have seen, some cannot believe that the Law was written so long ago by Moses, in spite of statements like Deuteronomy 31:24–26 and Numbers 33:2. Here Moses is represented as recording the 40 years' journeyings and the Law and Covenant and he does so in the legal style of Hittites 14 centuries BC and places it in the Ark, in the care of the priests. Yet sceptics believe that the scroll was not compiled until long after the exile by unknown scribes in a manner quite contrary to what archaeologists know to be the literary methods of the ancient Middle East.

More knowledge of ancient Hebrew styles, linked with the discovery of the Siloam inscription, reveals an affinity with the Samaritans' scroll written before the square Hebrew of Ezra's time and making it as old as Hezekiah.

Professor F. F. Bruce, supported by other scholars, writes, 'The script of the Samaritans is of the same general style as the script of the Siloam inscription, but rather more ornamental.'

Moreover, the Samaritans claim that their scroll was taken from a much earlier copy made by Abisha in Joshua's day. Indeed, it is written into the text. 'I, Abisha, son of Phinehas, made this copy'. Now a copy of The Law was made by Joshua at that very place – Mount Gerizim – according to Joshua 8:32–35, as God instructed in Deuteronomy 27:4–13. Abisha was alive at that time and, as a direct descendant of Aaron, would indeed be likely to make a scroll copy, as well as one on stone, from the original which was temporarily held by the priests in the Ark at Gerizim and Ebal.

Conclusion: the Bible Speaks for Itself

In this chapter, I have given a brief summary of the views held by the sceptical theologians regarding the books of Moses, the first five books of the Bible or Torah.

I have shown how these views, which arose a century or more ago, are still held by many despite the mass of evidence to the contrary. This evidence can be found essentially in the text of the Torah itself, which is entirely supported by the findings of archaeology and anthropology.

It remains a mystery why many theologians still adhere blindly to outdated views and persist in teaching them in their colleges.

In the next chapter, I will endeavour to show some of the evidence which supports the authenticity and factuality of the second and third sections of the Old Testament.

SUMMARY

THE BIBLE SPEAKS FOR ITSELF (1)

The Torah
Scroll called Torah (Law) is Moses' work (Genesis to Deuteronomy). Called Pentateuch when translated into Greek 288 BC at Alexandria meaning 'five books'. Was one scroll before division. Can see end and beginning of each was continuous originally. So when in Deut 31:24, Moses finished writing the Torah, it was the Pentateuch he placed in the Ark for safety. Hilkiah rediscovered it in 731 BC. 2 Chron 34:14–21.

Wellhausen (1860) said religion evolved. Not revealed to Moses as claimed. So he reshuffled it (JEDP) and said it was not completed until 400 BC. Hittite legal code 14 cent. BC shows Pentateuch was by Moses. Critics still ignore this and still cut up text according to God's names.

Anthropologists (Prof Evans-Pritchard) and archaeologists found religion did not evolve. Primitive early belief in Creator upheld, but degenerated to animism. Prof F. K. Kitchen finds ancient authors use 'Yaw' and 'El' in one text. e.g. Ebla Tablets.

Torah copied for Samaritan immigrants in 722 BC. So existed before 400 BC. Their copy matches style of Hezekiah's conduit tablet 701 BC.
Synagogues still keep their Torah scroll in an Ark cupboard, from Mosaic tradition.
Phinehas was Moses' scribe.
Themes in the Torah are worked out in rest of Bible.
Finalised in Revelation.

18 THE BIBLE SPEAKS FOR ITSELF (2)
THE PROPHETS AND THE SACRED WRITINGS

The second major section of the Old Testament is that of the prophets. This not only refers to the books by the prophets Isaiah to Malachi, but also to the sacred history of God's chosen people, Joshua to 2 Kings, which the prophets recorded because it was part of their duty to do so. These books were called the **Former Prophets**. They record the entry of Israel into the Promised Land where the Saviour would come and the rise of the royal lineage of David from whom the King-Messiah would descend. The history of this section ends with the exile of the nation 603 BC, in fulfilment of the warnings of Moses and the prophets.

The list of books contained in the 'Former Prophets' are Joshua, Judges, 1 and 2 Samuel and 1 and 2 Kings.

Contemporary Writers

There are clear indications that the writers were contemporary with the events of which they wrote. This is evident from such notes as the one which declares that Rahab was alive when the book of Joshua was being written (Joshua 6:25). She was an inhabitant of the city of Jericho when the walls collapsed at Israel's entry. 'But Rahab the harlot and her father's household and all who belonged to her, Joshua saved alive; and she dwelt in Israel **to this day**, because she hid the messengers whom Joshua sent to spy out Jericho' (RSV).

Similar contemporary notes occur throughout this section. Consider the following: the phrase 'unto this day' recurs over nine times in the books of Joshua and Judges, e.g. Joshua 6:25; 7:26; 8:28,29; 9:27; 13:13; 14:14; 16:10. Judges 18:1. See also 1 Samuel 6:18; 8:18; 1 Kings 12:19; 2 Kings 2:22; 8:22; 17:23–34.

Dr B. Atkinson drew attention to strong evidence that proves that all the history, before King David made Jerusalem his capital, was also written before the time of David. The evidence is that in that earlier history (Joshua to 1 Samuel), there is not the slightest idea that Jerusalem would acquire the fame and reverence of later history. When Jerusalem is referred to, it is as a little-known place of small importance, even a geographical note is added to say where it is.

Who were these contemporary recording prophets? We are told that they were Samuel, Nathan and Gad among others. (1 Chronicles 29:29; 2 Chronicles 9:29; 12:15; 13:22; 26:22; 32:32.) There was also the official court recorder (2 Samuel 20:24).

But who gathered these contemporary writings into consecutive history? Samuel would be the first. 'And Samuel told the people the manner of the kingdom and wrote it in a book, and laid it before the Lord.' This custom of adding the latest scriptures to those already in the sacred custody of the sanctuary was started by Joshua when he 'wrote these words in the book of the Law (Torah) of God' and set it by the sanctuary (Joshua 24:26).

Samuel would compile his account from existing records, with the background of the newly-founded kingship in mind. 'Samuel told the people the manner of the kingdom.' Hence the recurrent phrase in the book of the Judges of the times between Joshua and Samuel: 'For there was no king in those days and every man did what was right in his own eyes' (Judges 17:6; 21:25).

The foundation of a school of the prophets by Samuel would be a further assurance that records would be kept and a prophetic witness to the nation maintained. This school was still actively in existence 300 years later in the times of Elijah and Elisha (2 Kings 2:3–15; 2 Kings 6:1).

The Bible and Israel's Secular Records

Here we should draw attention to the difference between secular history and the inspired version of the prophets. The Bible is sometimes carelessly referred to as the Jews' history book, but Israel's secular records have long since perished, although referred to as sources for the Divine account. Secular sources were:

- The Book of the Wars of the Lord (Numbers 21:14)
- The Book of Jashar (Joshua 10:13)
- Solomon's Natural History (1 Kings 4:33)
- Acts of Solomon (1 Kings 11:41; 2 Chronicles 9:29)
- The Book of the Chronicles of the Kings of Israel (1 Kings 14:19)
- The Book of the Chronicles of the Kings of Judah (1 Kings 15:7)

(These last two are not the books of Kings and Chronicles contained in our present Bible, but are the official court records kept by all Middle East nations of those times which have perished, see 2 Kings 18:18.) The history written by the prophets is really God's viewpoint on secular history, e.g. Rehoboam II was a famous potentate, but if anyone was more interested in his worldly power rather than in God's estimation of his worth, he had better read 'The Book of the Chronicles of the Kings of Israel', 2 Kings 14:28 (i.e. the secular record). The Lord's own estimation of him was, 'He did evil in the sight of the Lord', 2 Kings 14:24; Amos 7:9–13.

Godly kings often appointed a faithful court prophet, whilst others merely tolerated one sent by God. (1 Kings 22:18: 'Did I not say he would prophesy no good of me?')

These court prophets also recorded history and for this reason their text was sacrosanct and quoted in 1 Chronicles 29:29. It is this which makes it possible to find styles, words and customs of their day still in the text, such comments as 'She dwells in Israel to this day'.

It is a Jewish tradition that it was **Jeremiah who collected together this history** recorded by the Former Prophets and compiled it into consecutive narrative. Archaeologists have learnt to take seriously the veracity of such traditions. Jeremiah's role in compiling Judges to Kings is recorded in the Babylonian Talmud.

Dr A. Hervey said, 'The series of historical books from Judges to the end of 2 Kings is formed on one plan, so that each book is a part of a connected whole' until the deportation of King Zedekiah. 'This would point to the time of Jeremiah the prophet' *(Speaker's Commentary)*.

Marks of identification supporting Jeremiah as compiler of this section (the Former Prophets) are seen in link phrases which he uses to link together those earlier records of the prophets.

The expression in Jeremiah 19:3 'his ears shall tingle' occurs elsewhere only in 1 Samuel 3:11 and 2 Kings 21:12. Another phrase 'filled this place with innocent blood' (Jeremiah 19:4) occurs in 2 Kings 21:16. Especially significant is the phrase, 'I have even sent unto you all my servants the prophets, daily rising up early and sending them' Jeremiah 7:25 and Jeremiah 29:19. This is recurrent in the book of Kings and is its climactic theme (2 Kings 17:13; 21:10). Among the writing prophets, only Jeremiah uses this expression, and that five times (Jeremiah 7:25; 25:4; 26:5; 29:19; 44:4). It would be because he was compiler of Kings that 2 Kings 24:18 onwards is repeated verbatim in Jeremiah 52, which records the deportation of King Zedekiah into exile.

The Latter Prophets

Still within the second main section referred to by our Lord are the individual books of prophecies written by the Latter Prophets. They are Isaiah through to Malachi.

Sometimes God had to raise up prophets independently of the school of the prophets. Amos was one and two others were Jeremiah and Ezekiel, priests whom God called to be prophets (Amos 7:14; Jeremiah 1:1–5; Ezekiel 1:3).

Isaiah's prophecy began in the reigns of godly kings, and so was accepted. Nevertheless, these prophets were not chosen by secular authority, but sent by God (2 Samuel 7:2–17). Usually their message was different from the ideas of the populace, who were always backsliding from God's truth. ' "My ways are not your ways, nor my thoughts your thoughts," saith the Lord' (Isaiah 55). It is therefore not correct to say that the Old Testament was a religion thought up by the Jewish nation. It was a revelation from above. Often the prophets wrote down words which they heard on events which they saw in a trance (Ezekiel 1:1; Jeremiah 1:9–11; Daniel 10:7–9).

These prophets lived mostly when God's judgment by exile was about to fall upon the northern and southern kingdoms of the twelve tribes (722 to 587 BC). They write of the coming of the Messiah to be our Saviour and foretell in great detail his birth, ministry, atoning death, resurrection and second coming at the end of the age.

One should beware of commentaries written by unbelievers who do not believe that God could foretell the future through his prophets. They say, therefore, that the prophecies must have been written after the events described and divide up books like Isaiah and Daniel accordingly. But this still does not get the sceptic out of his difficulty, because prophecies were fulfilled in detail in our Lord's first coming and are being fulfilled today as his second coming approaches. Indeed, their scepticism also fulfils prophecy, 'In the last days, sceptics will come saying, where is the promise of his coming . . .?'

They will be willingly ignorant that God created things by words (2 Peter 3:3) and will believe that things came into being of themselves.

Were There Two Isaiahs?

Two of the books of the prophets most attacked by critics are Isaiah and Daniel. The second half of Isaiah's work was attributed to another writer living later. In this way, the critics attempted to account for the fulfilment of the remarkable predictions of the emperor Cyrus. The critics did not want to believe that God could or would foretell and plan the future. Other critics even said there was a third Isaiah. But there are several clear indications of the unity of the whole book.

The Unity of Isaiah

First, there are over 300 words and expressions common to both sections – the former and latter part of Isaiah. Moreover, the exile and return are not only written about in the second section, but are also prophesied in the first section from chapter 11 verse 11 onwards. (See also Isaiah's words to Hezekiah in 2 Kings 20:16–18.)

Second, there is a phrase quite peculiar to Isaiah which runs through the whole book and is equally distributed between the two supposed halves. (The chapters of the supposed first Isaiah are 1 to 39 and the supposed second Isaiah are chapters 40 to 66.) The phrase is 'The Holy One of Israel' and it refers to God. This occurs 14 times in the first 39 chapters and 16 times in the last 27 chapters, making a total of 30. The phrase occurs only six times in the rest of the Old Testament and four of these are in that part of history, 2 Kings 19, for which Isaiah would be responsible. The other two are in Jeremiah, the compiler of that history. The phrase has certainly the Isaiah hallmark throughout his book.

Third, where there are new words in the later chapters, they are often associated with new subjects. There is no conflict here, since we must remember that Isaiah prophesied over many years, during the reigns of four kings and all writers know how their vocabulary develops.

Fourth, the Dead Sea Scroll of Isaiah shows no hint of any knowledge of a break at the end of chapter 39. The Bible was not divided up into chapters until the Middle Ages, so that it is significant that, in the Dead Sea Scrolls copied around 100 BC, not only does the text of our chapter 39 run right on into our chapter 40, but the first line of our chapter 40 actually starts on the bottom line of the column in the scroll! There would have been every incentive to start a new column if there had been any hint of a break in former copies.

Fifth, concerning the ability of God to prophesy the future, he tells Isaiah that this is the very reason he is giving the name of Cyrus whom he is going to use nearly 200 years later. It is to demonstrate that the Holy One of Israel is 'the first and the last . . . declaring the end from the beginning and from ancient times things not yet done . . .' saying of Cyrus, 'He shall fulfil all my purpose . . . I am God, there is none other . . . I made the earth and created man upon it' (Isaiah 44:6,7,28; 45:1–12; 46:9–11; 48:5–13). 'I declared them to you of old, before they came to pass I announced them to you.'

The conception of truthfulness by the critics is such that they deny God's prescience and imply that his prophets were frauds, saying that the prophecies were written after the event they so accurately describe. This gives point to 2 Peter 1:21, which declares that it was '**holy** men of God who were moved by the Holy Spirit to speak from God'.

The critics do not dispense with prophecy so easily, however. Isaiah foretells events fulfilled long after any supposed second or third Isaiah. For example, in chapter 9:6,7 'Unto us a child is born, unto us a son is given (already existing) for his name is Wonderful Counsellor, Mighty God, Everlasting Father, Prince of Peace.'

The whole life, atoning death, resurrection and preaching of the gospel is predicted in Isaiah 53, Jesus said he fulfilled Isaiah 61 and other prophecies are being fulfilled in our times.

Our Lord showed particular affection for the books of both Isaiah and Daniel and so we will now consider the book of Daniel.

Were Daniel's Predictions a Fraud?

A greater knowledge of archaeology and of Eastern literary methods show that the book of Daniel is not of later date, but written as indicated in 8:1, etc. by Daniel himself from 588 BC onwards.

There have been various objections to the genuineness of the authorship, but before considering them, it would be as well to acquaint ourselves with the real reason sceptics have for dating the book as late as 165 BC and claiming it was written by an unknown Jew.

It was assumed that, in spite of the book's claims, the future could not be foretold and therefore the 400 years of history down to Antiochus Epiphanes so accurately given must have been written after the event and then fraudulently presented as a prophecy. It leaves most critics unmoved to quote them that 'There is a God in heaven who reveals secrets' (Daniel 2:28) or 'I (the Lord) have even from the beginning declared it unto you before it came to pass lest you should say my idol has done this' (Isaiah 48:5).

To justify the later date, the critic contends that Aramaic, in which Daniel 2:4–7:28 are written, was not known until later. But as the *New Commentary* points out, Darius, in whose reign Daniel lived, introduced Aramaic to the Medo-Persians. Note also that, according to 2 Kings 18:26, the Assyrians used Aramaic (Syriac) two centuries earlier than Daniel's day. Arthur Gibson of Manchester University shows from the Dere Ala text (1968) that Aramaic was known in Palestine in Daniel's day before it reached Babylon.

Daniel's Choice of Language

Now Daniel was inspired to write 2:4–7:28, in Aramaic for a reason (see Volume 3: *Prophecy*). The prophecies and history of that section concern the Gentiles, whereas he returns to Hebrew for chapter 8 to the end because those prophecies concern the Jew, the sanctuary and the future of Palestine.

Professor Cyrus Gordon, an authority upon Middle Eastern styles, claims that the A-B-A form of the prologue and epilogue, being in a language of contrasting style to the body of the work, was according to the custom, e.g. the book of Job and Code of Hammurabi where we have prose-poetry-prose or vice-versa.

A further objection was that Babylonians were not called Chaldeans until much later, but Heroditus uses it in 440 BC as if it had already been long in use.

A historical objection was that no such king as Belshazzar was known, but only Nabonidus. Archaeology now reveals that there was a co-regency between the two, Belshazzar being subordinate; and in confirmation of this, Daniel is honoured by promotion next to Belshazzar, and yet is called 'third ruler in the kingdom' (5:29).

Sir Leonard Woolley's excavations revealed that a new style of buildings was introduced by Nebuchadnezzar to accommodate large assemblies. This shows the accuracy of chapter 3.

Critics entirely ignore the many prophecies which reach down to the Second Advent when 'the Son of Man comes with the clouds of heaven' (7:13) quoted by our Lord (Mark 14:62) and when the resurrection shall take place (Daniel 12:2-4) at the 'time of the end'. They also ignore our Lord's authority which identifies the abomination of desolation (Daniel 11:31) with the fall of Jerusalem, AD 70. Farrar and others admit that the prophecies of this second half of Daniel 11 do not coincide with Antiochus (165 BC), even if earlier verses do.

The Seventy Weeks

In order to force certain prophecies to terminate by 164 BC, critics telescope Daniel's 70 weeks and the four Gentile Empires in a manner which will not stand examination.

For example, F. W. Farrar acknowledges (*Int. Critical Commentary on Daniel*) that even commencing in Daniel's early years 588 BC, the 70 sabbatical weeks (490 years) do not terminate with Antiochus Epiphanes in 164 BC, during whose tyranny the unknown author is supposed to be writing. He says, 'It is true that from BC 588 to 164 only gives us 424 years . . . how is this to be accounted for?' He suggested it was the author's mistake of reckoning by 66 years, yet he ignores the divine statement that the starting date is not in Daniel's day but at what proved to be over 100 years later, when permission was granted first to Ezra, then to Nehemiah, to rebuild Jerusalem and the walls from about 460 to 440 BC (cf. Daniel 9:25, Ezra 4:5-7, Nehemiah 2:8). A reckoning from this time, the 490 years, brings us to the ministry and substitutionary death of Christ. 'He shall be killed, but not for himself' (Daniel 9:26).

This was clear enough to be understood in our Lord's time, for according to Dr Schonfield, the Jewish Dead Sea Scrolls expert, a discussion among the Pharisees is recorded puzzling out 'why the Messiah had not come – except for this Nazarene'.

The Four Empires

Likewise, the critics try to make the four empires terminate with the

Greek empire instead of the Roman empire. This they do by calling the Medo-Persian empire two successive empires. Such a treatment is unknown to history. The Medes and Persians were always one empire and are referred to as such in Daniel 5:28 and 6:8.

An independent and secular proof of this is the famous Ptolomy's canon of history which gives the four empires succeeding each other as Babylonian, Persian, Greek and Roman.

As Farrar ends his criticism of Daniel in the *Expositor's Bible*, he gets into worse confusion; having rehashed everything to suit critical agnosticism, he declares very little has been fulfilled and ends, 'Learn to say, "I do not know".'

'For Ever Learning but Never Understanding'

But God's words to Daniel tell us why people living in these latter day times will profess such agnosticism. He says the meaning of the prophecy is concealed 'and sealed until the time of the end . . . when none of the wicked shall understand, but the wise shall understand' (12:10).

God regards obstinate unbelief as wickedness (Luke 24:25) and wisdom in his sight is spiritual wisdom in contrast to worldly knowledge (Matthew 11:25, 1 Corinthians 2). 'For in the last days knowledge shall be increased' (Daniel 12:4) yet this science and education would be of a sceptical nature, as St Paul says, 'ever learning and never able to come to the knowledge of the truth' (2 Timothy 3:7).

The greatest of Daniel's prophecies are still to be fulfilled, for at the time of the end, Christ, the stone cut without hands, will strike the image of the world's empires on its feet. The symbolic 'iron legs' of Rome have stretched down the centuries to our modern mixture of weak and strong European nations of the clay and iron of the 'feet'.

Jeremiah – the Greatest!

The prophet Jeremiah was regarded by the Talmudic Jews as the greatest of the Latter Prophets, because he compiled the records of all the court prophets into one consecutive sequel to the Book of Joshua. He compiled all the Old Testament section from the Book of Judges, fourteen centuries BC, to the last king before the exile 587 BC (2 Kings 24). That is why this part of the record has one developing theme of the oscillating fortunes of king and people according to their allegiance to the Torah of Moses, and the challenge of the various prophets down these centuries until, by the irretrievable rejection of Jehovah's Law, the warnings in the Torah of dispersion and exile are fulfilled.

The recurring phrase, 'God rising up and sending his prophets from time to time to implore Israel to return to him; but they refused' is the dominant theme both of the book of the prophet and his compilation of the history, as we have mentioned above.

This knowledge of the part Jeremiah played in compiling Judges to 2 Kings has been forgotten by many modern scholars, but the testimony to it is to be found in the Talmudic writings (e.g. Seder Olam) and the tracate Baba Bathra Vol. 15.1. of the Gemara (Babylonian Talmud).

An example of history associated with a prophet's record is seen in the history of 2 Kings appearing word for word in the prophet Isaiah's book, chapters 36 to 39. Another example is seen with history recorded by Jeremiah. The text is regarded as sacred and not to be altered. 'Thus far are the words of Jeremiah,' they wrote before adding a chapter of history (Jeremiah 51:64).

They did not attempt even to alter the introduction which originally spoke only of his first prophecy, 'To whom the word of the Lord came in the days of Josiah, son of Amon, king of Judah', but when other oracles were added, they merely added, 'It came also in the days of Jehoiakim . . .' (Jeremiah 1:2,3). Josephus says, 'No one has been so bold as either to add anything or to take anything from them or to make any change in them.'

Jeremiah's scribe was Baruch and, as was customary for a scribe, would append the four verses at the end of 2 Kings 25 when he reached Babylon from Egypt after Jeremiah's death. He also received a personal word from God in Jeremiah 45, after the prophet's final word in chapter 44, and added earlier pronouncements of Jeremiah (46 to 51) and then the same epilogue (52:31).

Jeremiah and Baruch were dragged to Egypt against their will and were told by God to make a slab pavement before Pharaoh's palace as a sign that Nebuchadnezzar, king of Babylon, would erect his throne on it, which he did (Jeremiah 43). This pavement was actually discovered by the French.

Baruch accompanied Nebuchadnezzar back to Babylon where he would acquire from his brother Seraiah a copy of those pronouncements (46–51) which Jeremiah gave Seraiah to sink in the Euphrates. He would add them to Jeremiah's prophecies which he took with him and Daniel, 70 years later in Babylon, had copies of these prophetic books which guided his prayers (Daniel 9:2).

The Sacred Writings

The third and last section of the Old Testament is called the *Hagiographa* or sacred writings. This section includes 1 and 2 Chronicles, Ezra, Nehemiah, Esther, Daniel and also the Wisdom literature – Job, Psalms, Proverbs, Ecclesiastes and Song of Songs. This section is called the Psalms in Luke 24:44, because in the Hebrew

Bible it opens with the Psalms.

The sacred writings were compiled by Ezra and Nehemiah at the end of the exile in 445 BC. 2 Maccabees 2:13 refers to 'the writings and commentaries of Nehemiah and how he, founding a library, gathered together the acts of the kings and the prophets, of David and the epistles of the kings'.

Chronicles to Nehemiah is a complete recap of the Bible story from Adam's kindred tables down to the return of the Israelites from exile. Though divided into several books now, they are one book in the Hebrew Bible. They are the only post-exilic collection of history, written from the post-exilic viewpoint, with the lessons learnt from God's dealings with his people.

The sources of information are given and even these are original prophetic and royal records. They are named in 1 Chronicles 29:29, 'now the acts of David the king, first and last, behold, they are written in the book of Samuel the seer and in the book of Nathan the prophet, and in the book of Gad the seer' and other such acknowledgements as 2 Chronicles 32:32, 'Now the rest of the acts of Hezekiah and his goodness, behold, they are written in the vision of Isaiah the prophet . . . and in the book of the kings of Judah and Israel.' Again these are secular sources which have long since perished (see also Chronicles 9:29; 13:22; 26:22 and 29:22).

David's Royal House

The account follows the remarkable preservation of David's royal house which, in fulfilment of God's promises, never perishes until the family tree reaches 'King David's greater Son, our Lord Jesus Christ', whose genealogy opens the New Testament in Matthew's gospel. He fulfils God's promise that David's throne will be eternal, for 'Jesus shall reign where'er the sun doth his successive journeys run'.

What a contrast to the northern kingdom of Israel whose successive royal houses perished nine times and were supplanted one after another! As sources are so freely acknowledged, surely reference to the supposed JEDP documents (Chapter 17) would appear had they existed outside the imagination of higher critical theorists!

SUMMARY OF THE HUMAN AUTHORS OF THE OLD TESTAMENT

And Time of Writing According to Evidences Given in the Scriptures

The Old Testament	Writer or Compiler	Date written
The Pentateuch (Torah)	Written by Moses	14 – 15th century BC
Joshua	Written by Phinehas, son of Aaron	c. 1380 BC
Judges to the end of 2 Kings	Compiled by Jeremiah	c. 580 BC (Note 1)
The Latter Prophets (Isaiah onwards)	By the prophets named	8–5th century BC
1 and 2 Chronicles to Esther	By Ezra and Nehemiah	5th century BC (Note 2)
Wisdom literature	By those named	15th century BC to exile

Note 1. Jeremiah used the contemporary accounts of Samuel 'who wrote the manner of the kingdom' 1000 BC, Nathan, Gad, Ahijah, Iddo, Shemiah, Isaiah and others of the school of the prophets and official royal court chronicles.

Note 2. They used the contemporary records of Shemiah and Iddo (2 Chronicles 13:22), Isaiah (2 Chronicles 26:22), Nathan, Ahijah and Iddo (2 Chronicles 9:29).

S U M M A R Y

THE BIBLE SPEAKS FOR ITSELF (2)

1. The Former Prophets: Joshua to 2 Kings

Phrase '*unto this day*' indicates contemporary recording: Rahab rescued from Jericho 1400 BC was still alive 'unto this day' (Joshua 6:25). So book of Joshua was recorded by a contemporary writer. See also Judges 1:21; 1 Kings 8:8; 2 Kings 25:8,9.

Jerusalem, so famous after David's kingship, was virtually unknown when Judges was written. Judges 19:10.

The contemporary writers from Samuel to 2 Chron are named 6 times. They were Samuel, Nathan, Gad and Ahijah, Iddo, Isaiah, etc.

The Bible history is not the secular history which has perished (1 Kings 14:19) and which were the official court records, not the Kings and Chronicles of our Bible. Ezra named 22 writers of sacred history, but knows nothing of supposed JEDP compilers. Yet Ezra names everybody who did the least thing!

Evidence that Jeremiah used these sources to compile Judges to 2 Kings, e.g. 'ears tingle', phrases typical of Jeremiah, used in 1 Sam 3:11; 2 Kings 21:12; Jer 19:3.

2. The Latter Prophets: Isaiah to Malachi

Nearly all give date and reign of their prophecy, yet higher critics usually say it was someone else living hundreds of years later pretending it was a prophecy. Why? Because they did not believe that God could or would tell the future. Yet this is what proves he is God according to Is 46:9.

3. Isaiah

It enables Isaiah to prophesy Cyrus and exile 200 years later (Is 44:28), but a second Isaiah is postulated by critics as writing after the event, which detailed analysis disproves.

300 words common to all 66 chapters and phrase peculiar to Isaiah 'Holy One of Israel' occurs equally throughout. Therefore only one author.

4. Daniel

He notes who reigned when he wrote from 588 BC onwards, but critics say it was written after 165 BC when a prophecy was fulfilled. Yet Daniel had already been translated into Greek by 288 BC!

CONCLUSION

Subtle Deceptions

There has been good reason to give you information about how God brought about the writing of the sacred Scriptures. We know from experience that some whose faith has been strengthened by scientific evidence for the Bible have had that faith undermined later by a more subtle attack – the theories of 'higher critics'. In order to alert you to those dangers, I will tell you about two men.

The first one was Paul Kanamori of Japan. As a boy, he attended the Japanese village school. One of the boys found a Bible. He was fascinated as he read it, without the help of a missionary or a commentary. He was converted to Jesus Christ. He could not keep the good news to himself, and so he let others boys in his school read it. Many were converted and without any adult teachers they formed themselves into a fellowship until they numbered 100. Their ages ranged from 13 to 18 years.

The joy of salvation through Christ so thrilled them that they went into the market place to proclaim their good news.

Kanamori gradually took the leadership, but they were severely persecuted and Kanamori was cast into prison. He was searched, but hid the gospels of Matthew and John in the inner lining of his waistcoat.

When he was released, he wanted to become a pastor, so he went to a theological college. He was taught all the theories of higher criticism and, sadly what persecution could not do, this subtle deception accomplished. He was taught that the Bible was only a collection of myths and that God had not revealed his truth to the Old Testament prophets; religion had merely evolved; there was no Creator; the virgin birth was a myth and the resurrection was all imagination.

He lost his faith, but as a substitute became one of Japan's greatest social reformers. For 24 years, he continued in the darkness of unbelief. Then tragedy struck. His greatly loved wife died, leaving him with his nine children. He was shattered.

He did not know how to get comfort for his great grief. There was no resurrection, no hope of seeing her again and no living Saviour.

Then into his thoughts came scriptures he had learnt long ago. 'I am the resurrection and the life,' says the Lord. 'He who believes on me, though he were dead, yet shall he live.' He returned to the Saviour, the old joy returned and his eyes were opened to the clever deceptions which had tripped him up.

That same higher criticism is still taught today. It is compulsory for many of those who take preachers' courses, so that is why you have been given the opportunity of letting the Bible speak for itself.

He Was Taught Criticism

The second example is one who was a pioneer in correcting the assumptions of critics. He is the late Revd John Wenham. He became Vice-Principal of an evangelical college; many were surprised to read his story in *Themelios* published by Universities & Colleges Christian Fellowship. I quote it with permission.

He was a much valued friend of mine and I valued discussion with him when I visited Oxford for further science research. John Wenham says:

I came to active faith at the age of 16. I had been brought up in a loving, liberal Christian home and was being educated at a boarding school. I believed in God and respected Jesus, but I had a passionate interest in science and it seemed to me quite unreasonable that anyone in the 20th century should believe that the Creator of the universe had somehow become man and had lived in Palestine for 30 years. At school we were studying Daniel and the Maccabees as a subsidiary subject for the higher certificate. Our teacher (a brilliant man) used S. R. Drivers' Cambridge Commentary on Daniel and we used R. H. Charles' *Century Bible*. **I had lapped it all up** – the miracles were obviously legendary and the predictions were written after the events.

However, my sister had recently been converted and she and her friends prayed me to a Scripture Union holiday party in Switzerland, where I too asked Jesus to come into my heart. Having made a confession of faith before some boys from my school, the prospect of returning there was somewhat daunting. But the Bible had come alive to me and I found myself praying with great fervour. I soon found it necessary to get my ideas sorted out. A little book on Daniel (rather like Joyce Baldwin's *Tyndale OT Commentary*) convinced me that it was good history and genuine prediction. The next year we studied Genesis and I was initially persuaded of the JEDP analysis, till I read James Orr, 'The Problem of the Old Testament' which convinced me of its falsehood. I also read the biographies of Hudson Taylor and C. T. Studd with great delight, and I observed the fact (which appealed to my scientific outlook) that these men believed the Bible and found themselves empowered to evangelise the world. This straightforward belief in the Bible in the Word of God was given a firm theological foundation for me by reading B. B. Warfield's, *Revelation and Inspiration*.

In those days, the standard advice given to Evangelicals at university was: 'Whatever you do, don't read theology'. Though based on much painful experience, I could see that this policy had no future. It was essential that bad theology should be countered by good theology, so in my third year I took the plunge and read for the Cambridge theology tripos Part 1. At that time I had been made secretary of what became the Religious and Theological Students' Fellowship, and I tried in 1937 to organise our first conference. We got quite a good student attendance, but evangelical scholarship was at such a low ebb that we could not find a single senior scholar to come and defend the Bible for us. Three of us read student papers.

My paper was on 'Our Lord's View of the OT', which argued that Jesus regarded its history as true, its doctrine as authoritative and its wording as inspired. I was beginning to believe that this was the proper starting point for a sound Christian view of Scripture. This paper later became a Tyndale OT lecture.

Guidelines for Truth

The question is asked: How does one keep one's spiritual edge when immersed in much Bible study? I would suggest three things:

1. Get your basics clear – Christ is our teacher, believe his Scriptures. Don't let too many unsolved problems accumulate or cause doubts.

2. Keep prayer as a priority. Let him who thinks he stands take heed lest he falls. 'Lord, take not your Holy Spirit from us.'

3. Keep the vision of world evangelisation always in mind and witness to your neighbours – remember they need the Saviour – and we have a wonderful Word to pass on.